Deleuze and Guattari's Philosophy of Transformation

Plateaus – New Directions in Deleuze Studies

'It's not a matter of bringing all sorts of things together under a single concept but rather of relating each concept to variables that explain its mutations.'
Gilles Deleuze, *Negotiations*

Titles available in the series
Christian Kerslake, *Immanence and the Vertigo of Philosophy: From Kant to Deleuze*
Jean-Clet Martin, *Variations: The Philosophy of Gilles Deleuze*, translated by Constantin V. Boundas and Susan Dyrkton
Simone Bignall, *Postcolonial Agency: Critique and Constructivism*
Miguel de Beistegui, *Immanence – Deleuze and Philosophy*
Jean-Jacques Lecercle, *Badiou and Deleuze Read Literature*
Ronald Bogue, *Deleuzian Fabulation and the Scars of History*
Sean Bowden, *The Priority of Events: Deleuze's* Logic of Sense
Craig Lundy, *History and Becoming: Deleuze's Philosophy of Creativity*
Aidan Tynan, *Deleuze's Literary Clinic: Criticism and the Politics of Symptoms*
Thomas Nail, *Returning to Revolution: Deleuze, Guattari and Zapatismo*
François Zourabichvili, *Deleuze: A Philosophy of the Event* with *The Vocabulary of Deleuze* edited by Gregg Lambert and Daniel W. Smith, translated by Kieran Aarons
Frida Beckman, *Between Desire and Pleasure: A Deleuzian Theory of Sexuality*
Nadine Boljkovac, *Untimely Affects: Gilles Deleuze and an Ethics of Cinema*
Daniela Voss, *Conditions of Thought: Deleuze and Transcendental Ideas*
Daniel Barber, *Deleuze and the Naming of God: Post-Secularism and the Future of Immanence*
F. LeRon Shults, *Iconoclastic Theology: Gilles Deleuze and the Secretion of Atheism*
Janae Sholtz, *The Invention of a People: Heidegger and Deleuze on Art and the Political*
Marco Altamirano, *Time, Technology and Environment: An Essay on the Philosophy of Nature*
Sean McQueen, *Deleuze and Baudrillard: From Cyberpunk to Biopunk*
Ridvan Askin, *Narrative and Becoming*
Marc Rölli, *Gilles Deleuze's Transcendental Empiricism: From Tradition to Difference*, translated by Peter Hertz-Ohmes
Guillaume Collett, *The Psychoanalysis of Sense: Deleuze and the Lacanian School*
Ryan J. Johnson, *The Deleuze–Lucretius Encounter*
Allan James Thomas, *Deleuze, Cinema and the Thought of the World*
Cheri Lynne Carr, *Deleuze's Kantian Ethos: Critique as a Way of Life*
Alex Tissandier, *Affirming Divergence: Deleuze's Reading of Leibniz*
Barbara Glowczewski, *Indigenising Anthropology with Guattari and Deleuze*
Koichiro Kokubun, *The Principles of Deleuzian Philosophy*, translated by Wren Nishina
Felice Cimatti, *Unbecoming Human: Philosophy of Animality After Deleuze*, translated by Fabio Gironi
Ryan J. Johnson, *Deleuze, A Stoic*
Jane Newland, *Deleuze in Children's Literature*
D. J. S. Cross, *Deleuze and the Problem of Affect*
Laurent de Sutter, *Deleuze's Philosophy of Law*, translated by Nils F. Schott
Andrew M. Jampol-Petzinger, *Deleuze, Kierkegaard and the Ethics of Selfhood*
Nir Kedem, *A Deleuzian Critique of Queer Thought: Overcoming Sexuality*
Timothy Deane-Freeman, *Deleuze, Digital Media and Thought*
Axel Cherniavsky, *Deleuze and the Creation of Concepts: Philosophy and Methodology*, translated by Taylor Adkins
Edward Thornton, *Deleuze and Guattari's Philosophy of Transformation: Individuating the Line of Flight*

Forthcoming volumes
Sean Bowden, *Expression, Action and Agency in Deleuze: Willing Events*
Justin Litaker, *Deleuze and Guattari's Political Economy*

Visit the Plateaus website at edinburghuniversitypress.com/series/plat

DELEUZE AND GUATTARI'S PHILOSOPHY OF TRANSFORMATION

Individuating the Line of Flight

Edward Thornton

EDINBURGH
University Press

Edinburgh University Press is one of the leading university presses in the UK. We publish academic books and journals in our selected subject areas across the humanities and social sciences, combining cutting-edge scholarship with high editorial and production values to produce academic works of lasting importance. For more information visit our website: edinburghuniversitypress.com

Edinburgh University Press Ltd
13 Infirmary Street
Edinburgh EH1 1LT

First published in hardback by Edinburgh University Press 2025

Typeset in 11/13 Sabon LT Pro
by Cheshire Typesetting Ltd, Cuddington, Cheshire, and
printed and bound by CPI Group (UK) Ltd, Croydon, CR0 4YY

A CIP record for this book is available from the British Library

ISBN 978 1 3995 4804 5 (hardback)
ISBN 978 1 3995 4807 6 (paperback)
ISBN 978 1 3995 4805 2 (webready PDF)
ISBN 978 1 3995 4806 9 (epub)

Contents

Acknowledgements

According to Deleuze's own idiosyncratic account of writing, 'when you work, you are necessarily in absolute solitude ... But it is an extremely populous solitude. Populated not with dreams, phantasms or plans, but with encounters.'[1] My experience of writing this book was solitary in certain respects, but more than anything it was the product of a long series of encounters. Or, I might say that the years from 2013 to 2024 were one long encounter with Deleuze and Guattari, but this was an encounter that I could only have had through a thousand other encounters, some of which began earlier and many of which have continued after.

The list of the most proximate of these would include the personal, institutional and intellectual connections that coalesced during my PhD research: I was fortunate enough to be directed and provoked by two engaging and knowledgeable supervisors, Nathan Widder and Henry Somers-Hall; encouraged and challenged by peers at Royal Holloway and at reading groups in Senate House; stimulated by a wider network of intellectually inclined friends and family; and led productively astray by a yet broader cast of characters encountered at conferences and at the dual blessings of the A–Z group and the Network of Institutional Analysis. To name a few: David Ventura, Thomas Waterton, Josie Taylor, Christopher Thomas and Eric Harper.

This set of connections was in turn facilitated by an AHRC grant – and a university system slightly less damaged than it is today – without which I would not have been able to take the time to meet such unique people or to have thought through the ideas that are expressed in this book.

Less immediate in time and space lurk a broader set of encounters that are too long to list, but that played an equally vital role. An inventory of these encounters might include my interactions with those educators who knew nothing of the topics in this book, but

[1] Gilles Deleuze and Claire Parnet, *Dialogues*, 6.

who instilled in me a constant curiosity for learning and for discussion, ranging from Mrs English (my kindergarten teacher) to Mr Meadowcroft (who introduced me to philosophy at secondary school) to Dr Potter (who patiently read and responded to my undergraduate attempts to understand Wittgenstein).

Then, of course, there are those profound connections with the people closest to me, without whom I could never have made it through such a project, and whose personalities structure so much of what I do and think. The two most important of these are my partner, the inimitable Lotte Johnson, whose conviction, intellectual rigour and understanding are a constant source of strength; and my brother, Rich Thornton, whose ability to listen with care to what I say, and then to hand it back to me completely transformed, is as confounding as it is illuminating. Thank you to both of you, and to anyone else who has ever listened and responded to my attempts to make sense of things.

Introduction: Deleuze and Guattari's Philosophy of Transformation

A Philosophy of Transformation

> To what are we dedicated if not to those problems which demand the very transformation of our body and our language?[1]
>
> Gilles Deleuze

Before you picked up this book, when it was lying on the shelf, it seemed as if it was still. An inanimate object, unmoving and lifeless. However, we know that if we were to look closer – at a microscopic or even at a molecular level – this book is not still. It is a swarm of motion. It's apparent solidity and self-identity are in fact a kind of optical illusion produced by the fact that we are only aware of certain effects produced by the book and are not aware of the processes that give rise to these effects. For example, we see it as being a particular shape and as having a particular colour. To our eyes this shape and this colour seem relatively stable. What we do not see is that the apparently straight edges of the book are in fact jagged and are fluctuating with the constant jostling of the energetic processes that compose the book. Likewise, the book's colour only seems to be unchanging because we do not have the capacity to differentiate the myriad of different sections of the colour spectrum that compose it.

What happens if we apply the same logic to other kinds of entities? Not just physical or material objects, but abstract entities such as nation-states or psychical states, or to universals such as 'human beings' or 'power'? How might these entities appear differently to us if we were to look past their apparent unity to the forces that compose them? What if we were to do the same thing with the structure of experience, with the apparent unity of spatial locations and temporal moments? Taking our experiment one step further – and this is the really exciting move – what happens if we take the same approach to the very conceptual apparatus we are using to think and to perceive?

[1] Deleuze, *Difference and Repetition*, 192.

For example, what happens if we consider concepts, ideas, sensations, arguments and propositions in this way? Ultimately, what happens to our thought if we reapproach the activity of thinking in such a way that the tools we are using to think are, like the book in your hands, in a state of constant variation, fluctuating and adapting according to their environment and to their use?

There have been a number of admirable studies of Deleuze and Guattari's work which examine the potential for their writings to give birth to a new mode of science that can investigate the processes of transformation that underlie the effects of solidity and stasis that we experience as the physical world.[2] However, what interests me most – and what drives the argumentative structure of this book – is the way in which Deleuze and Guattari carry out something similar at the level of metaphysics and at the level of philosophical methodology. It is my contention that the real originality of Deleuze and Guattari's philosophy, and especially their experimental work in the two volumes of the *Capitalism and Schizophrenia* series, lies in their investigation of this optical illusion. What their work shows, I think, is that the building blocks of Western philosophy – the bricks with which the European canon has built the courthouse of reason – may seem solid to the touch, but they are alive at another level with processes of transformation that have remained beyond our analytic reach for as far back as philosophy can trace its history. In a certain sense, this book can be read as an attempt to uncover and express Deleuze and Guattari's response to the following problem: how can we think without misrepresenting thought as something essentially static? To summarise somewhat prematurely, we can abridge my conclusion as follows: in order to think the transformations of the world, thought must also be in a process of transformation.

In contrast to those who see Deleuze and Guattari's collaborations as a move away from philosophical rigour and towards a more artistic mode of experimental writing, this book argues that Deleuze and Guattari's *Capitalism and Schizophrenia* series contains a rigorous, methodical and comprehensive philosophy.[3] It takes seriously Deleuze's claim that his work should be read as 'philosophy, nothing

[2] See, for example, DeLanda, *Intensive Science and Virtual Philosophy*.

[3] While there are a number of publications that connect Deleuze and Guattari's work to other fields, and while there are a range of philosophical texts on Deleuze's individual work, the only recent book to approach either *Anti-Oedipus* or *A Thousand Plateaus* as a work of philosophy is Somers-Hall, Bell and Williams (eds), *A Thousand Plateaus and Philosophy*.

but philosophy' and that this does not change in his collaborations: 'philosophy is what Felix Guattari and I tried to produce in *Anti-Oedipus* and *A Thousand Plateaus*, especially in *A Thousand Plateaus*, which is a long book putting forward many concepts'.[4] Specifically, in this book I will aim to show how the system of concepts developed in *Anti-Oedipus* and *A Thousand Plateaus* responds to the philosophical problem of *transformation* with a philosophical methodology which is always in the active process of transforming itself.

While the majority of this study is restricted to the internal philosophical dynamics of Deleuze and Guattari's work, it is important to note that the *Capitalism and Schizophrenia* series also functions as an intervention in the historical norms of philosophical practice. The historical dominance of Plato's metaphysics of Forms and Aristotle's distinction between the essential and accidental attributes of a substance has tethered Western philosophy to a mode of thinking concerned with that which does not change. This philosophical lineage has concentrated its attention on the way things *are* and the properties of that which *exists*. Questions of genesis (how things came to be as they are) and change (how they become what they are not) have remained perennial problems. This focus on finding something static and unchanging on which to base one's thought runs right through the Western canon. Descartes' famous *cogito* argument is explicitly presented as an attempt to discover some solid 'foundation' on which a thinker can build a 'firm and permanent structure in the sciences'.[5] While Kant's metaphysics complicates that of Descartes, it also grounds philosophical thought on the 'abiding and unchanging' subject of 'pure apperception'.[6] What connects these central touchpoints in the history of philosophy – from Plato to Kant – is an enduring sense that in order to overcome the problematic changeability of things, we must find something unchanging that can provide us anchorage in the storm. In effect, truth – as the ultimate goal of this historical lineage of thinkers – is equated with what does not change. Deleuze and Guattari take an alternative tack, and I will try to show here that by accepting and working with the transformative nature of reality, Deleuze and Guattari provide us with a new set of concepts and a new methodology for doing philosophy.

In his early career, Deleuze attempted to reconstruct a hidden

[4] Deleuze and Clement, 'Entretien 1980'; Deleuze, *Negotiations*, 136.
[5] Descartes, *Meditations*, 6.
[6] Kant, *Critique of Pure Reason*, A123.

history of 'minor' philosophical figures – including Nietzsche, Spinoza and Bergson, among others – in order to overturn this Platonic dominance by affirming the primacy of *difference* over *identity* and by producing a new philosophical image of thought capable of thinking processes of transformation. At the same time, but in a different disciplinary field, Félix Guattari was working on two perennial problems of his own: how can Marxist theory think the radical revolutionary breaks that determine historical change and how can psychoanalytic theory recognise the essentially transformative nature of subjectivity. Making headway against the suffocating structuralism that dominated the intellectual scene at the time, Guattari developed an analysis of the 'machinic' processes that operate within both social and individual transformations, enabling him to conceptualise the material processes of transformation that constitute our lived reality.

When these two figures met, the convergence of their previous projects and conceptual apparatuses set the stage for their groundbreaking collaborative series, *Capitalism and Schizophrenia*. In two major works, Deleuze and Guattari develop a philosophical framework in which their own conceptual architecture is as mobile as the social, political, scientific and philosophical subjects on which it is brought to bear. No longer must they search for what is foundational and static beneath the moving currents of perception. Instead, they embrace transformation as a constitutive process and approach the world around them with the expectation that it is made of transformations all the way down.

Individuating the Line of Flight

In order to offer some orientation within Deleuze and Guattari's vast corpus, and in order to give this study a point of focus, I have decided to structure this book around the development of a single concept that emerges in Deleuze and Guattari's collective work. The concept in question is that of the 'line of flight' (*ligne de fuite*). Before diving into the substantive sections of this book, and before exploring the reasons why this concept is particularly important in Deleuze and Guattari's philosophy of transformation, it will be useful to say something about how Deleuze and Guattari use this concept, why I have chosen it, and how I will approach it.[7]

[7] For an extended account of some of the material contained here, see Thornton, 'On Lines of Flight'.

Deleuze offers us an instructive preliminary definition of the 'line of flight' in an interview he conducted with Claire Parnet while he and Guattari were writing *A Thousand Plateaus*. There, Deleuze explains that his work with Guattari is not interested in offering an analysis of 'things, but of a multiplicity of dimensions, of lines and directions', a collection of dynamic elements that they will name an 'assemblage'.[8] An assemblage is a set of connections that come together for a period of time and which, when taken together, produce a recognisable behaviour or effect. Each assemblage is a constellation of heterogeneous elements; however, these constituent elements are not to be taken as entities in themselves, but are also to be understood as processes or connections. Throughout their work, Deleuze and Guattari will refer to the connections that constitute an assemblage as 'lines'.[9] In the same essay, Deleuze states that according to their mode of thought: 'Whether we are individuals or groups, we are made up of lines and these lines are very varied in nature.'[10] If the world is made up of assemblages, and these assemblages are constituted by lines, then in order to give an account of phenomena encountered in the world it will be necessary to develop a theory of what these lines are, how they function and how they interact. Subsequently, the whole of Deleuze and Guattari's philosophical project becomes an attempt to do just that: 'What we call by different names – schizoanalysis, micro-politics, pragmatics, diagrammatism, rhizomatics, cartography – has no other object than the study of these lines.'[11]

As part of this project, Deleuze and Guattari differentiate between three different kinds of lines. For any assemblage to exist, it must be the case that some of the lines, or connections, that make up the assemblage serve to uphold its structure. These lines, which hold the assemblage together, are referred to as lines of rigid segmentarity, or molar lines. On the other hand, for the assemblage to reproduce itself in such a way that it survives over time, it must also be able to adapt or change. The lines which bring about these revisions are referred to as lines of supple segmentarity, or molecular lines. Finally, there are those lines that reach outside of the assemblage, those parts of

[8] Deleuze, *Dialogues*, 100.

[9] The concept of the 'line' goes through a number of transformations in Deleuze and Guattari's work. See Deleuze's comments on the 'line' and the 'vector' (*Difference and Repetition*, 290; *Logic of Sense*, 65, 125) and on the 'line' as an 'arrow' (*Difference and Repetition*, xiii; *Negotiations*, viii).

[10] Deleuze, *Dialogues*, 93.

[11] Deleuze, *Dialogues*, 94.

the assemblage that escape the structure of which they are a part and serve to connect such an assemblage to that which is outside itself. These lines are referred to as *lines of flight*. To clarify, for Deleuze and Guattari, lines of flight are not secondary to the assemblages that they escape. In direct opposition to this intuition, Deleuze and Guattari claim that lines of flight are constitutive and substantive. Assemblages can only come into existence through the creative capacities that lines of flight expose.[12] This is a complex and counterintuitive philosophical position to maintain, but it is not uncharacteristic of Deleuze and Guattari's philosophical style. In *Difference and Repetition*, Deleuze had argued that difference is the necessary precondition for the genesis of identity, and in *Psychoanalysis and Transversality*, Guattari had argued that group phenomena of desire logically precede individual desires. Once we have had a chance to explore these texts more closely, Deleuze and Guattari's claims in *Anti-Oedipus* and *A Thousand Plateaus* that lines of flight constitute the necessary preconditions for the genesis of assemblages will be much easier to swallow.

To say that this definition of the line of flight is a preliminary one does not go far enough. Given the fact that the concept of the line of flight undergoes transformations of its own as it moves through Deleuze and Guattari's work, any definition of it can only ever be partial. To overcome this problem, in this book I have attempted to utilise an original methodology of interpretation, one that traces out the *individuation* of the concept of the line of flight.[13] Instead of offering a simple definition of the concept of the line of flight – one which would treat the concept itself as something static and unchanging – I will try to show how the concept takes on an individuality of its own only through the various ways it transforms itself in relation to new problems.[14]

[12] Deleuze and Guattari, *A Thousand Plateaus*, 585; May, *Gilles Deleuze: An Introduction*, 137.

[13] The theory of individuation that I am drawing on here comes mainly from the work of Gilbert Simondon. In both *The Physico-Biological Genesis of the Individual* (1964) and *Psychic and Collective Individuation* (1989), Simondon's work is concerned primarily with the question of individuation. It is my decision to apply this theory to the individuation of a concept. Deleuze was heavily influenced by Simondon, praising his work as 'a profoundly original theory of individuation, which entails an entire philosophy' (*Desert Islands*, 43).

[14] I have decided to follow a methodology of mapping the individuation of a concept, over the better-known practices of archaeology and genealogy (in both the Nietzschean and Foucauldian senses), for two interconnected reasons. First, I

Another way to put this would be to say that I will treat the concept of the line of flight in its process of becoming. Instead of attempting to separate this concept out from the context in which it was created in order to offer an abstract definition, I will aim to put this concept into a dynamic relationship with a set of other concepts, such that they create an assemblage. This assemblage will bring together Deleuze and Guattari's critique of psychoanalysis, their interventions in Marxist political theory, and their reformulation of the insights of philosophers including Spinoza, Kant, Nietzsche and Bergson, not to mention the relationships they maintain with a heterodox set of authors, mathematicians and artists.[15] Through these connections, the concept of the line of flight will be individuated in a dynamic system of concepts that include 'the multiplicity', 'de/reterritorialization', 'transversality', 'the molecular' and the 'regime of signs', among others. By carrying out this process it will be possible to see not only what the concept of the line of flight signifies, but more importantly, how it functions in Deleuze and Guattari's philosophy of transformation.

We will see, for example, how the concept of the line of flight first begins to emerge in *Anti-Oedipus* in an attempt to think through the schizophrenic activity of pre-oedipal desire, later morphs into an essential feature of Deleuze and Guattari's analysis of universal political history, and eventually comes to play a specific role in their theory of material and immaterial assemblages. Rather than seeing any of these moments as of primary importance to the concept of the line of flight, this book investigates the constitution of the concept through the very transformations that it undergoes. This methodology is key to the book's conceptual project: it is by showing the transformations

do not treat Deleuze and Guattari's work as a 'discourse' in need of excavation, but as an open-ended system of thinking, for which we require entries and exits. Second, while my chapters do follow a chronological order, I am not conducting a historical analysis of the 'concept'. I do not wish to show what the concept meant at different moments in history, or to look at how it came to mean what it means today. Instead, I aim to show how the consistency of the concept emerges across its many variations. To borrow from Deleuze and Guattari, we could say that I aim to map the becoming-concept of the line of flight, and not the history of how it became a concept.

15 Of course, there will be many connections that I am unable to follow. One worth noting here is the reference that Deleuze and Guattari make to George Jackson's analysis of running from the police. See Jackson, *Soledad Brother: The Prison Letters of George Jackson*. See also the brilliant essay by Michelle Koerner titled 'Line of Escape: Gilles Deleuze's Encounter with George Jackson'.

that take place within the individuation of the concept of the line of flight that the book is able to express Deleuze and Guattari's philosophy of transformation. By way of this methodology, a new theory of the concept emerges. Following Deleuze and Guattari's own analysis of philosophy as the creation of concepts, it is a secondary intention of this book to offer a concrete demonstration of how the concepts created in philosophical practice are always actively incomplete and maintain themselves through internal processes of constant transformation.

A Map for What is to Come

This book proceeds through a series of chapters that trace the individuation of the concept of the 'line of flight' through the chronological development of Deleuze and Guattari's publications. The first two chapters analyse the works produced separately by Deleuze and Guattari before 1972. Chapter 1, titled 'Deleuze and the Metaphysics of Difference', examines the conceptual precursors to the concept of the line of flight arising in Deleuze's early attempts to transform the history of the philosophical canon. It offers a focused reading of Deleuze's magnum opus, *Difference and Repetition* (1968), with special attention being paid to his analysis of spatial relations. The chapter analyses Deleuze's use of the concept of the 'multiplicity', and his use of the terminology of linear perspective, and thereby uncovers the concept of the 'abstract line' as one of the forerunners of the 'line of flight'. Chapter 2, titled 'Guattari's Psychotherapeutic and Militant Escapes', turns to Guattari's works of the 1950s and 1960s, especially as they are collected in *Psychoanalysis and Transversality*, to demonstrate the theoretical innovations that he brought to bear on the practical activities of psychotherapy and political activism. It shows how Guattari utilised Institutional Psychotherapy and Marxist theory to produce the concept of the 'machine', allowing him to foreground the role of 'escape' in all formations of desire. While there have been a number of useful studies of Guattari's work, there has been no significant analysis of the way in which this work informs the *Capitalism and Schizophrenia* series.[16] The research presented here

[16] See Watson, *Guattari's Diagrammatic Thought*, and Genosko, *The Guattari Reader*, *Félix Guattari: An Aberrant Introduction* and *Félix Guattari: A Critical Introduction*.

provides a necessary and significant corrective to this blind spot in the literature.

Chapters 3 and 4 concentrate on *Anti-Oedipus*, and on the emergence of the concept of the 'line of flight' in this book. Chapter 3, titled '*Anti-Oedipus* and Desiring-Machines', explores Deleuze and Guattari's first use of the concept of the line of flight in *Anti-Oedipus* and shows how it originates as a response to the problem of schizophrenic desire. Crucially, it also shows that the transformational impact of the concept of the line of flight has been systematically overlooked in the literature because the accepted translations of Deleuze and Guattari's two most important books – *Anti-Oedipus* and *A Thousand Plateaus* – render the French *ligne de fuite* as 'line of escape' and 'line of flight' respectively. When it is recognised that a single concept underlies these two translations, and when the many allusions contained in the French phrase *ligne de fuite* are brought to light, a connection emerges across Deleuze and Guattari's works concerning the problem of transformation. The second chapter on *Anti-Oedipus* – titled '*Anti-Oedipus* and Social Machines' – shows how Deleuze and Guattari's theory of desire is linked to a philosophy of historical transformation in which the line of flight is reconceptualised as a moment in revolutionary political change. Here we see that Deleuze and Guattari's analysis of the 'schizophrenic line of flight' and their analysis of the 'revolutionary line of flight' ultimately result in four different senses of this concept, whose interrelationships determine their whole project in *Anti-Oedipus*.

Chapters 5 and 6 turn to *A Thousand Plateaus* and to the various ways the concept of the line of flight is transformed in this text. Chapter 5, titled '*A Thousand Plateaus* and the Metaphysics of Transformation', demonstrates how the first explicit introduction of the 'rhizomatic image of thought' and the role of the 'assemblage' in the constitution of reality allow the concept of the line of flight to take on a new level of consistency. This chapter also explores the relationship between the metaphysical and the ethical dimensions of *A Thousand Plateaus*, and shows how they are connected by the concept of the line of flight. My hope is that this chapter will also offer a useful overview of the metaphysical framework of Deleuze and Guattari's project. The final chapter, titled '*A Thousand Plateaus* and Political Pragmatics', ties together the metaphysical and ethical concerns of the previous chapter with Deleuze and Guattari's political philosophy and shows how it is the concept of the line of flight which allows these elements to combine into a comprehensive philosophy of transformation. The chapter ends by demonstrating how the four senses of the line of flight discussed in Chapter 4 are transformed in *A Thousand Plateaus* to produce a mobile philosophical methodology which is general enough to apply to all forms of material and immaterial transformation.

In the conclusion, I return to the broad project of Deleuze and Guattari's philosophy, reading it alongside the more reflective analysis offered in the pair's final collaboration, *What is Philosophy?* Here I suggest that as well as producing a *philosophy of transformation* – in the sense that their work attempts to think about transformative processes – their collective writings can be seen as a *transformation of philosophy* – in the sense that their methodology is one which puts the discipline of philosophy into a state of continuous variation.

This book is not intended to offer a definitive interpretation of Deleuze and Guattari's philosophy. On the contrary, my hope is that it offers one route through their work; one possible orientation of thought that connects Deleuze and Guattari's works prior to their meeting with their major collaborations in *Anti-Oedipus* and *A Thousand Plateaus*. By following this route, I do not mean to rule out any others. For those who already have their own maps – those who have previously devised their own ways of navigating Deleuze and Guattari's oeuvre – this book is intended to offer another dimension that can be overlaid on theirs. For those who are relatively new to Deleuze and Guattari's writings, this book is intended as a first pass; a navigation that runs from *Difference and Repetition* and *Psychoanalysis and Transversality* through *Anti-Oedipus* to *A Thousand Plateaus*, and that can be treated as an initial mapping exercise, which will hopefully suggest new explorations in the future.

1

Deleuze and the Metaphysics of Difference

Depth, Flight and Transformation

At the time of publishing *Difference and Repetition* (1968) and *Logic of Sense* (1969), Deleuze had not yet begun to use the concept of the line of flight. His work from this time does, however, contain a number of clues as to the origins of this concept. Furthermore, at this stage in his career, and without explicitly framing it in these terms, Deleuze begins to grapple with the problem of transformation. The purpose of this chapter is therefore to track down these clues and to provide a strong basis for subsequent chapters, where the examination of the concept of the line of flight and the possibility of transformation, as they appear in the *Capitalism and Schizophrenia* series, will begin in earnest.

I have chosen to concentrate the majority of my analysis in this chapter on *Difference and Repetition*, not only because it is the text that contains the most comprehensive account of Deleuze's metaphysical programme, but also because it contains his most sustained comments on the problematics of traditional philosophical conceptions of space. As we will see, part of what animates Deleuze's engagement with the philosophy of space is his desire to conceptualise spatial relations as both generative and transformative, rather than as static and conditioning. This focus on the nature of spatial relations is also important because it is here that Deleuze will brush up against the terminology of the 'line of flight' as it appears in other intellectual domains.

As we will see, *Difference and Repetition* is scattered with critical references to traditional methods for representing space. Specifically, we find a large number of references to the way in which painters use techniques of linear perspective to simulate depth in their work. For Deleuze, these techniques can tell us a great deal about the kinds of assumptions that Western thought has made about the nature of space. Crucially, the phrase *ligne de fuite* is a common piece of terminology used in French to describe one feature of perspectival painting. This connection has been almost completely missed by Anglophone commentators and translators of Deleuze and Guattari's work: while many have noted that the French term *ligne de fuite* might have some connection to the French term *point de fuite*, a concept conventionally translated into English as 'vanishing point', there is an almost complete lack of recognition in the secondary literature that the phrase *ligne de fuite* is used in linear perspective to designate a specific line. Brian Massumi's note to his translation of *A Thousand Plateaus* is typical: '*Fuite* covers not only the act of fleeing or eluding but also flowing, leaking, and disappearing into the distance (the vanishing point in a painting is a *point de fuite*). It has no relation to flying.'[1]

Similarly restrained references to the possible connection with the concept of the vanishing point are made by Massumi elsewhere, and are echoed by Ronald Bogue, Jean-Michel Rabate, Janae Sholtz, Meaghan Morris and Edward Kazarian, among others.[2] The connection with linear perspective is only made in these instances to clarify what kind of escaping or disappearing might be implied by the French word *fuite*, and no direct reference is made to the technical meaning of the *ligne de fuite* in linear perspective.[3] In the latter sections of this chapter I will give a full account of the use of this term among theorists of linear perspective and will aim to show how Deleuze's critiques of the model of space that these techniques assume contain an implicit reworking of the concept of the *ligne de fuite*.

Deleuze's comments on linear perspective are, however, only given within the much broader context of his attempt to overturn many of the assumptions embedded in the philosophical canon. Before attempting to comment on his specific critiques of linear perspective it will therefore be useful to give a more comprehensive account of what is going on in *Difference and Repetition*. This analysis will also allow us to touch on a number of key pieces of terminology that will be useful in our analysis of both *Anti-Oedipus* and *A Thousand Plateaus*, including the distinction between the virtual and the actual,

[1] Deleuze and Guattari, *A Thousand Plateaus*, xvii.

[2] Kazarian, 'Line of Flight', 219; Morris, *Identity Anecdotes*, 195–6; Sholtz, *The Invention of a People*, note 18; Bogue, *Deleuze's Way*, 130; Bogue, *Deleuze on Literature*, 156; Bogue, *Deleuze and Guattari*, 110; Rabate, *Crimes of the Future*, 43; Lamarre, 'Diagram, Inscription, Sensation', 162.

[3] Bonta and Protevi are a notable exception (*Deleuze and Geophilosophy*, 106–7). This text references the importance of the *ligne de fuite* in linear perspective; however, the implications of this are not followed up.

the concept of the multiplicity, the distinction between intensive and extensive differences, and the individuation of spatio-temporal dynamisms.[4]

The Dogmatic Image of Thought

Deleuze's self-professed project in Chapter 1 of *Difference and Repetition* is '[t]o rescue difference from its maledictory state'.[5] The 'maledictory state' Deleuze is referring to here is the state of being subordinate to identity, such that 'difference' is only understood as the difference *between* two entities, which each possess their own identity. The problem, as Deleuze puts it, is that '[t]he difference "between" two things is only empirical, and the corresponding determinations are only extrinsic'; however, properly understood, '[d]ifference is the state in which one can speak of determination *as such*'.[6] His point here is that any conception of difference that relies on a prior distinction between objects of our judgement, which are said to differ from one another, has already assumed that each of these objects can be determined as individual objects, and such a procedure already requires them to have been *differentiated* from their surroundings. To avoid the circularity of this presupposition, Deleuze argues that philosophy must find a way of thinking the concept of 'difference-in-itself' as something positive, which differs not from other things, but only from itself.

In the first chapter of *Difference and Repetition*, after working through the various methods used by a number of canonical Western thinkers for conceptualising difference, Deleuze picks out Aristotle and Hegel as those who typify the main forms of philosophy's traditional misrecognition of difference most clearly.[7] According to Deleuze's reading, Aristotle defines difference in terms of contrariety, which he asserts, over contradiction or privation, to be the most

[4] While the majority of the conceptual framework presented in *Difference and Repetition* will be radically altered in Deleuze's collaborations with Guattari, it is also the case that much of Deleuze and Guattari's collaborative work can be read as a direct response to problems raised in *Difference and Repetition*. See Deleuze's preface for the English translation of *Difference and Repetition* (*Difference and Repetition*, xvii). See also Deleuze, *Desert Islands*, 238.

[5] Deleuze, *Difference and Repetition*, 37.

[6] Deleuze, *Difference and Repetition*, 36.

[7] Deleuze discusses Plato, Aristotle, Descartes, Leibniz, Spinoza, Kant, Hegel and Heidegger, among others (*Difference and Repetition*, 38–58).

perfect form of difference, because '[c]ontrariety alone expresses the capacity of a subject to bear opposites while remaining substantially the same'.[8] Hegel takes contrariety as his starting point but he 'extends it to the infinite' by requiring of absolute difference that it entails the identity of contraries. However, according to Deleuze's critique, both of these methods for defining difference rely on some prior understanding of identity, which itself requires an understanding of difference for its determination. We will never escape the vicious circle of definition by finding 'stronger' forms of difference, because the problem does not lie in the fact that Aristotle's or Hegel's conceptions of difference are somehow too weak, but in the fact that they only consider difference from the point of view of identity. The problem is not one of degree, but one of kind. Insisting on the need for a new kind of understanding of difference, Deleuze writes that 'a more profound real element must be defined in order for oppositions of forces or limitations of forms to be drawn'.[9]

In the central chapter of the book, Deleuze claims that conceptual philosophical thought has 'as its implicit presupposition a pre-philosophical and natural Image of thought'.[10] What this means is that, even though philosophers have often defined their practice by the way in which they banish all previously held assumptions, the very practice of philosophising has retained a set of implicit presuppositions concerning thought itself. What philosophers have taken for granted is 'not a particular this or that but the form of representation or recognition in general'.[11] This image of thought contains two distinct presuppositions that Deleuze will attempt to overturn, namely those of *good sense* and *common sense*. Good sense is the assumption that each of the faculties of the mind is faithful in principle and naturally tends towards truth. Common sense is the assumption that these faculties cohere in a common subject and share a common object. Despite his appreciation for the Kantian project, Deleuze picks out Kant as having taken both common sense and good sense for granted. He writes that 'the Kantian critique is ultimately respectful: knowledge, morality, reflection and faith are supposed to correspond to natural interests of reason, and are never themselves called into question', and the purpose of Kant's work is only to

[8] Deleuze, *Difference and Repetition*, 39.
[9] Deleuze, *Difference and Repetition*, 61.
[10] Deleuze, *Difference and Repetition*, 167
[11] Deleuze, *Difference and Repetition*, 166.

declare each of the faculties 'legitimate or not in relation to one or other of these interests'.[12] The acceptance of the two presuppositions of good sense and common sense has led philosophers to characterise thought as inherently representative, so that the quality of thought has been judged on its ability to represent the world accurately.[13] This representative image of thought presupposes a certain distribution of the empirical and the transcendental, resulting in an 'inability to conceive of difference in itself'.[14] Deleuze's task in *Difference and Repetition* is therefore to critique this distribution of the empirical and the transcendental to produce a 'thought without image' capable of thinking difference-in-itself.[15]

The fallout from rejecting both good sense and common sense as the foundation for thought is considerable. No longer can the apparent individuality of the subject of thought, or the individuality of the object of thought, be taken for granted. To give an indication of the consequences of this move I will give two quick examples of the kind of philosophical problems that arise. First, with neither good sense nor common sense on our side, it is no longer possible to take the agreed-upon sense of language for granted. If language appears to have a sense, so that individual words have individual referents, and individual signifiers correlate with individual signifieds, then this ordered and individualised reality of sense is what needs to be explained. Deleuze tackles this problem in *Logic of Sense*, where he reads Stoic philosophy alongside the writings of Lewis Carroll to offer a genetic account of the way in which sense arises out of non-sense. Here he argues that a 'surface' of sense is produced as a mediating boundary between the pre-conscious and pre-individual depths of nonsense and the transcendental and structuring force of the 'voice

[12] Deleuze, *Difference and Repetition*, 173. Deleuze's reading of Kant is not straightforward. While he recognises that for Kant, 'Ideas lead us into false problems', he does not attribute this error to the faculties themselves, but to their misapplication (*Difference and Repetition*, 214).

[13] For Deleuze, this model of representation relies on Plato's theory of the Forms, and his theory of recognition as anamnesis. Following Nietzsche, Deleuze therefore writes that 'the task of modern philosophy has been defined: to overturn Platonism' (*Difference and Repetition*, 71). For Deleuze's engagements with Plato, see *Difference and Repetition*, 154–6, and *Logic of Sense*, 145–4, 219–302.

[14] Deleuze, *Difference and Repetition*, 174.

[15] Deleuze, *Difference and Repetition*, 208.

of the heights'.[16] Deleuze's arguments in this book are organised as a series of paradoxes in which he describes both the dynamic genesis of sense, from the perspective of psychoanalytic development, and the static ontological genesis of sense.

Second, without good sense or common sense being assumed, the framework of spatio-temporal reality and the individuality of the here-and-now can no longer be taken for granted. If it is the case that experience is organised in such a way that space and time appear as regular and rationally ordered, and that the current moment appears to have its own individuality, then this structuring of phenomena is what needs to be explained. If the 'here and now' are presupposed 'as empty identities' and 'as abstract universalities', then the identity and universality of these categories must be accounted for.[17] This problem, concerning the given spatio-temporal structure of phenomenal reality, is what Deleuze attempts to respond to in *Difference and Repetition*. To a certain degree, Deleuze's response to this problem follows from Kant, who also recognises that the spatio-temporal structure of experience must not be assumed to organise the world as it is in itself, but only our phenomenal experience of it. However, Deleuze aims to go further than Kant by attempting to give an account of the categories of experience that is both transcendental and genetic. What makes both of these problems even more challenging is that in each case the apparent orientation of experience along a subject–object axis is also problematised and is taken to require an explanation.[18] In order to introduce Deleuze's solution to this problem, and to prepare us for his critiques of linear perspectival conceptions of space, we will first need to comprehend the distinction that he makes between the virtual and the actual aspects of reality.

The Virtual and the Actual

Commenting on a passage from Plato's *Republic*, Deleuze makes a statement that describes his project in *Difference and Repetition*: 'This text distinguishes two kinds of things: those which do not

[16] Deleuze, *Logic of Sense*, 271.

[17] Deleuze, *Difference and Repetition*, 63.

[18] Deleuze's characterisation of his philosophy as a 'transcendental empiricism' is defined by exactly this problem. While Kant's problem was 'How can the given be given to a subject?' and Hume's problem was 'How is the subject constituted within the given?', his own problem is 'How can a subject transcending the given be constituted in the given?' (*Expressionism in Philosophy*, 86).

disturb thought and ... those which *force* us to think.'[19] That which does not disturb thought is given by representation and includes all that appears to us in an actual and constituted reality composed of individual objects of thought. That which forces us to think is the problematic dimension of reality. If we are to think difference-in-itself, then we must learn to think these problems, which are real and yet do not present themselves to us in what is actual. To name those aspects of reality that are real without being actual, Deleuze uses the term 'virtual'. Deleuze's ontology is therefore composed of two aspects: the first includes what is given (including the subject to whom the given is given) and the second includes that which explains how the subject is constituted and how the given is given to such a subject. For Deleuze, 'the virtual and the actual are two mutually exclusive, yet jointly sufficient, characterisations of the real'.[20] While the actual aspects of reality are extended in space and time, the virtual aspects of reality are defined by the problems that such an extended entity has been actualised to solve.

In his article, 'Deleuze's Secret Dualism?', Dale Clisby offers us the useful example of a knot to explain the relationship between the virtual and the actual:

> [W]hat is 'actual' is that which appears to us in spatio-temporal reality. A knotted rope is one such example of an actual object. The virtual, on the other hand, explains the development of the actual object. In this case, a knot exists as the solution to a problem, perhaps, 'how do we fasten one object to another?'

What is key in this example is that the problem 'exists independently of the various actualised forms of objects that provide a solution to it'.[21] The virtual field may determine all the possible solutions to a problem, but the structure of the problematic field is not only possible, but real. For this reason, Deleuze is very clear that the virtual 'is opposed not to the real but to the actual. The virtual is fully real in so far as it is virtual.'[22] Because this virtual problematic field exists not only in possibility, but in reality, Deleuze describes the virtual as the structure of the object. He states: 'The reality of the virtual is structure.'[23]

19 Deleuze, *Difference and Repetition*, 175.
20 Boundas, 'Virtual/Virtuality', 300.
21 Clisby, 'Deleuze's Secret Dualism?', 128.
22 Deleuze, *Difference and Repetition*, 260.
23 Deleuze, *Difference and Repetition*, 260.

Let us take the example of a block of ice. There are certain things that are true about the structure of a block of ice, but that are not located anywhere in the extended spatio-temporal actuality of the object. The melting point of ice is a real and determinate point defined by the temperature and pressure at which the ice will change from a solid to a liquid. This point is not located anywhere in the actual space and time of reality, but it is nonetheless a real aspect of the block of ice. The 'structure' that Deleuze describes as virtual is not the extended spatial structure of the object, but the structure of the singular points, like the melting point of ice, that define its conditions. It is important to note here that, for Deleuze, the virtual, problematic structure of an object and the actual, extended qualities of an object are in constant interaction, and mutually presuppose each other, such that the reality of the object is produced by the relation between these two aspects.[24]

For Deleuze, the virtual does not resemble the actual, just as problems do not resemble their solutions. Instead, responding to Kant's understanding of an Idea as that which is not instantiated in actual reality and yet 'must be thought' according to certain categories, Deleuze describes the virtual as being populated by Ideas.[25] Unlike Kant, however, Deleuze takes these Ideas to be multiple and to operate as the structuring principle which gives rise to actual objects. We have already seen that Deleuze produces his theory of the virtual to combat the representational and dogmatic image of thought. This means that his conception of virtual Ideas must not take good sense, common sense or the category of individuality for granted. To avoid these potential pitfalls, Deleuze argues that virtual Ideas are not individual and that they are not self-identical. Instead, virtual ideas are composed of 'a continuum of differential relations' which differ from themselves, and which therefore contain their own difference.[26] This form of logical structure is what Deleuze will call the 'multiplicity'.

[24] It is a common misreading of Deleuze's work to assume that the virtual simply precedes the actual and gives rise to it. See, for example, Hallward, *Out of This World*. For correctives to this misreading, see Seigworth, 'Little Affect: Hallward's Deleuze', and Protevi, Review of Peter Hallward's *Out of This World*.

[25] Kant, *Critique of Pure Reason*, A245/B302; Deleuze, *Difference and Repetition*, 263.

[26] Deleuze, *Difference and Repetition*, 315.

Riemann and the Multiplicity

The concept of the multiplicity is used to designate a substantive and numerical property that is opposed to both the many and the one.[27] For Deleuze, the substantive categories of the 'one' or the 'many' are both aspects of the representational image of thought, which reduces reality to either a complete individual or a series of individuals. Neither of these options can capture the problematic nature of virtual Ideas. The concept of 'multiplicity' is important for Deleuze because it 'denounces simultaneously the One and the many, the limitation of the One by the many and the opposition of the many to the One'.[28] Simply put, a multiplicity is a collection of elements in which the elements themselves are completely indeterminate, are reciprocally determining in their relation to one another, and give rise to the complete determination of a virtual object. Speaking of virtual Ideas, Deleuze states that 'Ideas are pure multiplicities which do not presuppose any form of identity' and that 'Ideas are multiplicities: every idea is a multiplicity.'[29]

Deleuze borrows this concept from the work of the nineteenth-century mathematician Bernhard Riemann, a figure who became a regular point of reference for him.[30] Riemann's work is important for Deleuze because he sees it as the first successful attempt to formally describe how a collection of elements could be held in a relationship with one another, such that these elements would be indeterminate in themselves and yet wholly determined by their relations.[31] Such a collection would thus be constituted not simply by a set of individuals, but by the interrelations of a set of relations. Riemann's major contribution to the study of geometry came with his use of integral calculus to construct a theory of multiplicities, which could explain

[27] Deleuze, *Difference and Repetition*, 230.

[28] Deleuze, *Difference and Repetition*, 254.

[29] Deleuze, *Difference and Repetition*, 230, 243.

[30] Deleuze, *Bergsonism*, 39–40, 79, 117; *Foucault*, 14; *The Fold*, 179; *A Thousand Plateaus*, 36, 157, 532–6; *What is Philosophy?*, 124, 161.

[31] We might assume that Deleuze would champion Spinoza as the first to have achieved this feat. However, Deleuze never takes up Spinoza's terminology of attributes, substances and modes to talk about the transcendental field. This decision can probably be attributed to Deleuze's claim that the only fault in Spinoza's philosophy is that he defined the modes in relation to substance, rather than making 'substance turn around the modes' (*Difference and Repetition*, 377).

the properties of a space without giving a designation of the locations of points within that space.[32] When giving an exposition of the logical form of virtual ideas, Deleuze states specifically that he is using the 'Riemannian usage of the word "multiplicity"'.[33] Given the fact that both Edmund Husserl and Henri Bergson also developed the concept of the multiplicity, and given the fact that Deleuze also writes extensively on Bergson's use of the concept, it will be useful here to provide a careful analysis of Riemann's specific understanding of the concept of the multiplicity.[34] This will also allow us to give

[32] Riemann, 'On the Hypotheses which Lie at the Foundation of Geometry'. The term used by Riemann was not multiplicity, but *Mannigfaltigkeit*, which is most often translated into English as *manifold* or *manifoldness*. However, in French, it is most often translated as *multiplicité*, while the accepted English translation of the term *multiplicité* in Deleuze's work is *multiplicity*.

[33] Deleuze, *Difference and Repetition*, 230.

[34] While I will be taking Deleuze at his word when he says that he is relying on the Riemannian use of the concept of the multiplicity, it is worth sketching out Deleuze's reasons for choosing to follow Riemann here over Bergson. In *Time and Freewill* and *Duration and Simultaneity*, Bergson developed the concept of the multiplicity to elaborate the structure of the experience of time, or duration, as opposed to that of space. Here Bergson will argue that while space can be understood as a quantitative and discrete multiplicity, time, or duration, must be understood as a qualitative and continuous multiplicity. In his book on Bergson, Deleuze laments the fact that 'too little importance has been attached to the use of this word "multiplicity"', which in Bergson's work 'is not there as a vague noun corresponding to the well-known philosophical notion of the Multiple in general' (*Bergsonism*, 38). According to Deleuze, Bergson was aware of Riemann's concept, and the book *Duration and Simultaneity* should be seen as an attempt on Bergson's part to distinguish his own ideas from relativity theory by opposing his own concept of the multiplicity to that of Riemann (*Bergsonism*, 39). Unfortunately, for Deleuze's purposes, there is one fatal flaw in Bergson's understanding of the concept of the multiplicity. Bergson's mistake, according to Deleuze, was to align the distinction between continuous and discrete multiplicities with two further distinctions, namely the split between the qualitative and the quantitative and the split between the intensive and the extensive. While Bergson will say that duration is a continuous, qualitative, intensive multiplicity and space is a discrete, quantitative, extended multiplicity, Deleuze will keep these distinctions separate while also putting forward the argument that Bergson reintroduces quantity into continuous multiplicities. As we will see in the rest of this chapter, Deleuze will argue that both continuous and discrete multiplicities can be understood as quantitative because the relation between them is 'static and purely ideal' and 'implies no more than number' (*Difference and Repetition*, 218–19). On the other hand, Deleuze will argue that the question of intensity does not concern the relation between the kinds of multiplicity directly, but instead informs the process of individuation, which occurs between the virtual

a more precise account of how Deleuze attempts to define virtual ideas in such a way that they will contain difference in themselves.

Riemann's work responds to a particular problem that arose at the beginning of the nineteenth century. At this point, several mathematicians, including Carl Friedrich Gauss, Ferdinand Karl Schweikart, János Bolyai and Nikolai Ivanovich Lobachevsky, had all shown that it was possible to construct internally consistent geometries that contravened Euclid's fifth axiom. What these mathematicians had shown, contra Euclid, was that there was no way of proving *a priori* that parallel lines will not intersect when they are extended. In fact, these mathematicians had shown that the opposite was true: that it was possible to construct coherent geometrical systems in which, for any straight line, and for any point not on that line, there are either zero or multiple other straight lines that run through the point that are parallel to the initial line. In brief, space need not be 'flat' but could be 'curved' in several different ways. The problem facing Riemann was the following: if there are multiple possible, consistent geometries, then how are we to know for sure which of them is applicable in reality? While it is possible to use experience as a guide and to select the geometry which seems most applicable to space as it is experienced, this will lead the truths stated by geometry to lose their rigorous mathematical basis and become 'not necessary, but only of empirical certainty'.[35] In order to overcome this challenge, Riemann developed a new and particular form of non-Euclidean geometry, which aimed to provide a mathematical description of all possible spaces, or 'multiply extended manifolds', of which Euclidean space

continuous and the actual discrete multiplicity. For this reason, Deleuze will ultimately argue that 'the Bergsonian critique of intensity seems unconvincing' (*Difference and Repetition*, 299, 329). Craig Lundy is therefore incorrect to claim that 'Deleuze's understanding of intensity draws from Bergson's heterogeneous multiplicity' ('Emerging from the Depths', 74). Ansell-Pearson makes a similar error in claiming that Deleuze is entirely consistent in his acceptance of Bergson's theory of multiplicities (*Germinal Life*, 155). In his later works, Bergson sees the relationship between the two forms of multiplicity as a Russellian-style paradox: is the difference between qualitative multiplicities and quantitative multiplicities a qualitative or quantitative difference? In answer to this problem, Bergson talks about a qualitative multiplicity that represents a higher-order difference, which subsumes the difference between the two. In *Creative Evolution* the qualitative multiplicity becomes both 'a unity that is multiple and a multiplicity that is one'. See also Mullarkey, *Bergson and Philosophy*, 142–4.

35 Riemann, 'On the Hypotheses which Lie at the Foundation of Geometry', 380.

and the non-Euclidean spaces that had now been proved possible would be particular limit cases.

Up until the point at which Riemann tackled this problem, there was one method for representing curved spaces geometrically, namely by embedding these non-Euclidean spaces in a Euclidean space with an added dimension. For example, a two-dimensional surface with constant positive curvature can be represented as the surface of a three-dimensional sphere. The problem with using this process to overcome the metaphysical problem of how to select a single geometry out of the many internally consistent geometries available is that it begs the question: if we have abandoned Euclid's fifth axiom following the proofs that show that it cannot be taken as a necessary truth, then to assume the framework of a higher-dimensional *Euclidean* geometry will simply reintroduce the contingency of this form of geometry at a higher level. If Riemann wanted to define a geometry that could account for all possible, consistent geometries, without having to assume the applicability of Euclid's fifth axiom, then he would have to do so without also assuming the existence of any higher-dimensional Euclidean space.[36]

Riemann required a way to express the curvature of a space immanently. To do this, he turned to differential calculus. Differential calculus is a field of mathematics that concerns itself with the study of the rates at which quantities change. In practical terms, differential calculus does this by discovering the properties of singular points that lie on a curve. To take an example, in order to determine the speed of an accelerating object at a specific point in time, calculus can be used to measure the angle of the curved line used to represent the acceleration of the object at a specific point. Because this line is curved, it is not possible to determine the speed of the object by comparing the distance covered over a set period with the time taken to cover this distance. Instead, differential calculus solves this problem by *initially* considering the average velocity of the object over a period of time. By then slowly decreasing the duration used, our equation will approach the instantaneous velocity of the object at the point we want to consider. The shorter the duration we consider, the closer our result will be to the instantaneous velocity of the object. By making

[36] In Deleuze's attempt to define depth without simply assuming a 'fictitious third dimension' we can see an echo of this problem. Both Riemann and Deleuze recognise that to explain the extended dimensions of space a non-extended spatial thinking is required.

the duration tend to zero, we can discover the exact instantaneous velocity of the object. This is written in differential calculus using the symbols *dx* and *dy*, where each of these refer to the ever-decreasing, or infinitesimal, quantities used to determine the rate of change at the point. The most important thing to note here is that while the *dx* and the *dy* are indeterminate in themselves, by their mutual determination they fully determine the rate of change at a singular point.

Carl Friedrich Gauss, one of the originators of non-Euclidean geometry, and under whom Riemann had studied, had proved that it was possible to use calculus to analyse two-dimensional curved spaces without the need to embed them in a non-curved three-dimensional space.[37] Gauss showed that the curvature of a particular surface could be derived from the way that distances relate to each other on that surface, just as the curvature of a particular point on a line can be derived from the relations between two differentials on that line. Riemann developed Gauss's proof in order to apply it to multiply extended manifolds, or multiplicities, with any number of dimensions, so that a curved, n-dimensional manifold could be defined without embedding it in an n^{+1}-dimensional Euclidean space. By using this method, Riemann had showed that a multiplicity of n-dimensions, and with any possible curvature, could be analysed using a combination of n-dimensional geometry and differential calculus.

What Riemann found, however, was that when space is treated according to this form of differential geometry, and when curvature is understood intrinsically, it has several striking features that distinguish it from Euclidean space. Spaces whose curvature is expressed extrinsically, or whose curvature is expressed as a variation in another dimension, can be defined using a grid of regular points, which are metrically determined. Riemann refers to these multiplicities as *discrete manifolds* because relationships within the manifold occur between points whose location can be determined irrespective of the location of other points, and that hence form a discontinuous sequence. A discrete manifold of three dimensions, for example, can be defined using a Cartesian coordinate system, in which any point in that space can be determined by 'x', 'y' and 'z' values, which each define the distance of the point from one of the three axes. However, multiplicities in which curvature is expressed intrinsically cannot be defined by such a regular grid because the 'curvature' of the space is manifested as the variability of distances within the space. In a

[37] Greenberg, *Euclidean and Non-Euclidean Geometries*, 373–4.

curved three-dimensional space, the distances defining the 'x', 'y' and 'z' values would vary depending on their position in the manifold. Manifolds or 'multiplicities' of this type are called *continuous manifolds* because relationships within the manifold occur continuously throughout the space.[38]

In continuous multiplicities, unless curvature can be determined as regular, measurements of distance cannot be generalised across the space. This is due to the way in which the concept of quantity is applied here. Riemann explains that 'quantity comes in discrete magnitudes by counting, in continuous magnitude by measurement'.[39] While discrete manifolds are defined by regular points, so that the length of a line can be measured by counting the number of points it passes through, in a continuous manifold there is no such regular grid. As magnitudes can only be quantified by comparing one against another, in a continuous manifold this can only be done when one length constitutes a part of the other length. These measurements are only locally defined and cannot therefore be generalised across the manifold.

Riemann is clear that in the case of continuous multiplicities, all quantities can only be measured relative to one another, and this makes it impossible to give magnitudes any absolute quantity:

> Measuring consists in superposition of the magnitudes to be compared; for measurement there is requisite some means of carrying forward one magnitude as a measure for the other. In default of this, one can compare two magnitudes only when the one is a part of the other, and even then, one can only decide upon the question of more and less, not upon the question of how many.[40]

Here it is only possible to discuss quantity in relative terms. For example, it is possible to determine that a straight line A is longer than another straight line B, if B is included in A, and that B is

[38] Riemann offers the following definition: 'Notions of quantity are possible only where there exists already a general concept which allows various modes of determination. According as there is or is not found among these modes of determination a continuous transition from one to another, they form a continuous or a discrete manifold' ('On the Hypotheses which Lie at the Foundation of Geometry', 412). I have given my own definition above to highlight the importance of expressing curvature internally for the determination of curvature in continuous manifolds.

[39] Riemann, 'On the Hypotheses which Lie at the Foundation of Geometry', 413.

[40] Riemann, 'On the Hypotheses which Lie at the Foundation of Geometry', 413.

longer than another straight line C, if C is included in B. In this case, it is also possible to say that A is longer than C and therefore that the order of the lines in terms of their length is A, then B, then C. However, we cannot determine by how much each of these lines varies in length from the other two. For this reason, our method of measurement is restricted to the use of ordinal numbers, such as 1st, 2nd and 3rd, and we cannot legitimately apply any cardinal numbers to lengths, such as 1 cm, 2 cm and 3 cm. Riemann sums up the results of this investigation into the legitimacy of the use of measure in the case of continuous manifolds, stating that: 'the metric relations of the manifold are completely determined by the measure of curvature' and that given the impossibility of proving mathematically the necessary curvature of space, it is quite conceivable that 'the spatial relations of size are not in accord with the postulates of geometry'.[41]

The ultimate result of Riemann's work on the foundations of geometry was a radically new understanding of the nature of geometrical space. Riemann had shown that it was possible to describe curved spaces in any number of dimensions without relying on the assumptions made by Euclidean geometry.[42] In doing this, Riemann also showed that space should be considered fundamentally as a continuous, curved multiplicity, of which regular, Euclidean space is only one particular limit case. He also showed that space, when understood as such a continuous multiplicity, is necessarily non-metric, as relationships can only be measured comparatively rather than absolutely, using an ordinal number system and not a cardinal one. Most importantly, however, Riemann had shown not only that such an understanding of geometry was possible, but that it was the only way that geometry could be practised without assuming Euclid's fifth axiom, and without subordinating mathematics to physics, by

[41] Riemann, 'On the Hypotheses which Lie at the Foundation of Geometry', 421, 424. Riemann's argument at this point turns on the question of whether it is possible for us to assume 'flatness in the smallest parts' of space. Riemann follows up both possibilities, while Deleuze is specifically interested in the consequences of *not* making such an assumption. For a detailed account of Deleuze's interpretation of this aspect of Riemann, see Widder, 'The Mathematics of Continuous Multiplicities'. It is also due to arguments in this article that I have followed White's translations of Riemann over the more widely circulated Clifford translation.

[42] This application of differential geometry in n-dimensional spaces allowed Einstein to produce his theory of general relativity and the associated concept of space-time.

forcing mathematicians to justify the truth of their mathematical analyses on the basis of their applicability to experienced reality.

The Virtual Idea as Multiplicity

As we have already discussed, Deleuze claims that the virtual is populated by 'Ideas' that are composed of 'a continuum of differential relations', which differ from themselves and which therefore contain their own difference.[43] With Riemann's concept of the continuous multiplicity in hand, we are now able to give a clear picture of the logical structure of these virtual Ideas. Here we will see that Deleuze borrows from Riemann's use of differential calculus, but applies its insights outside of the strict field of geometry.[44]

The relevance of the differential *dx* in calculus, as that which is completely undetermined in itself but determinable in relation to another infinitesimal, *dy*, is profound for both Riemann and Deleuze. It was calculus that allowed Riemann to develop his own form of differential geometry and to develop his concept of the multiplicity. For Riemann, it is calculus that allows us to define a geometry that can account for a non-metric conception of space. For Deleuze, the *dx* is important at a conceptual level as that which is indeterminate in itself, but which is determinate when it is put in a relation.[45] The *dx* and the *dy* are each indeterminate but determinable elements, which are given a reciprocal determination in their relation, and which together absolutely determine a singular point. For Deleuze, it is this differential relationship between the indeterminate, the reciprocal determination and the absolute determination that defines the virtual Idea, and it is for this reason that he names

[43] Deleuze, *Difference and Repetition*, 315.

[44] It was Russell's view that Riemann's quantitative conception of the multiplicity restricted him to the field of mathematics (*An Essay on the Foundations of Geometry*, 25). However, in the lecture where he first presented the concept of the continuous multiplicity, Riemann offered the experience of colour as an example of a non-mathematical use of the continuous multiplicity. Deleuze's use of Riemann's concept of the multiplicity is certainly not constrained to mathematical examples.

[45] Deleuze's interpretation of the calculus is a contentious one. Deleuze wants to consider differentials not as having a minimal (but determinate) positive value, but as genuinely undetermined. For a comprehensive elaboration of Deleuze's discussion of differential calculus in *Difference and Repetition*, see Somers-Hall, *Deleuze's Difference and Repetition*, 131–43.

the structure of the Idea a multiplicity. Deleuze makes this explicit when he writes:

> The symbol *dx* appears as simultaneously undetermined, determinable and determination. Three principles which together form a sufficient reason correspond to these three aspects: a principle of determinability corresponds to the undetermined as such (*dx, dy*); a principle of reciprocal determination corresponds to the really determinable (*dy/dx*); a principle of complete determination corresponds to the effectively determined (values of *dy/dx*). In short, dx is the Idea.[46]

As a formal definition of the virtual multiplicity that does not rely strictly on differential calculus, Deleuze offers three distinct criteria. First, that a multiplicity is a variety of elements that are not determinate prior to the relations that they form with one another: 'the elements of the multiplicity must have neither sensible form nor conceptual signification, nor therefore, any assignable function'. Second, that in a multiplicity the elements come to be determined by the relationships that form between them: 'the elements must in effect be determined, but reciprocally, by reciprocal relations which allow no independence to subsist'. Third, that the structure of the multiplicity must be applicable to a number of different states of affairs: it 'must be actualised in diverse spatio-temporal relationships, at the same time as its elements are actually incarnated in a variety of terms and forms'.[47] For Deleuze, the Idea cannot be split into a number of elements that can be said to have any existence, or any sense, independent of their relation. The definition given by James Williams in his guide to *Difference and Repetition* highlights the way in which the multiplicity, as it is defined by Deleuze, prioritises relationships over pre-existing elements: 'The multiplicity is, therefore, a structure of elements defined as: things in continuous variation resistant to identification; relations between those elements; relations between those relations and actual relations; and relations between the elements and actual forms and terms.'[48] Following from the recognition that differential calculus is only a method for thinking such a structure, Williams is right to observe that our structural definition of the multiplicity should not be restricted to a mathematical reading

[46] Deleuze, *Difference and Repetition*, 217.
[47] Deleuze, *Difference and Repetition*, 183.
[48] Williams, *Gilles Deleuze's Difference and Repetition*, 146.

and that Deleuze's definition of the Idea as a multiplicity is 'allied to the statement that everything is a multiplicity'.[49]

While the mathematics of differential calculus provides the context for Deleuze's definition of the multiplicity, he is also clear that the structure of the virtual is not strictly mathematical in nature. Echoing his earlier comment about the fact that any space presupposes a problematic structure of primary depth, be it 'geometrical, physical, biophysical, social ... [or] linguistic',[50] Deleuze states that the virtual, understood as a problematic field, is not mathematical, but dialectic: '*Problems are always dialectical.*' In an attempt to clearly distance himself from what he sees as the pitfalls of the Hegelian dialectic, Deleuze is careful to state that by 'dialectic' he does not mean 'any kind of circulation of opposing representations which would make them coincide in the identity of a concept', but instead 'the problem element in so far as this may be distinguished from the properly mathematical element of solutions'.[51] Differential calculus is a method that allows us to think the differential nature of the virtual Idea, but the structure of the virtual problematic field is in no sense mathematical. Instead, 'What is mathematical (or physical, biological, psychical or sociological) are the solutions.'[52]

Before moving on from this discussion of the multiplicity of the Idea and its differential structure, it is worth making two clarificatory points. First, that the virtual Idea is not indeterminate or underdetermined, but completely determined. When discussing the virtual, Deleuze writes: 'We have seen that a double process of reciprocal determination and complete determination defined that reality: far from being undetermined, the virtual is completely determined.'[53] Second, that since the virtual is real, it is not a negative or inert transcendent field, but a positive and productive immanent one. In his work on Bergson, Deleuze is clear on this point:

> One only has to replace the actual terms in the movement that produces them, that is bring them back to the virtuality actualized in them, in order to see that differentiation is never a negation but a creation, and that difference is never negative but essentially positive and creative.[54]

[49] Williams, *Gilles Deleuze's Difference and Repetition*, 145.
[50] Deleuze, *Difference and Repetition*, 62.
[51] Deleuze, *Difference and Repetition*, 226–7.
[52] Deleuze, *Difference and Repetition*, 226–7.
[53] Deleuze, *Difference and Repetition*, 260.
[54] Deleuze, *Bergsonism*, 103.

This is a point reiterated by a number of interpreters of Deleuze's work and is captured by Michael Hardt when he writes that 'virtual being is not abstract and indifferent, and neither does it enter into relation with what is other than itself – it is real and qualified through the internal process of differentiation'.[55]

The task of giving an exposition of the differential structure of virtual Ideas is particularly important for Deleuze because it allows him to offer an alternative to the dogmatic image of thought, with its reliance on the subjective presuppositions of common sense and good sense. To put it bluntly, we might say that under the regime of the dogmatic image of thought it is not possible to think processes of transformation. By challenging this image, Deleuze is able to show that the apparent differences that we apprehend between actual entities rely on a virtual realm, which is real without being actual. Here, virtual Ideas form 'an n-dimensional, continuous, defined multiplicity'.[56] The differential relations between the elements of this multiplicity are the internal difference which gives rise to the structure of the world of actual, differenciated objects. It is this realm of virtual Ideas which allows Deleuze to define difference as logically prior to identity. We might also say that it is Deleuze's account of the differential nature of virtual ideas that allows him to think of transformation at a transcendental level. Here, the differential relations between virtual elements 'make the difference' between those actual entities that appear to us to differ from one another.

To be clear about the relationship between the differential relations that exist between and within virtual Ideas, on the one hand, and the differences that we perceive between actual objects, on the other, Deleuze utilises two different spellings of the word differen*t*iation/differen*c*iation. According to this distinction, we can say that there are differential relations (spelled with a 't'), which hold between the pre-individual elements of virtual Ideas. These compose the internal or immanent difference which explains the existence of differences (spelled with a 'c') that exist between actual entities in experience.[57] In his essay 'How Do We Recognize Structuralism', Deleuze gives the following explanation of these terms:

55 Hardt, *Gilles Deleuze: An Apprenticeship in Philosophy*, 14.

56 Deleuze, *Difference and Repetition*, 230.

57 Deleuze's concept of 'internal difference' comes from his reading of Bergson. He defines it as the 'unity of the thing and the concept' (*Desert Islands*, 33).

> Of the structure as virtuality, we must say that it is still undifferentiated (c), even though it is totally and completely differential (t). Of structures which are embodied in a particular actual form (present or past), we must say that they are differentiated, and that for them to be actualized is precisely to be differentiated (c).[58]

In brief, it is the virtual process of differentiation that explains the genesis of the actual process of differenciation.

Individuation, Intensity and Dynamism

There is one final aspect of Deleuze's metaphysical project in *Difference and Repetition* that we must clarify before we can offer a coherent outline of his critique of linear perspective, and before we can see how the concept of the line of flight is prefigured in this text – namely his account of the dynamic genesis of the individuation and dramatisation of 'spatio-temporal dynamisms'. While Deleuze's use of the concept of the multiplicity has shown how the structural relations of actual terms rely on the differential relations that are internal to virtual Ideas, these relations are static, while the world is dynamic and our experience of it is durational. To account for this, and to complete his genetic account of actual experience, Deleuze claims that we still require a dynamic and generative process to animate actualisation, by which a virtual structure can give rise to a set of actual differences. To put this point in more general terms, we could say that while the actual/virtual relation can give us an account of *difference in itself*, we are still lacking the requisite account of *repetition for itself*, which will offer a description of the process that drives the genesis of experience. To put this back into our conversation about transformation, we might say that while Deleuze's analysis of the virtual allowed him to think transformation at the level of the transcendental, it is his account of spatio-temporal dynamisms that allows him to think transformation in the empirical.

To appreciate why Deleuze believes it is necessary to offer an account of the dynamic and intensive nature of experience, it will be useful to remind ourselves why he characterises his philosophy

[58] Deleuze, *Desert Islands*, 179. For more information on the ways in which Deleuze uses these terms in 'How Do We Recognise Structuralism', *Difference and Repetition* and *Logic of Sense*, and more on how his understanding of structure changes when he begins to work with Guattari, see Thornton, 'The Rise of the Machines'.

as a 'transcendental empiricism'. At the point of writing *Difference and Repetition*, Deleuze was attempting to answer the traditional Kantian problem, namely 'How can the given be given to a subject?', by utilising a form of transcendental philosophy.[59] This can be seen in the preceding sections where Deleuze shows that the differential relations of virtual Ideas are the necessary preconditions for the possibility of the differences that exist in experience between actual entities. In other words, internal difference is the condition for external differences. Deleuze is also, however, grappling with what he sees as the traditional question of empiricism, namely 'How is the subject constituted within the given?'[60] It is to this latter problem that Deleuze's analysis of the intensive and dynamic nature of experience is directed.[61] His philosophical project does not stop here, but aims to synthesise these questions by posing the more complex problem, 'How can a subject transcending the given be constituted in the given?'[62]

In order to answer the empiricist's question of the constitution of the subject, Deleuze begins by recognising what he calls the 'privilege of sensibility as origin', which he claims 'appears in the fact that, in an encounter, what forces sensation and that which can only be sensed are one and the same thing'.[63] It is an encounter with pure sensation that instigates thought, so it is through an analysis of sensation that Deleuze will provide an empirical ground for his transcendental philosophy. What strikes Deleuze about thought's encounter with pure sensation is that, despite what Kant had claimed concerning the *a priori* nature of the structures of space and time, sensation is not necessarily extended spatio-temporally. Instead, sensation is intensive. What can only be experienced in sensation is its intensity. The level of intensity of a colour, or the intensity of a sound or a temperature, are not thinkable outside of sensation itself, that is to say, that they cannot be represented. The intensity of a colour is not necessarily experienced as covering a determinate space, or lasting for

[59] Deleuze, *Expressionism in Philosophy*, 86.

[60] Deleuze, *Expressionism in Philosophy*, 86.

[61] Deleuze's most direct answer to the question of the constitution of the subject is given in Chapter 2 of *Difference and Repetition*. Deleuze shows how, starting with the passive synthesis of habit, and via a process of repetition in which what is repeated is not the same but different, the subject–object relation is generated as an integral axis of actual experience.

[62] Deleuze, *Expressionism in Philosophy*, 86.

[63] Deleuze, *Difference and Repetition*, 182.

a measurable length of time. These intensities constitute a form of difference unlike that of the differential relations internal to virtual Ideas. Here, differences are always degrees of difference and are constantly changing in a dynamic field of intensity. Deleuze will claim that it is through an analysis of this 'intense world of differences' that we can account for the extended nature of experience. For this reason, intensity 'is precisely the object of a superior empiricism'.[64] Following this, Deleuze will try to show how this sensory field of difference, which is quantitative and intensive in itself, can give rise to the qualitative and the extended nature of both thought and experience.

The qualitative nature of experience relies on the differences in intensity expressed, for example, in colour, light, sound and heat. According to *Difference and Repetition*, sensation is simply the contraction of intensive differences. To put this another way, while sensory experience is qualitative, that which is within sensation and gives rise to sensation, and which transcendental empiricism attempts to capture, is a pure intensive quantity. However, Deleuze is not only interested in the intensive nature of sensation as a transcendental ground for the possibility of quality, but also as the explanation of extension. To understand this point we will need to recognise some of the key features of intensive differences. One such defining feature is the fact that while extensive differences are additive, intensive differences are not. Differences such as those of length, area and volume are extensive because they can be increased by adding to them and can be decreased by subtracting from them or by dividing them. For example, when a length of one metre is added to another length of one metre, the total length is two metres, and when this length is divided into two, we will have two one-metre sections again. The defining feature of intensive differences, on the other hand, is that they cannot be increased by adding or decreased by subtracting or dividing. Taking temperature as an example of an intensive difference, we can see that if we add one litre of water at 40°C to another litre of water at 40°C we do not get a body of water that is 80°C. Similarly, if we divide a body of water in two, the intensity of the temperature is not halved. The same can be said for colour or sound. Another distinctive feature of intensive differences it that here, increases or decreases in difference will result in a change of nature. For example, if a body of water is heated, it will alter its movement, eventually being transformed into a gas.

[64] Deleuze, *Difference and Repetition*, 69.

According to Deleuze, it is because changes in intensity lead to changes in nature that the explication of intensity also gives rise to extension as such. It is the intensities of heat internal to a body of water that determine the way that such a body is extended in space and time, and not the other way around. Manuel DeLanda sums up this position with the slogan, '*intensive differences are productive*', which he explains by writing that 'wherever one finds an extensive frontier ... there is always a process driven by intensive differences which produced such a boundary'.[65] The boundary distinctions used to measure differences in extension are themselves the result of intensive differences that have no spatio-temporal extension of their own. Deleuze writes that intensity is 'the uncancellable in difference of quantity, but this difference of quantity is cancelled by extension', going on to clarify that extension is nothing other than 'the process by which intensive difference is turned inside out and distributed in such a way as to be dispelled, compensated, equalised and suppressed in the extensity which it creates'.[66] Deleuze's analysis of intensity is central to his philosophical project, ultimately accounting for both the apparently qualitative nature of things and the way they are extended in space and time. He writes that 'there would no more be qualitative differences or differences in kind than there would be quantitative differences or differences of degree, if intensity were not capable of constituting the former in qualities and the later in extensity'.[67] It is intensity that generates extended differences and not the other way around.

According to *Difference and Repetition*, the aforementioned intensive field is populated by 'spatio-temporal dynamisms' and its explication goes by way of two distinct moments, namely 'individuation' and 'dramatization'.[68] In the first of these moments, bundles of intensity known as 'spatio-temporal dynamisms' become individual objects of thought. Here Deleuze is drawing heavily on Gilbert Simondon's explanation of the process of individuation to explain the genesis of individuated forms from a pre-individual field.[69] In the

[65] DeLanda, 'Space: Intensive and Extensive, Actual and Virtual', 81.

[66] Deleuze, *Difference and Repetition*, 292.

[67] Deleuze, *Difference and Repetition*, 299.

[68] Deleuze, *Difference and Repetition*, 313.

[69] Deleuze was heavily influenced by Simondon, referencing him in *Nietzsche and Philosophy*, *Difference and Repetition* and *Logic of Sense*, and then with Guattari in both *Anti-Oedipus* and *A Thousand Plateaus*, praising his work as 'a profoundly original theory of individuation, which entails an entire philosophy' (Deleuze, Review of Gilbert Simondon's *L'individu et sa genese*

second moment, spatio-temporal dynamisms dramatise virtual Ideas to produce the actual. To describe the relationship of spatio-temporal dynamisms to actualisation, Deleuze writes that '[t]hey are precisely *dramas*, they dramatize the Idea'.[70] This process of dramatisation does not occur within a metric structure of time and space, because these metric qualities only refer to extended entities.[71] Instead, it is through the dynamic unfolding of individuation and dramatisation that the very framework of extended space and time is created. According to Deleuze's analysis, the category of extensity 'does not account for the individuations that occur within it', and is only accounted for by the spatio-temporal dynamisms.[72]

Talking of this procedure, Deleuze writes that any difference of intensity 'is cancelled or tends to be cancelled in this system, but it creates this system by explicating itself'.[73] What is key for Deleuze here is that, in the process of cancelling themselves out, intensive differences create the extended structure in which this process occurs.[74] In this way, the process of dramatisation 'incarnates the two traits of the Idea, differential relations and corresponding singular points'.[75] It is through this incarnation that the virtual can eventually be fully differenciated, and can appear in the form of the actual. While some interpretations of *Difference and Repetition* assume that the process of individuation is actual, and must therefore presuppose the process of actualisation, Deleuze explicitly warns against making this mistake.[76] In Chapter 5, he writes that 'any reduction of individuation to a limit or complication of differenciation, compromises the whole of the philosophy of difference', and that individuation 'does not presuppose any differenciation; it gives rise to it'.[77] It is important to note here that Deleuze does not separate the two processes completely, or say that one is completely conditional on the other. Instead, these

physico-biologique, 43). See also Simondon, *L'individu et sa genèse physico-biologique*.

70 Deleuze, *Difference and Repetition*, 268.

71 Deleuze begins his analysis of dramatisation with Nietzsche, whose method, he claims, is precisely one of dramatisation because it relates all (actual) values back to an (intensive) will to power (*Negotiations*, 93–4).

72 Deleuze, *Difference and Repetition*, 288.

73 Deleuze, *Difference and Repetition*, 287.

74 See DeLanda, 'Space: Intensive and Extensive, Actual and Virtual', 81.

75 Deleuze, *Difference and Repetition*, 270.

76 For a full discussion, see Clisby, 'Deleuze's Secret Dualism?', 145.

77 Deleuze, *Difference and Repetition*, 308–9.

two processes embody a complex relation in which the process of individuation can only be understood in the context of the process of differenciation, or actualisation, to which it also gives rise.[78]

The intensive realm does not operate of its own accord. It is understood as a kind of theatre that requires stage-direction from the virtual Ideas. Taking the generative processes contained in an egg as inspiration, Deleuze writes: 'The world is an egg, but the egg itself is a theatre: a staged theatre in which the roles dominate the actors, the spaces dominate the roles and the Ideas dominate the spaces.'[79] So, while intensively defined spatio-temporal dynamisms drive the process of individuation, this process is directed by virtual Ideas to the extent that we can say that these Ideas are 'dramatised'.[80] Ultimately, Deleuze will combine the different processes discussed here into the combination 'differentiation–individuation–dramatisation–differenciation', which describes the production of actual experience: a process of individuation in an intensive field of depth produces spatio-temporal dynamisms in accordance with the virtual structure of the Idea; these dynamisms are then dramatised to produce an extended field of actual, differenciated elements that stand in relations of opposition and limitation to one another.[81]

The four different moments involved in this process are distinct and they do not play out in a linear order. Deleuze is careful to

[78] This form of complex causation between two different processes is not unusual in Deleuze's work. For example, it might be worth reading this relationship with reference to the 'quasi-cause' as it is discussed in *Logic of Sense*. The static process of actualisation and the dynamic process of individuation in *Difference and Repetition* could then be read alongside the static and logical ontological geneses that Deleuze discusses in the context of Leibniz and the dynamic genesis that he discusses in the context of psychoanalysis (*Logic of Sense*, 126–44, 214–20). These two texts do not, however, offer analogous readings of individuation, which is characterised as dynamic in *Difference and Repetition* but as the product of the static ontological genesis in *Logic of Sense* (*Logic of Sense*, 137).

[79] Deleuze, *Difference and Repetition*, 269.

[80] In an echo of Kant's famous claim that 'Thoughts without content are empty, intuitions without concepts are blind' (*Critique of Pure Reason*, A51/B 75), we could say that for Deleuze, 'Virtual Ideas without spatio-temporal dynamisms are empty, spatio-temporal dynamisms without virtual Ideas are blind.' However, Deleuze's account differs from Kant's, especially because, for Deleuze, the subject is not required to apply concepts to intuitions. On the contrary, the subject is created as a side-effect who experiences the process, without playing an active role.

[81] Deleuze, *Difference and Repetition*, 213.

clarify that the previously discussed process of differen*t*iation–differen*c*iation, which relates virtual Ideas to actual entities, relies on the activity of individuation–dramatisation. As Deleuze puts it: 'Individuation always governs actualisation.'[82] This means that while there are 'the differential relations which constitute the pre-individual field to be actualized', the actualisation of these differential relations is driven by the individuation and dramatisation of spatio-temporal dynamisms.[83] Returning to the example of the developmental process undergone by an egg, Deleuze explains that while the virtual aspect is defined by a set of differential relations, 'their actualisation is determined only by the cytoplasm, with its gradients and its fields of individuation'.[84] For Deleuze, the process of individuation is carried out in an 'intensive field' where pure intensities explicate themselves, and through this process individuate the differential relations of the virtual Idea. As Deleuze writes: 'Intensity creates the extensities and the qualities in which it is explicated; these extensities and qualities are differenciated', which is to say that they are actualised.[85]

Depth in Linear Perspective

As previously mentioned, even though he does not mention the concept explicitly in the text, Deleuze's work in *Difference and Repetition* approaches the concept of the 'line of flight' obliquely via his engagement with linear perspective. Now that I have outlined Deleuze's metaphysical project, I will give a short account of linear perspective, including a discussion of the use of the French phrase *ligne de fuite* in this context. Following this descriptive section, I will show why Deleuze finds the tendency in the history of philosophy to use linear perspective as a model for our understanding of space problematic, and exactly how he aims to critique such a tendency. Here we will see how Deleuze's discussion of the four-part process of differentiation–individuation–dramatisation–differenciation provides an alternative account of the genesis of the spatial structure of actual experience. Finally, putting all the previous work together, I will offer my own analysis of the somewhat spectral presence of the concept of the line of flight in *Difference and Repetition*.

[82] Deleuze, *Difference and Repetition*, 313.
[83] Deleuze, *Difference and Repetition*, 313.
[84] Deleuze, *Difference and Repetition*, 313.
[85] Deleuze, *Difference and Repetition*, 317.

We must begin with linear perspective itself. In the graphic arts, linear perspective is a technique for representing three-dimensional shapes or spaces on a two dimensional plane, such as a painting on canvas.[86] The techniques associated with linear perspective reach back to Greek and Roman painting,[87] but they were first studied and codified during the Renaissance by painters such as Piero della Francesca and Paolo Uccello.[88] The historical development of the linear perspectival technique during the fourteenth and fifteenth centuries is well documented, as are the ways in which this technique was closely tied to a new understanding of the nature of space.[89] The mathematical form of linear perspective was most clearly conceived in 1425 by Filippo Brunelleschi and later codified as *perspectiva artificialis*, or artificial perspective, by Leon Battista Alberti in his work *Della pittura* (*On Painting*), published in 1435.[90] For the artist, linear perspective is intended to provide a rational, geometrical technique for the systematic representation of objects in space. It does this by replicating the visual illusion that the parallel edges of rectilinear bodies converge at a singular point on the horizon. During his discussion of perspective painting in *Mathematics in Western Culture*, Morris Kline explains that, by developing this technique, theorists were 'motivated by far more than the desire to attain verisimilitude. The greater goal was understanding of the structure of space.'[91]

86 Here I will attempt to explain the theory of linear perspective in the language used by its progenitors. This requires the acceptance of a particular model of space, as it is thought in extension. We will see later that Deleuze's critique of linear perspective is tied to his critique of this understanding space.

87 For example, Agatharcus is thought to have used perspective in his *skenographia*, or stage sets. It is this sort of technique that Plato mistrusts in the arts: 'Thus (through perspective) every sort of confusion is revealed within us; and this is that weakness of the human mind on which the art of conjuring and of deceiving by light and shadow and other ingenious devices imposes, having an effect upon us like magic ... And the arts of measuring and numbering and weighing come to the rescue of the human understanding – there is the beauty of them – and the apparent greater or less, or more or heavier, no longer have the mastery over us, but give way before calculation and measure and weight' (Plato, *The Republic*, 602c-d).

88 For a discussion of the ways in which ancient perspectival techniques prefigured the development of geometric linear perspective in the renaissance, see White, *Perspective in Ancient Drawing and Painting*.

89 Kline, *Mathematics in Western Culture*, 150–69; Panofsky, *Perspective as Symbolic Form*.

90 Alberti, *On Painting*.

91 Kline, *Mathematics in Western Culture*, 157.

Linear perspective works by placing the canvas on an imaginary plane between the eye of the artist and the objects perceived. This plane, called the picture plane, sits at right angles to the point of view of the artist and acts as a screen on to which the light from the objects is projected. When a viewer takes up the point of view of the artist, by standing in front of the painting, the painted image forms an approximation of the artist's view. As the perceived size of an object decreases the further it is from the viewer, linear perspective reproduces this effect through foreshortening. The result is that two parallel lines in space are represented on the picture plane by two converging lines. As these lines recede infinitely into the distance they intersect at a singular point on the horizon. The point at which any two parallel lines converge is known as the *point de fuite* in French, and as the 'vanishing point' in English. This point does not have a specific location in the space being represented, but in the painting it is a singular point that orientates the eye of the viewer. A painting in linear perspective can have any number of vanishing points, depending on the number of pairs of parallel lines in the scene being represented. While a vanishing point or *point de fuite* refers to the point at which any two parallel lines on a plane will converge if they are extended until they intersect, the vanishing line or *ligne de fuite* refers to the line at which any two parallel planes will converge if extended until they intersect. The horizon line is the most common *ligne de fuite*, which represents the intersection of any two planes that are parallel with the ground plane (and are thus perpendicular to the eye of the viewer). However, an infinite number of other *lignes de fuite* are possible, corresponding to the existence of any two parallel planes in the space being represented. While two parallel lines on a plane that is not parallel to the ground plane will form a *point de fuite* that is not on the horizon, two parallel planes that are not parallel with the ground plane will form a *ligne de fuite* that is not coextensive with the horizon line.

The ability of linear perspective to accurately reproduce the experience of vision has been comprehensively contested. For example, in his systematic review of linear perspective, Erwin Panofsky noted that perspective painting makes a number of assumptions about vision, such as the stillness of the eye, that are rarely fulfilled in experience, and that the technique is not able to deal with either the stereoscopic nature of vision or the curvature of the retina. He states that,

> In order to guarantee a fully rational – that is, infinite, unchanging and homogenous – space, this 'central perspective' makes two tacit but essential assumptions: first, that we see with a single and immobile eye, and second, that the planar cross section of the visual pyramid can pass for an adequate reproduction of our optical image. In fact these two premises are rather bold abstractions from reality.[92]

For the purposes of our discussion, it is also worth noting one further point about linear perspective, which restricts the technique to the formation of an *approximation* of a scene as it is viewed by the eye, namely that while two parallel planes in our field of view seem to converge under certain circumstances, in the three-dimensional space being represented these planes do not converge and will therefore never intersect. While the *ligne de fuite* has a definite and located existence in the picture, it is defined by the position of the viewer and does not correspond to any line in the 'reality' of the space depicted.

Following the numerous critiques of linear perspective as a mimetic technique, a number of thinkers have also questioned the social or political neutrality of perspective painting.[93] Panofsky addresses the ways in which linear perspective was a kind of visual corollary of the Renaissance conception of the human being as a disengaged, individual and rational observer.[94] The historical question of the relationship between linear perspective and the development of modern subjectivity has also been addressed by thinkers as diverse as Marshal McLuhan, who claims that 'far from being a normal mode of human vision, three-dimensional perspective is a conventionally acquired mode of seeing',[95] and Michel Foucault, who offers an analysis of the mode of subjectivation carried out by the viewing of a perspectival painting.[96]

92 Panofsky, *Perspective as Symbolic Form*, 28–30.

93 One of the only current writers to offer a philosophical defence of linear perspective is Hubert Damisch, a student of Merleau-Ponty. Damisch offers a Lacanian reading of perspective and claims that the visual grammar of perspective painting is integral to the symbolic formation of subjectivity, in the same way that the grammar of indexicals in speech is necessary for the formation of the self-reflexive subject. See Damisch, *The Origins of Perspective*; and Wood, Review of *The Origin of Perspective*.

94 Panofsky, *Perspective as Symbolic Form*, 67.

95 McLuhan, *Counterblast*, 16.

96 See Foucault's analysis of *Las Meninas* by Velásquez, in *The Order of Things*, 3–18.

Difference contra Linear Perspective

As we might expect, Deleuze is strongly critical of the image of human experience, and the image of thought, contained in this theory of linear perspective. Put most simply, for Deleuze, the problem is that this way of speaking about vision makes several unfounded assumptions: we must assume a fully constituted viewing subject, already distinct from a fully constituted three-dimensional spatial reality; and we must assume that such a subject has an organised two-dimensional field of vision, from which he or she must deduce the existence of a third dimension. For Deleuze, it is precisely these assumptions that need to be explained. How is the subject generated? How is the object of experience constituted? How does experience come to be organised? In more general terms, we can also say that Deleuze critiques the model of linear perspective for its representational form and for its consistent attempts to cover over difference-in-itself and to reduce difference to the false differences of opposition and limitation. Deleuze's critique of linear perspective is therefore quite different from that of Panofsky, McLuhan and Foucault, as it is based on a metaphysical disagreement concerning the nature of space and the nature of the subject, rather than an empirical or directly political disagreement. He does not simply want to show that linear perspective is inaccurate, or that it is a historically located form of subjectivation, but that it is part of an image of thought tied up with the Euclidean model of space and the Cartesian model of the thinking subject.[97] Theories of linear perspective, assuming that vision is in some way analogous to the projection of an image on to a screen or canvas, take for granted the organisation of objects in a field of vision and try to deduce depth. Deleuze argues that depth, as a form of difference, must be thought independently of vision, and of experience, so that the genesis of such experience can be accounted for.

Perhaps Deleuze's most direct criticism of linear perspective concerns the way in which depth is supposedly generated in a field of view via the opposition between two forms that represent parallel planes. As Deleuze points out, the opposition between these planes,

[97] Descartes' discussion of the projection of light on to the retina in optics leads him directly to a theory of geometric space (*Discourse on Method*). For more on this problem, see Henry Somers-Hall's discussion of Merleau-Ponty's critique of the impact of Descartes' optical thinking on the development of linear perspective in *Hegel, Deleuze, and the Critique of Representation*, 115.

organised by their orientation towards a shared *ligne de fuite*, can only be understood if it is assumed that in vision they are 'spread out upon a flat surface' and 'polarised in a single plane'. The problem with this model is that it requires the implicit assumption of 'a fictitious third dimension' in which height and breadth can be differentiated from each other.[98] To put this another way, to interpret the apparent location and orientation of the two planes in question *as converging*, we must first recognise that this orientation can only exist in depth. During a discussion of the Hegelian dialectic, Deleuze extrapolates from this line of argument by claiming that philosophers have traditionally misunderstood difference as 'traced or projected on to a flat space' only when they have forced it 'into a previously established identity'. Deleuze goes on to state that the form of the identity that is all too often taken for granted is specifically the identity of the 'here and now'. He writes that 'the here and now are posited as empty identities, as abstract universalities which claim to draw difference along with them'. In direct contrast to this, Deleuze states that 'difference does not by any means follow and remains attached in the depths of its own space, in the here-now of a differential reality always made up of singularities'.[99] This comment returns us to one of the central problems of *Difference and Repetition*, namely how to think the genesis of the actual, without assuming in advance anything that is given in the actual. While actual entities are structured in an extended space and an extended time, the process that produces these actual entities cannot be structured in such a way. Talking specifically about the apparent separation of space and time as a duality of structures that contain all actual experience, Deleuze writes that this duality 'does not exist in the process of actualisation itself, but only in its outcome, in the actual terms, species and parts'.[100] What this section makes clear is that, when it comes to the question of space, a differential metaphysics requires a way of thinking the here-now, not as an empty identity to be filled by oppositions and limitations, but as a differential and pre-individual reality.[101]

[98] Deleuze, *Difference and Repetition*, 61.

[99] Deleuze, *Difference and Repetition*, 63.

[100] Deleuze, *Difference and Repetition*, 270.

[101] The assumption of the identity of the here-and-now is nothing other than the assumption of good sense and common sense, namely the assumption that different representations relate to the same object and that they cohere in a single subject.

We can now begin to see how Deleuze will offer his own, positive response to the problem of depth. Deleuze's recasting of the nature of difference in terms of a relation between the differential relations internal to the virtual Idea and the differences that exist between actual entities will provide a way of thinking the here-now as a form of differential reality, which does not presuppose any spatio-temporal extension. The difference that exists between the two planes in my field of view is formally determined by a set of differential relations that are purely virtual. It is possible to articulate this response in the terms of Riemann's theory of multiplicities. Just as Riemann had shown how we could avoid any assumption about the geometrical nature of space by creating an immanent geometry using differential calculus, Deleuze produces a metaphysical explanation of the genesis of space, while avoiding any assumptions about the structure of such a space, or of the structure of experience in general. Via a form of transcendental argument, Deleuze is able to define virtual ideas as having no identity, but only internal difference among pre-individual elements. This virtual field is a form of the here-now construed as a continuous multiplicity, which can be thought without imposing any particular spatial extension upon it.

Intensity contra Linear Perspective

Deleuze's critique of linear perspective does not, however, concentrate solely on the problem of difference, and it does not respond only with a theory of virtual multiplicities. On the contrary, perhaps the most consistent critique that Deleuze levels at linear perspectival forms of thinking is that they take for granted an organisation of the visual field. It may be the case that, given a two-dimensional representation of an extended space, it is possible to simulate depth, but the question remains, how would such a representation be given to a subject in the first place? Taking the most basic operation of linear perspective as an example, in which two parallel planes seem to converge on the horizon, Deleuze asks how each of these planes appear as distinct and individual entities in my field of vision in the first place. To answer this question, we will not only need to mobilise Deleuze's theory of the virtual, but we must return to his comments on intensity and the dynamic individuation and dramatisation of spatio-temporal dynamisms.

For Deleuze, before any form can be compared or opposed to other forms, it must become determinate in experience. In vision, we can say that the form must separate itself from an indeterminate background. In direct contrast to the way in which linear perspective relies on the mutual differentiation of two things from each other, Deleuze recommends that, 'instead of something distinguished from something else, imagine something which distinguishes itself – and yet that from which it distinguishes itself does not distinguish itself from it'.[102] Deleuze also writes here that 'form distinguishes itself ... from the ground, but not the converse, since distinction itself is a form'.[103] The point Deleuze is making here is deceptively simple; in order to claim that two planes in my field of view are parallel, or that they are converging, I first need to be able to make them out, and this requires a dynamic process by which they come to stand out in my field of view. Deleuze argues that such a process requires a primary dimension of depth. He writes: 'The law of figure and ground would never hold for objects distinguished from a neutral background or a background of other objects unless the object itself entertained a relation to its own depth.'[104] To put it another way, no figure could show up for me unless it did so out of the depth of my vision. Deleuze concludes that the relation between figure and ground 'is only an extrinsic plane relation' and that this relation presupposes 'an internal, voluminous relation between surfaces and the depth which they envelop'.[105] The question here concerns not actualisation as such, but specifically the individuation of figures in a field of view. As we have already seen, it is through the process of individuation that intensive differences are dramatised and ultimately generate extension. Thus, the individuation of figures must be explained by the relation between intensity and extension.

Framing the problem in this way, Deleuze claims that linear perspective assumes that space is extended, but extensity 'can emerge from the depths only if depth is definable independently of extensity'.[106] This means that we cannot use an operation that takes place in extension to give an account of the dimension of depth. Instead, we must understand that an intensive depth pre-exists the act of vision, in which the dynamic nature of the visual field is distributed before it takes on an extended spatial form. While the extended space of

[102] Deleuze, *Difference and Repetition*, 36.
[103] Deleuze, *Difference and Repetition*, 36.
[104] Deleuze, *Difference and Repetition*, 289.
[105] Deleuze, *Difference and Repetition*, 289.
[106] Deleuze, *Difference and Repetition*, 289.

actual entities is named the *extensum*, the intensive depth that is its transcendental ground is named the *spatium*:

> The extensity whose genesis we are attempting to establish is extensive magnitude, the *extensum* or term of reference of all the *extensio*. The original depth, by contrast, is indeed space as a whole, but space as an intensive quantity: the pure *spatium*.[107]

The *spatium* referred to here is the intensive space of spatio-temporal dynamisms, and the *extensio* is the space generated by their dramatisation. There are four key ways in which these two spaces differ; while the *spatium* is intensive, continuous, unlimited and immanently defined, the *extensio*, which is simply assumed in the linear perspectival model, is extended, discrete, bounded and defined transcendentally by an external measure. Instead of thinking of the extended forms as a surface which completely covers the depths of the *spatium*, the intensive relationship between determinate forms and their indeterminate background means that they are in a constant process of individuation. The result of this constant tension is that intensive space and extended space can never be fully separated from each other.[108]

It is interesting to note here the similarity between Deleuze's critique of linear perspective and that of Merleau-Ponty. Although Merleau-Ponty is only mentioned twice by name in *Difference and Repetition*, the influence of his phenomenological critique of linear perspective is hard to ignore.[109] Deleuze's claim that '[i]t is no use rediscovering depth as a third dimension unless it has already been installed at the beginning, enveloping the other two and enveloping itself as third', echoes almost exactly the wording used in 'Eye and Mind', where Merleau-Ponty writes of traditional conceptions of depth that: 'Once depth is understood in this way, we can no longer call it a third dimension. In the first place, if it were a dimension, it would be the first one.'[110] Although articulated in different terms, Merleau-Ponty's argument is based on the same form of critique as that of Deleuze, namely that any attempt to define depth through the opposition of forms is logically undermined by the fact that these forms cannot be determined apart from their relation in depth.

[107] Deleuze, *Difference and Repetition*, 289.
[108] Deleuze, *Difference and Repetition*, 37.
[109] Deleuze, *Difference and Repetition*, 77, 209.
[110] Deleuze, *Difference and Repetition*, 62; Merleau-Ponty, 'Eye and Mind', 140.

He states this by noting that 'there are forms and definite planes only if it is stipulated how far from me their different parts are'.[111]

Unlike in Deleuze's account, Merleau-Ponty is concerned with the ability of linear perspective to accurately describe our experience of vision, and unlike Deleuze he aims to recapture an originary and 'spontaneous' vision. Despite this difference, the influence of Merleau-Ponty's critique of depth on Deleuze is interesting to us here for two reasons. First because, unlike Deleuze, Merleau-Ponty specifically discusses the concept of the *ligne de fuite*:

> In spontaneous vision, things rivalled one another for my look and, being anchored in one of them, I felt the solicitation of the others which made them coexist with the first ... In perspective, I renounce that ambiguity and agree to let only that figure in my drawing which could be seen from a certain reference point by an immobile eye fixed on a certain 'vanishing point' [*point de fuite*] of a certain 'vanishing line' [*ligne de fuite*], chosen once and for all.[112]

The distinction made here by Merleau-Ponty, between the fluid and ever-changing experience of 'spontaneous vision' and the structured space of linear perspective with its dominating 'vanishing line' or *ligne de fuite*, shares much with Deleuze's approach. Both thinkers also refer to the error made by the linear perspectival model as a transcendental illusion.

There is, however, a second reason why Merleau-Ponty's influence on Deleuze is interesting to us here. While Deleuze is ambivalent towards the phenomenological project in general, the similarities between Deleuze's and Merleau-Ponty's critiques of linear perspective highlight a mutual commitment to a philosophy concerned primarily with a metaphysics of immanence. What they share is the recognition that the structure of reality cannot be considered from an imaginary, external, Archimedean point, from which it would be possible to provide the prior conditions for the possibility of that experience. For example, in his comments on the genesis of space, as we have considered them here, Deleuze is critical of any attempt to discover the spatial conditions for experience from a transcendent, non-spatial perspective. Instead, like many thinkers within the phenomenological tradition, Deleuze is committed to a philosophy that accepts its own

111 Deleuze, *Difference and Repetition*, 62; Merleau-Ponty, 'Eye and Mind', 140.

112 Merleau-Ponty, *The Prose of the World*, 52 (my parentheses). See also Merleau-Ponty, *The Visible and the Invisible*, 34, 119, 222.

inherently perspectival nature. This is worth clarifying in the context of his critique of linear perspective.

Deleuze's critique of linear perspective is not based on the way in which such a theory considers the genesis of space in relation to the perspective of a particular point of view. On the contrary, his criticism is that linear perspective assumes that any individual perspective is only one of many possible perspectives on an otherwise non-perspectival world. With Deleuze's theory of intensive space, perspective will not only be considered as an aspect of our perceptive apparatus, but as an essential element of the world.[113] Returning to Deleuzian terminology, we can say that both Merleau-Ponty and Deleuze show that the *extensio* must presuppose a *spatium*, because the difference that exists between a form and its background is an intensive and not an extensive difference.

The ligne abstrait *and the* ligne de fuite *in* Difference and Repetition

Given Deleuze's comprehensive critique of linear perspective, we might think that there is no way that the concept of the *ligne de fuite*, as it is used in perspective painting, could be recuperated by a Deleuzian metaphysics. However, to prefigure some of the ways in which the concept will appear later in his collaborative work with Guattari, I will offer two possible methods for such a recuperation. The first involves maintaining the sense of the *ligne de fuite* as a vanishing line, or horizon line, while detaching it from the frame of the visual field and relocating it as a transcendental condition for the emergence of such a field. For the second method, I will introduce the

113 Deleuze's perspectivism is worked out in *Difference and Repetition* through his attempt to 'reverse' Platonism, where the power of the *simulacra* is considered as the primary force that constitutes reality, over and above the power of the representative image (*Difference and Repetition*, 81). For more on Deleuze's imaginative reworking of Plato's use of the *simulacrum*, see *Logic of Sense*, 291. This critique of Platonism is closely aligned with much of the phenomenological project, but Deleuze departs from Merleau-Ponty in his attempt to give a positive account of the genesis of experience by broadening his philosophical view beyond the *actual* world, to the *virtual*. For a more detailed discussion of Deleuze's debt to Merleau-Ponty, and the way in which his perspectival account of the conditions of experience attempts to overturn Platonism, see Somers-Hall, 'Deleuze and Merleau-Ponty: The Aesthetics of Difference', and Somers-Hall, *Hegel, Deleuze, and the Critique of Representation*, 111.

concept of the abstract line (*ligne abstrait*), as it appears in *Difference and Repetition*, and show how these two concepts might relate, and might ultimately collapse into each other. By sketching out these two options, and by analysing them side-by-side, I hope to give an account of the role that the missing concept of the line of flight might play in our reading of *Difference and Repetition*. This reading will also give us one final opportunity to examine the precise relationship between the four different moments of differentiation–individuation–dramatisation–differenciation.

In standard accounts of linear perspective, the *ligne de fuite* is taken as a line that orientates the viewer within the visual field, by providing a line, nominally located at infinity, towards which parallel planes seem to converge. The problem with this account, according to the Deleuzian critique, is that it is also taken to appear within an already orientated visual field. If the *ligne de fuite* is a necessary condition for the orientation of vision, then it cannot also appear within an orientated vision. This problem might, hypothetically, be resolved by rethinking the *ligne de fuite* as a virtual line. Such a line would be real, in the sense that it marks something that really is significant, without being actual, in the sense that it is not located within an extended spatio-temporal framework. To rethink this line as virtual, we must recognise that it is not given in experience but acts as a necessary precondition for the genesis of experience. We previously examined the three criteria that Deleuze provides as a formal definition of the virtual multiplicity. First, in the virtual, elements are not determinate prior to the relations that they form with one another: 'the elements of the multiplicity must have neither sensible form nor conceptual signification'. Second, that these virtual elements come to be determined by the relationships that form between them: 'the elements must in effect be determined, but reciprocally, by reciprocal relations which allow no independence to subsist'. Third, that the structure of this virtual multiplicity must be applicable to a number of different states of affairs: it 'must be actualised in diverse spatio-temporal relationships, at the same time as its elements are actually incarnated in a variety of terms and forms'.[114]

If we take the horizon line as our example of a *ligne de fuite*, then we can see how it fulfils each of these criteria. A *ligne de fuite* is nothing other than a line that runs through, and connects, all *points de fuite* for a given plane. Each of these vanishing points is an

[114] Deleuze, *Difference and Repetition*, 183.

indeterminate element, defined only by the relation between parallel lines on a single plane. These indeterminate elements reciprocally determine one another to form a straight line, which can be actualised in any number of spatio-temporal relationships. That is to say, the horizon is actualised whenever and wherever such a reciprocal relation between vanishing points is generated. It is not the case that parallel objects define the location of the *ligne de fuite*, but that the *ligne de fuite* opens the possibility of parallelism.[115] In this way, it is possible to detach the *ligne de fuite* from the visual field and to conceptualise it as a virtual precondition for the genesis of any actual visual field. As a line that connects virtual elements, it should also be understood as the line that separates, and connects, the virtual and the actual. Only when a selection of virtual elements resonate with one another in this way will a field of vision be actualised. To draw such a line is an act of differentiation–differenciation. It is double-edged; it is both the point of convergence and the point of divergence between the virtual and the actual.[116]

A second method for recuperating the *ligne de fuite* can be accomplished by comparing it with the alternative concept of the *ligne abstrait*. In opposition to his criticisms of the practice of using linear perspective in painting to simulate depth, Deleuze writes positively about painters such as Odilon Redon, who prefer to use the *chiaroscuro* technique.[117] This technique uses only shading and continuous gradations of colour to convey a sense of depth. It does not rely on the distinct borders of objects, but on the way in which the intensity of light defines the relative positions of bodies. While no border lines

[115] By 'parallelism' here I only mean to denote the condition of being parallel. However, this discussion of the way in which parallel planes are generated might also apply to Deleuze's reading of Spinoza's famous 'parallelism' between extension and thought.

[116] The fact that this line is a convergence opens the possibility that it is here that the virtual can be glimpsed in the actual. Deleuze explores the possibility of escaping the actual through the contours of actual forms via an analysis of the subjects in Francis Bacon's paintings, who attempt to 'pass through the syringe and to escape through this hole or vanishing point functioning as prosthesis-organ' (*Francis Bacon*, 11–14).

[117] In the original French, Deleuze does not use the Italian *chiaroscuro*, but the French term *clair-obscur*. This resonates with Deleuze's critique of Descartes' distinction between 'clear and distinct' ideas and 'obscure and confused' ideas, to which Deleuze contrasts the 'clear-confused' and the 'distinct-obscure'. These alternative pairings are borrowed from Leibniz (*Difference and Repetition*, 315).

are drawn, 'abstract lines' are created by the divisions of light and dark. For example, if a body is lit from the side, so that one side of the body is in shadow, the edge of the shadow, where light fades into dark, will create a line that cuts across the face of the body. In a passage that beautifully reflects Deleuze's claim that forms can only be determined in relation to an indeterminate ground, he quotes Redon as stating:

> No plastic form will be found in my works, I mean any form perceived objectively, for itself ... All of my art is confined solely to the resources of chiaroscuro, and also owes much to the effects of the abstract line, that agent from a profound source, acting directly on the spirit.[118]

For Deleuze, an abstract line of this kind is neither virtual, nor actual, but intensive. It is a line that connects zones of intensity – here, intensities of light – to allow for the emergence of a determinate form against an indeterminate background. It is a line that individuates a form, and dramatises it, to allow for the actualisation of an object of experience. What is of extra interest to us here is that, in Deleuze's collaborations with Guattari, the abstract line, or *ligne abstrait*, will become synonymous with the line of flight.[119]

As an alternative example of the abstract line, Deleuze discusses the dynamics of a lightning strike. Deleuze calls the abstract line, 'the determination absolutely adequate to the indeterminate, just as the flash of lightning is equal to the night'.[120] Unlike a line that marks the border between two determined forms, the abstract line is described as a determination, 'which is not opposed to the indeterminate and does not limit it'.[121] The flash of lightning is of special interest to Deleuze, not only because it seems to differentiate itself from a dark sky, while the sky remains indeterminate, but because it is a connection brought about as a result of an intensive difference between points of differing electrical charge, and made between a set

[118] Deleuze, *Difference and Repetition*, 37. Deleuze cites the following reference: Odilon Redon, *A soi-meme: Journal, 186--1915* (Paris: Fleury, 1922), 63.

[119] Deleuze and Guattari, *A Thousand Plateaus*, 10, 218, 224, 226, 305.

[120] Deleuze, *Difference and Repetition*, 345. Deleuze also writes that 'like thunder and lightning ... spatio-temporal dynamisms come to fill the system' (*Difference and Repetition*, 144). The line of flight can also be understood in relation to the concept of the 'dark precursor' which Deleuze develops while discussing lightning as an example of actualisation (*Difference and Repetition*, 145–51).

[121] Deleuze, *Difference and Repetition*, 345.

of singular points.[122] By defining the abstract line in this way, and by using both the abstract line in a *chiaroscuro* painting and a lightning strike as his examples, Deleuze gives us a concept that differentiates, or 'makes the difference' between, the intensive field, or *spatium*, and extended space, or the *extensio*. It is a line that connects zones of intensity to allow for the distribution of an individuated entity in space and time, and thus allows for the distribution of space and time themselves. It is also a line of double orientation at which the intensive and the extensive simultaneously converge and diverge.

What I would like to suggest at the close of this chapter is that these two lines, the *ligne de fuite* and the *ligne abstrait*, are not wholly distinct, and that by thinking them together we can gain a clearer understanding of the four moments in the process of 'differentiation–individuation–dramatisation–differenciation'. As previously discussed, Deleuze's metaphysical project in *Difference and Repetition* is a kind of transcendental empiricism. Deleuze aims to show how the intensity of sensation, and the intensity of an encounter in thought, can provide the transcendental ground for the genesis of actual experience, with its subject–object orientation and its extended spatio-temporal structure. Showing how the *ligne de fuite*, once detached from the visual field, and the *ligne abstrait* relate to each other in the context of our experience of visual space can help us to see this process in action. A field of varying intensities of light, seen from no particular perspective and given no particular extension, begins to individuate as zones of intensity start to resonate with one another. The line that connects these zones of intensity is the *ligne abstrait*. The formation of this line is not, however, totally independent. The individuation of the line is directed by the structure of a virtual multiplicity. This is to say that a collection of indeterminate points reciprocally determine one another to create a complete determination of the line. This is the *ligne de fuite*, taken as a transcendental precondition for the genesis of vision. It is the virtual that directs the individuation and dramatisation of

[122] Somewhat surprisingly, the mechanics of lightning are not clearly understood by modern science. The basic process involves the polarisation of positive and negative charges within a storm cloud and a corresponding polarisation of charges in the ground below the cloud. When the electrical potential between the cloud and the ground reaches a certain threshold, the electrical energy passes through the atmosphere separating the two bodies, equalising the polarisation. See Rakov and Uman, *Lightning: Physics and Effects*, 4–12.

spatio-temporal dynamisms, and it is spatio-temporal dynamisms that dramatise the virtual Idea. As such, we can say that it is the *ligne de fuite* that directs the *ligne abstrait*, and it is the *ligne abstrait* that dramatises the *ligne de fuite*. It is through this interaction that actual forms take shape, become distinct from their background, and orientate themselves to determine the position of the subjective viewer.

The analysis I have provided here must be contextualised. Deleuze does not use the concept of the *ligne de fuite* in *Difference and Repetition* and does not compare the *ligne de fuite* to the *ligne abstrait*. However, by sketching out the possibility of this reading, I have aimed to show how it is possible to find a significant precursor for Deleuze and Guattari's later use of the concept of the 'line of flight' in Deleuze's earlier work. By doing this, the following chapters will be better positioned to show exactly what changes in the shift from *Difference and Repetition*, and to a lesser extent from *Logic of Sense*, to *Anti-Oedipus* and *A Thousand Plateaus*.

In brief, what we have seen here is that, below some of Deleuze's more explicit concerns in *Difference and Repetition*, his metaphysical innovations are designed to grapple with the possibility of transformation. His account of the virtual allows for a picture of a transcendental field that is transformative in nature, while his account of the dramatisation of spatio-temporal dynamisms allows for a conceptualisation of transformation at the level of the empirical. The metaphysical framework provided here is one that allows us to think not only processes of change that occur within a static spatio-temporal structure, but also to think of more fundamental processes of change in which the formation of the structure of reality and the transformation of this structure are coextensive.

Before moving on to see the effects of this metaphysics in Deleuze's work with Guattari, it will be useful to give an account of some of the themes in the intellectual and practical work that Guattari completed before he began his collaboration with Deleuze. This will allow us to give a full account of the problems that both thinkers were dealing with when they created the concept of the line of flight.

2

Guattari's Psychotherapeutic and Militant Escapes

The Militant Psychoanalyst

Guattari was, first and foremost, a political militant, and his theoretical work was all produced in an attempt to grapple with questions of political praxis. Unlike Deleuze, whose work aimed to solve long-standing philosophical problems, Guattari wrote that '[t]he whole fabric of my inmost existence is made up of the events of contemporary history'.[1] Shortly after Paris was liberated from the Nazis in 1944, Guattari joined the Student Hostel organisation, where his high school social science teacher Fernand Oury – a leftist activist and a great influence on the young Guattari – was in charge of recreational activities.[2] Guattari soon started to attend meetings of the French Communist Party, with whom the Student Hostel organisation had close ties.[3] From this point on, and until his death, Guattari would always be involved with communist groups. After his time in the youth wing of the French Communist Party, where he worked on its newspaper *Tribune de discussion*, and in the Union Nationale des étudiants de France, Guattari participated in alternative Trotskyist groups and on the subversive journal *La Voie communiste*.[4] He was greatly influenced by Trotsky's autobiography *My Life*,[5] and most of his early adult life was spent as an organiser of communist splinter groups. Always on the fringes of authority, and permanently uncomfortable with conformity, Guattari preferred the Trotskyist model of permanent revolution and self-emancipation. He maintained Trotsky's concern for the way in which party bureaucracy could stifle a genuinely proletarian movement and worked constantly to ward off the emergence

1 Guattari, *Psychoanalysis and Transversality*, 209–10.
2 Dosse, *Gilles Deleuze and Félix Guattari: Intersecting Lives*, 24–5.
3 Dosse, *Gilles Deleuze and Félix Guattari: Intersecting Lives*, 26.
4 Genosko, *Félix Guattari: An Aberrant Introduction*, 11.
5 Guattari, *Psychoanalysis and Transversality*, 209–10.

of Stalinist-style dictatorships at any level of the communist programme.[6]

At university, Guattari initially studied pharmacology before switching to study philosophy at the Sorbonne. However, he never settled into university life and in December 1950 Fernand Oury suggested that he escape the university and visit the psychiatric clinic at Saumery, where his brother Jean Oury was the director.[7] Jean, in turn, suggested that Guattari read Lacan's recent works, and then asked Guattari to attend Lacan's lectures on his behalf. In 1954 Guattari was invited by Lacan to attend his seminar at the Sainte-Anne psychiatric hospital in Paris, where he was the first non-psychiatrist to be a regular member.[8] Guattari would soon go into analysis with Lacan, ultimately qualifying as a Lacanian analyst and joining Lacan's psychoanalytic school, of which he remained a member for life. Jean Oury, who had previously worked at the famous St Alban clinic with the celebrated François Tosquelles, left Saumery to set up his own psychiatric clinic at La Borde in 1953. La Borde was founded on communist ideals as an asylum for psychotic patients, where the model was anti-bureaucratic and where the staff would alternate between manual and intellectual work.[9] Oury invited Guattari to work at La Borde, and in 1955 he moved there to take up a permanent organisational and therapeutic role. In what follows, it will be important to keep in mind that, as a Trotskyist political activist with an academic background in both pharmacology and philosophy, Guattari was working in a therapeutic clinic for psychotic patients. Here, as a follower and analysand of Lacan, Guattari was primarily concerned with putting psychoanalytic theory to work in the context of a psychiatric asylum operating under a communist model.

By the time he met Deleuze in 1969, Guattari had already developed a complex and distinctive conceptual style that utilised political, psychoanalytic and philosophical thinking to tackle the practical issues arising in his life as a militant psychotherapist. However, much of the secondary literature discounts Guattari's role in the collaborations

6 Guattari, *Psychoanalysis and Transversality*, 348–56.
7 Dosse, *Gilles Deleuze and Félix Guattari: Intersecting Lives*, 37.
8 Dosse, *Gilles Deleuze and Félix Guattari: Intersecting Lives*, 38.
9 Oury wrote a constitution for his new clinic under the title 'Year I' (Dosse, *Gilles Deleuze and Félix Guattari: Intersecting Lives*, 44).

with Deleuze, either by paying little attention to his writing[10] or by actively deriding Guattari's influence on his more philosophically accomplished counterpart.[11] The majority of Anglophone readers of Deleuze and Guattari therefore lack the resources to see how the conceptual innovations presented in the *Capitalism and Schizophrenia* series, including that of the line of flight, respond to problems that arise in Guattari's work prior to 1969.[12]

While Guattari does not refer to the *ligne de fuite* before his work with Deleuze, and while he only uses the term *fuite* a small number of times in his writing prior to 1972,[13] he does develop a number of theoretical devices that rely on the concept of an *escape*.[14] During the course of this chapter I will try to show the relevance of these references, and demonstrate how they become integral to Deleuze and Guattari's later project. The ten subsections in this chapter can be divided into two groups. The first five explore Guattari's psychotherapeutic work and his theory of group subjectivity. Here I will show how Guattari borrowed from Lacan and Sartre to rethink subjectivity as a

[10] For example, while Buchanan does reference some of Guattari's preparatory notes for *Anti-Oedipus* in *Deleuze and Guattari's 'Anti-Oedipus': A Reader's Guide*, he does not consider any of the essays written by Guattari prior to 1972. This is odd given Buchanan's comment that 'the secondary criticism on the work of Deleuze and Guattari has tended to overlook his contributions altogether or consign them to a merely secondary role' ('Deleuze, Gilles and Félix Guattari', 248). Holland fares slightly better in *Deleuze and Guattari's Anti-Oedipus: Introduction to Schizoanalysis*, where he includes mention of *Molecular Revolution*, which contains a concise selection of Guattari's work prior to 1972.

[11] See Žižek, *Organs Without Bodies*, 20. Also see Buchanan's comments on Žižek and Badiou's critique of Guattari in *Deleuze and Guattari's 'Anti-Oedipus'*, 135–6.

[12] See Watson's characterisation of Guattari's early work in *Guattari's Diagrammatic Thought*, 23. Guattari had his own form of Freudo-Marxism (*Psychoanalysis and Transversality*, 248, 278), and used the concepts of 'machine' (318–28), 'deterritorialization' (341) and 'war machine' (242, 262).

[13] In the English publications the French term *fuite* is translated variously as leak, escape or evasion. See *Psychoanalysis and Transversality*, 8/ii, 16/viii, 32/14, 87/61 and 202/148 (English/French pagination).

[14] Guattari regularly uses the French term *échappe* to refer to escape, for example when he talks about 'madness as something that escapes social determination' (*Psychoanalysis and Transversality*, 62/41). For other uses of *échappe*, see *Psychoanalysis and Transversality*, 59/37, 89/61, 89/62, 91/63, 123/88, 126/90, 129/93, 134/96, 153/111, 188/137, 236/174, 239/177, 337/255, 360/278 (English/French pagination).

group phenomenon, adding his own concept of the 'transversal line' to explain how the ability of such groups to interact with their milieu is determined by something that cuts across them, *escapes* them, and connects them with their outside. By paying attention to these lines, Guattari aimed to empower both therapeutic and revolutionary groups to affect the worlds in which they were embedded. Here we will also be able to take note of a general thematic in Guattari's practical work: as a psychotherapist and as a political militant, he was concerned with transformation. As a therapist, he is continually frustrated by the failure of psychoanalytic theory to account for personal and psychic transformation, finding that it always reads such conversions as if they were nothing but repetitions of previously discovered models of desire. As a militant, Guattari will also find himself agonising over the inability of Marxist discourse to think through the transformative nature of political action, always planning the next revolution according to the model of the previous one.

The five subsequent sections will explore Guattari's concept of the 'machine', defined as that which *escapes* structural relations. These sections can be read as a positive account of Guattari's attempts to devise a new conceptual language capable of expressing the real, transformative practices experienced in psychotherapy, in political revolution, and in their interaction. In these sections I will show how, in his essay 'Machine and Structure', Guattari used his concept of the machine to respond to Deleuze's work in *Difference and Repetition* and *Logic of Sense*. Finally, I will show how Guattari's machinic conception of desire arises from a combination of certain insights from Marx and Lacan. These two broad aspects of Guattari's work – the transversal line and the machinic nature of desire – will provide us with everything we need to explain the emergence of the concept of the line of flight in *Anti-Oedipus* and *A Thousand Plateaus*.

Sartre and Group Subjectivity

Guattari's development of a robust theory of group subjectivity can be understood as a reaction to the mismatch between the psychoanalytic theories he had acquired in his Lacanian training and the practical context of working with psychotic patients at La Borde. This mismatch occurred because while both Freudian and Lacanian psychoanalytic theory are interested in psychosis as an object of study, ultimately they agree that the traditional method of psychoanalytic treatment in the form of a 'talking cure' cannot be used to treat psychosis. Freud argued that the analyst–analysand relationship is at root a contractual one, and the psychotic patient has neither a strong enough ego nor a strong enough grasp on reality to uphold such a contract.[15] Despite the fact that Lacan wrote extensively on the question of psychosis, his explanation of it as a form of psychic 'foreclosure' led him to side with Freud, and to claim that any attempt to apply the therapeutic technique of psychoanalysis to psychosis is 'as stupid as to toil at the oars when the ship is on the sand'.[16]

Despite these warnings, this is exactly what Guattari would try to do. To sidestep the issue of the individual psychotic's inability to maintain a therapeutic relationship, Guattari developed a form of psychoanalysis that did not require a one-to-one relationship between the doctor and the patient, but which could operate at the level of the relationship between a large group of patients and the hospital as a whole. In this form of therapy, which, along with Jean Oury, Guattari would name 'Institutional Psychotherapy', the institution becomes an analytic tool capable of working simultaneously with all the patients in the hospital.[17] The aim here is to foster group subjectivity of a particular kind. The theory of group subjectivity used by Guattari relies on a distinction between 'subject groups' and 'subjugated groups'. To understand this distinction, it will be necessary to explore Sartre's theory of groups as it is developed in *Being and Nothingness* and *Critique of Dialectical Reason*, and Lacan's theory of the Symbolic as it is deployed in his early seminars.

Guattari admitted on a number of occasions that his conceptual work owed a great debt to Sartre, whom he idolised in the years before he took up his more long-standing Lacanian affiliation.[18]

[15] Freud, 'An Outline of Psychoanalysis', 26–37.

[16] Lacan, *The Seminar of Jacques Lacan, Book III*, 34.

[17] For more on the impact of the practices of Institutional Psychotherapy and Institutional Pedagogy on Guattari's work, see Thornton, 'Thinking and Writing Together'.

[18] 'Everything I said or did was obviously affected by him. His reading of annihilation, of detotalization, which became becoming for me, deterritorialization, his idea of seriality, of the pratico-inert, which informed my idea of the group-subject, his understanding of freedom, and of the commitment and responsibility of the intellectual, which he embodied, all of these remained imperatives or at least immediate givens for me.' Félix Guattari, 'Plutôt avoir tort avec lui', *Libération*, 23–24 June 1990, in Dosse, *Gilles Deleuze and Félix Guattari: Intersecting Lives*, 29. See also Guattari, *Psychoanalysis and Transversality*, 210. Guattari interviewed Sartre in February 1961; see Dosse, *Gilles Deleuze and Félix Guattari: Intersecting Lives*, 28–31, 33.

Perhaps surprisingly, Guattari does not draw any explicit connection between Sartre's critique of Freud and his own deviations from psychoanalytic orthodoxy.[19] Instead, most of Guattari's interactions with Sartre concern the question of the relation between subjectivity and communism.[20] In the *Critique of Dialectical Reason*, Sartre aimed to create a synthesis of his earlier existentialist position and that of his burgeoning Marxism by reconciling the concept of freedom that he had developed in *Being and Nothingness* with the concrete social context of the subject. Here Sartre moves away from his model of the human being as a distinct and isolated object of study and considers the relevance of the economic, political and social structures in which the individual exists. Sartre aims to immerse the subject 'in a material world which radically conditions and limits it'.[21] The result is that one of the central themes that runs through the *Critique* is 'the nature of our bond to each other'.[22]

In the first chapter of part three of *Being and Nothingness*, Sartre had explored the way in which the relation between the act of looking at another person and recognising their subjectivity, and the subsequent act of being looked-at by the other, and thus seeing oneself from the perspective of the other, allows for one to see oneself as an object in the world. Following this, Sartre also comments on how a similar process can occur for groups: '[T]here are two radically different forms of the experience of the "we", and the two forms correspond exactly to the being-in-the-act-of-looking and being looked-at.'[23] In the *Critique of Dialectical Reason*, Sartre returns to the process of group formation in more detail, now more aware of the ways in which group interactions form the conditioning environment for the emergence of the individual. Here Sartre describes first the process by which a selection of individuals come together to from a group and then goes on to explain the different ways that this group can develop and eventually break down. I am going to concentrate on

19 Sartre's accusation is that Freud's metapsychology initially splits the mind into distinct parts to overcome the problem of self-knowledge, but then treats at least some of these parts as capable of self-knowledge. See Sartre, *Being and Nothingness*, 50. See also Gardner, *Sartre's 'Being and Nothingness'*, 123.

20 For example, where Sartre aims to establish 'whether the principles and truths that constitute Marxism allow subjectivity to exist and have a function' (Sartre, *What is Subjectivity?*, 3).

21 Anderson, *Sartre's Two Ethics*, 88.

22 Catalano, *A Commentary on Jean-Paul Sartre's Critique of Dialectical Reason*, 31.

23 Sartre, *Being and Nothingness*, 415.

the distinction Sartre draws between a selection of individuals loosely united around the same object, or what Sartre calls a 'series', and the first form of group cohesion, which he calls a 'group-in-fusion'.

A 'series' is a collection of individuals who have no common connection other than the fact that they are part of a particular gathering. There is no internal connection between the members of the series and, as such, each of the members is effectively alone among others. Sartre gives the example of people waiting in a queue, who form a group only in the most basic sense, because they all have a similar relation with something outside the group, namely whatever it is they are queuing for. As other, more politically motivated examples, Sartre mentions the workers in a factory and the consumers in a market.[24] A series is constituted by an external determination in which each of the members is 'looked at' by something outside the group.[25] As such, each of the members of the series is defined in contradistinction to the surrounding others. In a series, I am simply that which is not the other; my place in the queue, the market or the factory is defined in opposition to the place of the others. As Sartre writes:

> In the series, however, everyone becomes himself (*as Other than self*) in so far as he is other than the Others, and so, in so far as the Others are other than him ... every member is serial by virtue of his place in the order.[26]

The series is only a group in the sense that it is defined as such by something external to it. Due to this reliance on an external 'common object', the series is incapable of acting as a group. In the case of the queue, this 'third' or 'common object' would be the item being queued for, and in the case of the factory the 'common object' could be the commodity being produced, or even the capitalist who owns the factory, to whom each of the workers sells their labour. As Sartre writes: 'I have described *serial being* as the determination of the bond of alterity as a unity of plurality by the exigencies and structures of the common object which in itself defines this plurality as such.'[27] It is this reliance on an external common object that constrains the series to inactivity.

[24] Sartre, *Critique of Dialectical Reason*, 256, 277.
[25] Anderson, *Sartre's Two Ethics*, 96–7.
[26] Sartre, *Critique of Dialectical Reason*, 262.
[27] Sartre, *Critique of Dialectical Reason*, 303.

In the *Critique of Dialectical Reason*, Sartre attempts to explain the possibility of agency by making a distinction between what he names 'praxis', which is free, self-conscious, purposive or active consciousness working on matter, and what he names the 'practico-inert', which is the worked matter, the matter in which past praxis is embodied, or sedimented praxis. For Sartre, the series is incapable of acting as a community and taking up a praxis, and as such it is said to be embedded in the practico-inert. He states that the series is defined by 'relations which are established in the practico-inert field between the *individual* activities of men', and that 'this serial being is constituted as a *negative unity*'.[28] As an alternative to this powerlessness, according to Sartre, it is possible for the members of a group to join in common action and to form a 'group-in-fusion'. This occurs when, instead of each defining themselves by their relationship with an external object, the members of the group turn to one another and recognise themselves in one another. Describing the change in relation between members of a series and members of a group-in-fusion, Sartre writes: 'Through the mediation of the group, he is neither the Other nor identical: but he comes to the group as I do; he is *the same* as me.'[29]

If a queue of people is a good example of a series, then a group-in-fusion is formed when the people in the queue recognise their shared grievance, overcoming their mutual alienation. Now the position of each member of the group is no longer defined negatively by its alterity to the other members, but reciprocally.[30] Those in the queue can now work together to take what they are waiting for, or work to produce it themselves. Subsequently, each individual becomes defined by his or her place in the group; the group is no longer defined by its position of 'being looked at', and the group appears *as a group* from its own perspective.[31] According to Sartre, the act

[28] Sartre, *Critique of Dialectical Reason*, 303.

[29] Sartre, *Critique of Dialectical Reason*, 377.

[30] In a striking similarity with Deleuze's distinction between continuous and discrete multiplicities, Sartre claims that the distinction between a cardinal and an ordinal number system is analogous to that between a series and a group-in-fusion (*Critique of Dialectical Reason*, 262–3).

[31] In these cases, Sartre claims the 'third party' can be each member for the others, or the praxis of the group (*Critique of Dialectical Reason*, 377). These different forms of group determination produce a 'group-in-constraint' or a 'pledged group' (*Critique of Dialectical Reason*, 420). See also Santori, *Sartre on Violence: Curiously Ambivalent*, 41–5. Sartre applied this model to the question of

of entering into a group-in-fusion increases the power and freedom of each individual, because it provides a context in which to become active.[32] Utilising the language of *Being and Nothingness*, we can say that in the formation of a group-in-fusion, the members turn away from 'bad faith', escape their embeddedness in the practico-inert, accept the responsibility of their radical freedom, and become capable of taking up a praxis.[33]

Guattari was taken by Sartre's distinction between the series and the group-in-fusion and would try to apply it in the psychiatric hospital as a model for the production of group subjectivity among patients. If psychotics are those who have been excluded from society and from action, and if those in the hospital are defined by the act of being looked at – most commonly by the doctors – then perhaps if they could turn to one another and define themselves via a form of group praxis, thus becoming a group-in-fusion, they could overcome the marginalisation which they face and could work to reshape the institutions that subjugate them. We can see here why Guattari's development of Institutional Psychotherapy had both a therapeutic and a political dimension. The production of group subjectivity among the patients could never remain a personal affair, as their group action would need to be turned against the practico-inert structures that conditioned them, including the state, the legal system, and all structures of power. However, for Guattari, it is not enough to simply produce group subjectivity in the hospital; instead it must be done in a particular way, to guard against the possibilities of destructive group identifications. To understand how Guattari attempted to apply this theory of groups *in a particular fashion*, it is important to recognise the ways in which it came to be embedded within a strictly Lacanian psychoanalytic framework.

psychoanalysis, claiming that the analyst can become the 'third party' by which the subject of the analysand can relate to itself, See Gardner, *Sartre's 'Being and Nothingness'*, 186.

32 Anderson, *Sartre's Two Ethics*, 97–8.

33 There may be a linguistic connection here between Sartre's definition of bad faith, or 'la Mauvaise foi', as a fleeing from freedom, or 'la fuite devant la liberté', and Guattari's use of the word *fuite* in his work with Deleuze.

Lacan, the Symbolic and 'Full Speech'

Guattari was ultimately critical of Sartre's theory of groups because it failed to recognise the crucial difference between group identification and group subjectivity. To overcome this issue, Guattari would incorporate Lacan's distinction between the Imaginary and the Symbolic into his own theory of group subjectivity. Lacan's distinction between the Imaginary and the Symbolic is explained clearly in his first three seminars, given between 1953 and 1956, at exactly the time Guattari was first working on his theories of group subjectivity.[34] According to this model, the process of ego formation begins in the mirror stage, when an infant first recognises its own reflection. Lacan contends that before this point the child is not able to differentiate between itself and the world around it, but that by seeing an image of itself it becomes aware that it is an individual thing separated from the world. However, in this moment, the infant feels threatened by its image. Unable to control its own body, the child feels inferior to the image, which is clearly constituted and appears complete. To compensate for this inferiority the child appropriates the image it sees in the mirror as the image it has of itself: this constitutes the birth of the ego. The contest that initially defines the ego's relation with its mirror image recurs throughout life in the relation that the individual holds with the 'other'; specifically, the ego is always defined against the image of the other and by internalising the image of the other.[35] As this whole process occurs at the level of images – the ego is the *image* one has of oneself that is generated in contrast to the *image* of the other – Lacan names this register of reality the 'Imaginary'.

For Lacan, this process of ego formation at the level of the Imaginary is very different from the process of subject formation, which occurs only with the child's entry into language. In his early seminars, Lacan argued that the social field is essentially linguistic and that, as a social being, the subject only emerges within the structure of language.[36] According to this model, it is by saying the word

[34] In 'An Introduction to Seminars I and II' Miller writes: 'The imaginary/symbolic distinction is the main thrust of the seminar' (13).

[35] See 'The Mirror-Stage as Formative of the I as Revealed in Psychoanalytic Experience', in Lacan, *Écrits*, 75–81.

[36] 'Prior to signifying something, a sign signifies to someone. Lacan thereby emphasised the fact that a patient speaks *to* someone ... He stressed the social function of language – language as a social link' (Miller, 'An Introduction to Seminars I and II', 17).

'I' that one can represent oneself with a signifier and locate oneself within the structure of language, and subsequently in the wider social field. Following Saussure, Lacan claims that the subject, like the signifier, is not defined by its relation to a signified (some object for which it stands), but instead by its relation to other signifiers. The subject is constituted by its social relation with other people, in and through language. For Lacan, 'the subject is the agency that understands meaning, the agency correlated with meaning', and as such, '[w]e call "subject" that instance or agency which understands meanings or is correlated thereto, such that there is no meaning without a subject'.[37] While the ego was defined at the level of the Imaginary by its relation with an 'other', in what Lacan calls the 'Symbolic' register of reality the subject of language is defined by its relation to the whole structure of language, which predates it and conditions it. This structure of language, which Lacan also equates with the 'law' and ultimately the oedipal law of the father, and which is what one addresses oneself to when one speaks, Lacan calls the 'big Other'. For Lacan, the ego and the subject are not the same thing: they are generated out of two different processes, and they do not necessarily cohere in reality. Lacan clearly states that 'the *ego* is never just the subject'.[38] Guattari follows Lacan here almost to the letter, but leaves open the possibility of applying this distinction to group formations when he writes: 'A subject is not necessarily the individual or even *one* individual.'[39]

While Lacan is careful to distinguish the ego, as a feature of the Imaginary, and the subject, as a feature of the Symbolic, he does not separate the two absolutely, but attempts to describe their interaction by way of a diagram he names the L-Schema. If the ego is constituted by its relation to an 'other' and the subject is constituted by its relation with the 'big Other', these relations form two different axes, namely the Imaginary axis and the Symbolic axis. These two axes 'are situated in such a way as to intersect and constitute a cross' and '[t]he imaginary relationship – in other words, the relationship that derives from the mirror stage – is an obstacle to the establishment of a truly symbolic relationship'. This means that one must 'trespass upon or cross over the imaginary in order to pave the way to the

37 Miller, 'An Introduction to Seminars I and II', 22.
38 Lacan, *The Seminar of Jacques Lacan, Book II*, 177.
39 Guattari, *Psychoanalysis and Transversality*, 69.

symbolic'.[40] For Lacan, in the process of psychoanalytic treatment, the analyst is tasked with helping the patient form a cohesive subject position. What matters here is the relation that the analyst holds with the subject and not with the ego of the analysand. The analyst and the analysand must work to 'cross over' the Imaginary axis of the ego and constitute their relationship in the register of the Symbolic – this is why Lacan was so staunchly opposed to ego-psychology. While the ego is purely imaginary and based on phantasy, the subject is able to speak and to communicate, and thus to interact. Stressing the difference between the imaginary nature of the ego and the symbolic nature of the subject, Miller states that:

> The imaginary level is fundamentally characterized by aggression, so we have to distinguish the level of language, where understanding and dialogue are possible, from the level of the imaginary ... The imaginary is war; the symbolic level of speech is language, and its fundamental phenomenon appears to be peace.[41]

Guattari, at this point a loyal follower of Lacan, found that Sartre's theory of groups did not distinguish between the Imaginary and the Symbolic registers of reality. For Guattari, this meant that Sartre's theory of groups, based as it is on an explanation of the differing dynamics of the act of looking at and the act of being looked at, would be unable to distinguish the Imaginary effects of group phantasy and group identification from the Symbolic effects of group subjectivity. Following Lacan's emphasis on the importance of the Symbolic register for the production of subjectivity, but applying it to the question of groups, Guattari states: 'The concept of group subjectivity implies the development of a theory of the signifier in the social field.'[42] To put Guattari's insight another way, we can say that Sartre's category of 'groups-in-fusion' is too broadly construed because it does not distinguish between group identifications, at the level of the Imaginary, and group subjects, at the level of the Symbolic.

One clarificatory point is required here concerning the relation of language to the Imaginary and the Symbolic in Lacan's early seminars. Despite the fact that the Symbolic is understood as essentially linguistic, while the Imaginary is not, our use of language, and the

[40] Miller, 'An Introduction to Seminars I and II', 29.
[41] Miller, 'An Introduction to Seminars I and II', 21.
[42] Guattari, *Psychoanalysis and Transversality*, 128.

analysand's use of language, is not confined to the Symbolic realm. It is also possible for speech to be used along the Imaginary axis, as a tool for the antagonistic mirroring that defines that relation. Lacan codifies this by stating that the ego only has access to 'empty speech' in which true desire is avoided or repressed in favour of imaginary identifications. Here language is used only to determine the ego in its relation to an 'other'. On the other hand, when a subject is engaging with another on the level of the Symbolic, this subject has access to 'full speech', which is performative and which allows access to desire.[43] In this case, the speaking subject is addressing himself not only to an 'other', but to the 'big Other' of language itself. The subject is taking part in a collective discourse in which communication and dialogue are possible.[44]

Subject Groups

In his group-therapeutic work at La Borde, Guattari was aware that the formation of groups is not always productive: 'Group life can have harmful effects: when people use the other as a pretext to quietly turn inward and let things happen.'[45] In order to aid in the formation of groups in the hospital, while avoiding the pitfalls of group identifications and obstructive group phantasy, Guattari produced his own theory of group subjectivity that took Sartre's theory of groups from the *Critique of Dialectical Reason* as a model, but reinscribed it within a Lacanian framework. Guattari's theory of group subjectivity relies on a distinction between subject groups and subjugated groups. Just as the collection that Sartre named a 'series' was defined by an external determination, Guattari's 'subjugated groups' are those that 'receive their law from the outside'.[46] Like those in a 'series', subjugated groups are unable to take up a praxis and are conditioned by the inertia of the practico-inert. They form 'a subjectivity which is lost to view in the otherness of society', and consequently they 'are only something passive for themselves'.[47] Just as Sartre claims that a series will become a group-in-fusion when it is

[43] Lacan, *The Seminar of Jacques Lacan: Freud's Papers on Technique*, 107.

[44] For more on full and empty speech, see Soler, 'The Symbolic Order (II)', 43–7.

[45] Guattari, *Psychoanalysis and Transversality*, 345. See also Guattari's comments on 'dependent groups' in *Psychoanalysis and Transversality*, 119.

[46] Guattari, *Psychoanalysis and Transversality*, 64.

[47] Guattari, *Psychoanalysis and Transversality*, 107, 71.

able to define itself by an internal relation between its members, for Guattari, the formation of a subject group is 'based on the assumption of an internal law', which gives the group a 'vocation' and allows it 'to control its own behavior and elucidate its object'.[48]

However, Guattari's distinction diverges from Sartre's on several crucial points. First, Guattari explains that subject groups differ from subjugated groups because the former relate to one another at the level of the Symbolic, while the latter relate to one another at the level of the Imaginary: 'the subject group is articulated like a language and links itself to the sum of historical discourse, whereas the dependent group ... has a specifically imaginary mode of representation, that is the medium of the group phantasies'.[49] Guattari is consistent here in using Lacanian terminology to explain the essential differences between subject and subjugated groups, often using the Lacanian concept of *méconnaissance*, which characterises the child's relationship with its image in the mirror stage, to describe the dynamics of the subjugated group.[50] Second, unlike Sartre, Guattari is keen to stress the fact that the distinction between subject and subjugated groups is not absolute; the two coexist in any group situation. Guattari's distinction is 'not so much with two sorts of group, but two functions, and the two may even coincide'.[51] Just as Lacan uses the L-Schema to explain how subject formation at the level of the Symbolic must 'cross over' the Imaginary relation between the ego and the 'other', subject groups must always contend with their potential subjugation on the axis of group phantasy. Third, while Sartre spoke of the agency of the group-in-fusion in terms of 'praxis', following Lacan Guattari defines the agency of the group in relation to its ability to engage with speech. For Guattari, the subject group 'hears and is heard' and is defined by 'a subjectivity whose work is to speak'.[52] To be more precise here, we should say that the subject group has access to 'full speech' while the subjugated group cannot get beyond the barrier of 'empty speech'.[53]

48 Guattari, *Psychoanalysis and Transversality*, 64, 107.
49 Guattari, *Psychoanalysis and Transversality*, 224.
50 Guattari, *Psychoanalysis and Transversality*, 79, 258.
51 Guattari, *Psychoanalysis and Transversality*, 224.
52 Guattari, *Psychoanalysis and Transversality*, 107.
53 As we will see, Guattari's theory of semiotic relations differs significantly from Lacan's semiotics, based as it is on structural linguistics. For the moment it is enough to note that unlike Sartre, but like Lacan, Guattari concentrates on the semiotic relations of groups.

Applying this Guattarian-Lacanian development to our previous Sartrean example of the queue, we can say that the group that is formed when those standing in the queue turn to one another can either be a subject group or a subjugated group. Imagine that the group produce banners and badges with a chosen slogan, which they chant at the shop owner to express their frustration. It might be the case that the only effect of this act of collective speech is to unite the members of the group. It provides a way for the members to align their group phantasy at the level of the Imaginary by defining who is in the group and who is outside it, but it does not allow for the production of discourse in the Symbolic. Guattari would call this group a subjugated group with access to 'empty speech' only. Alternatively, the group might use language to address their demands to the shop owner, or to organise an alternative access to the product. This requires them to relate to one another symbolically, through a shared language in which they can listen and have dialogue. In this case Guattari would say that the group have access to 'full speech' and constitute a subject group.[54]

As well as these numerous Lacanian adaptations of Sartre's analysis of groups, Guattari also makes at least two further modifications that are not borrowed from Lacan. First, unlike Sartre, Guattari does not give any precedence to the role of the individual over that of the group. While Sartre starts from the assumption that a collection of fully individuated subjects exists, and then goes on to explain how they can come together to form a group, Guattari is interested in how subjectivity at the level of the group and the level of the individual are co-produced. Guattari's group practice at La Borde works in the opposite direction to that of Sartre. Institutional Psychotherapy functions precisely by producing a group subject in the hospital, within which psychotic patients will be given the necessary structure to define their own subject positions. As Guattari's theory of groups progresses, he will dismiss the concept of individual subjectivity completely and claim that all subjectivity is always group subjectivity. In 'We are all Groupuscules', he writes: '[t]he model of the individual ... is too fragile' and we must therefore 'build a new form of subjectivity that no longer relies on the individual and the

[54] The key distinction between full speech and empty speech does not concern the content of speech, but whether it engages in social discourse and whether it is heard. Guattari would readily admit that political chants and slogans fulfil the conditions of full speech in many cases.

conjugal family'. Coining a term that will later be used regularly with Deleuze, Guattari names these new units of group subjectivity, 'collective agents of enunciation'.[55]

Second, because Guattari recognises that subjugated groups and subject groups are not different general categories, but that subjectivity and subjugation exist as the two sides of any group formation, it is not simply the case that a group will be defined either by an external or an internal determination, but instead that any group will be defined by the level of internality/externality of its determining relations. For Guattari, a group is made up of a multiplicity of relations, some of which exist between members of the group while others connect a member of the group with something outside the group, while both internal and external connections may be either Symbolic or Imaginary. Group subjectivity is produced when a relative stability is attained between the internal and external relations in the group, which Guattari names 'the notion of *subjective consistency*'.[56] For Guattari, the elements that make up any subject group must relate to one another internally; however, the subject group is defined as much by those connections and relations that escape the group structure as by those that uphold it. This is a line of thought that Guattari takes up with Deleuze in *Anti-Oedipus* and *A Thousand Plateaus*, where the question of how a group relates to that which escapes it becomes of central ethical and political importance. Interestingly, one of the first occurrences of the concept of the 'line of flight' in Deleuze and Guattari's work comes in Deleuze's preface to *Psychoanalysis and Transversality*, where he praises Guattari's theory of group subjectivity for 'pursuing the flows that constitute myriad *lines of flight*' and allowing 'collective agents of enunciation to emerge'.[57]

Transversality and Escape

In his role at La Borde, Guattari aimed to find ways of transforming subjugated groups into subject groups by altering the institutional operations of the hospital. To do this, Guattari would turn once again to his Lacanian training and adapt the conceptual tools he found there, in this case reworking the traditional psychoanalytic concept

[55] Guattari, *Psychoanalysis and Transversality*, 368–9.
[56] Guattari, *Psychoanalysis and Transversality*, 346.
[57] Guattari, *Psychoanalysis and Transversality*, 16.

of transference into that of transversality.[58] For Freud, transference refers to the process by which an analysand redirects previously repressed emotions and desires towards the analyst, projecting the role of another person on to the analyst, usually the mother or father. According to Freud, this process can be useful for analysis when, by taking on the projected role, the analyst is able to help the analysand work through unresolved family relationships. However, it can also interrupt analysis when the love or hate that the analysand ends up feeling towards the analyst blocks the possibility of progress. Lacan, who dedicated his 1960–61 seminar to the concept and named it as one of the 'four fundamental concepts' of psychoanalysis in his seminar of 1963–64, recast the double-edged nature of transference using his own distinction between the Imaginary and the Symbolic.[59] For Lacan, transference is ineffective when the analyst becomes a mirror for the analysand's ego. Here the relation is imaginary and the analysand treats the analyst like an 'other' with whom he or she has an antagonistic relationship. Alternatively, transference can be effective when the analysand treats the analyst not as an 'other', but as the 'big Other', or what Lacan also calls the 'subject-supposed-to-know'.[60] As Miller explains: 'As long as Lacan defined transference as imaginary, it remained a moment of inertia in psychoanalytic experience ... His theory of transference changes when he tries to offer a *symbolic* definition of transference.'[61] Where the transference operates in the Symbolic it can be used to foster subject-formation in the analysand.

Guattari borrows this latter, Symbolic understanding of transference from Lacan, but takes it out of the analyst's office, where the relation can only ever be enacted by two people, and puts it to work in the hospital.[62] At first, Guattari describes how a relation

[58] For a full discussion of the ways in which the concept of transversality evolved over the course of Guattari's career, see Genosko, 'The Life and Work of Félix Guattari', and Goffey, 'Guattari and Transversality'.

[59] Lacan, *The Seminar of Jacques Lacan, Book VIII*; and 'The Transference and the Drive' and 'The Field of the Other and back to the Transference', in Lacan, *The Seminar of Jacques Lacan, Book XI*, 123–262.

[60] For more on transference, see Lacan, *Écrits*, 184, 503.

[61] Miller, 'An Introduction to Seminars I and II', 23.

[62] For Guattari's description of the difficulties involved in reworking this concept for use in group therapy, see *Psychoanalysis and Transversality*, 123–4: 'In this somewhat eclectic way, we came to recast a series of notions from various sources for our institutional use ... Some of these notions, like the superego and fantasy,

exists between the institution as a whole, which plays the role of the analyst, and the group of patients in the hospital, who play the role of the analysand. However, as Guattari is aware that group subjectivity is not produced by any single relation but by the 'subjective consistency' that is produced out of a multiplicity of interacting relations, he proposed 'to replace the ambiguous idea of the institutional transference with a new concept: *transversality* in the group'.[63] In geometry, a transversal is defined as a line that crosses any two lines in the same plane at two distinct points.[64] Adapting this usage, Guattari states: 'Transversality is a dimension that tries to overcome both the impasse of pure verticality and that of mere horizontality' and that describes 'communication among different levels and, above all, in different meanings' within the hospital.[65] As we have seen, Guattari's distinction between subjugated groups and subject groups recognises the ways in which various internal relations, which tend to be horizontal, and various external relations, which tend to be vertical, exist for the group simultaneously. The degree of openness of this web of relations is what mediates between that side of the group which achieves its own subjectivity and the reverse side which remains subjugated. The overall degree of openness of the group is what Guattari names the 'coefficient of transversality'.[66]

In the hospital, a wide range of relationships exist between the patients, the doctors, the nurses and the other staff, all of which play a role in determining the 'coefficient of transversality' in the hospital.

were easier to adapt due to the ambiguities of Freudian doctrine, which does not differentiate between their use at the level of individuals or groups. Other notions, like transference, involved a deeper reassessment.'

63 Guattari, *Psychoanalysis and Transversality*, 112.

64 Transversals are used in Euclidean geometry to determine whether two lines are to be considered as parallel to one another. According to Euclid's fifth postulate, Deleuze's critique of which I discussed in the previous chapter, if two lines are parallel then the consecutive interior angles produced by the transversal that crosses them will be supplementary, the corresponding angles produced will be equal, and the alternate angles will also be equal.

65 Guattari, *Psychoanalysis and Transversality*, 113.

66 Guattari, *Psychoanalysis and Transversality*, 113. For more on the role of 'openness', see Guattari, *Psychoanalysis and Transversality*, 108. Here Guattari imagines the effects on a group of horses in a field who are all wearing blinkers. If the blinkers are set too tightly then the horses will not be able to see one another and will not move around freely. However, if one were to open the blinkers too quickly, this could frighten the horses. Guattari equates the degree of openness of the blinkers with the group's coefficient of transversality.

The analyst's job is to work with all of these different groups to maximise communication between the various levels of language that exist there and the different meanings that they produce. As Guattari states: 'it is possible to change the various coefficients of unconscious transversality at the various levels of an institution'.[67] Most of the time the technical language of the doctors, the social discourse of the cleaning staff and the schizophrenic speech of the patients do not connect with one another. However, by fostering communication between these different levels, these groups can interact, and group subjectivity can be produced. For example, Guattari explains how 'the overt communication that takes place within the circle consisting of the medical superintendent and the house-doctors may remain on an extremely formal level, and it may appear that its coefficient of transversality is very low', while the 'coefficient existing at department level may be found to be much higher: the nurses have more genuine relationships among themselves, in virtue of which the patients can make transferences that have a therapeutic effect'.[68]

Guattari also argued that the formation of subject groups was central to the practice of Marxist politics. According to his analysis, the communist movement can be understood as an attempt to transform the proletariat from a subjugated group into a subject group. Like the factory workers that Sartre gave as an example of a 'series', the working classes under capitalism are organised as a group only by a form of external determination by capital. To break out of this subjugation, the proletariat must escape the Imaginary identification which organises them *as workers* and enter the Symbolic register as a cohesive group subject. One effect of Guattari's psychoanalytic evaluation of communist struggle is that it gave him a fundamental distrust of the concept of the avant-garde, or of the centralised Party which claims to act on behalf of the people. Guattari is clear on this point when he states: 'A subject group is not embodied in a delegated individual who can claim to speak on its behalf.'[69] The problem with

[67] Guattari, *Psychoanalysis and Transversality*, 113.

[68] Guattari, *Psychoanalysis and Transversality*, 113–14. There is an echo here of Guattari's later distinction between macro- and micro-politics: 'Everyone knows that the law of the State is not made by the ministries; similarly, in a psychiatric hospital, de facto power may elude the official representatives of the law and be shared among various sub-groups.'

[69] Guattari, *Psychoanalysis and Transversality*, 219.

the Party structure is that while '[i]t is always the mass of the people who have created new forms of struggle ... the Party and the unions have systematically retreated from the creativity of the people'.[70] For this reason, Guattari always aligned himself with the ideas of permanent revolution and self-emancipation, and aimed to ward off the possibility of dictatorships establishing themselves in communist circles.

While Guattari was a member of the French Communist Party he was constantly critical of it, claiming that 'revolutionary organization has become separated from the signifier of the working class's discourse ... the subject groups spoken of by Marx'.[71] He was especially critical of those intellectuals who proposed to interpret Marx's texts on behalf of the people, claiming that, '[u]nlike Althusser, the subject group is not a theoretician producing concepts'.[72] As an alternative to this intellectualism, Guattari helped set up a number of splinter groups which aimed to dislodge the hegemony of the Party line. Pushing against both the idea of the 'mass movement' and that of the 'avant-garde', Guattari spoke of these groups as 'analytical groups', defined as 'a group that positions itself against the "normal" order of things'.[73] In order to produce subject groups consisting of workers, intellectuals and young people, capable of producing their own statements and locating themselves in the symbolic order, Guattari helped set up collaboratively written communist newspapers, including the *Tribune de Discussion* which he described as 'an internal dissident organ within the French Communist Party'.[74] In both his psychotherapeutic work and his political militancy, Guattari had discovered that to produce transformations in the normal order of things it was necessary to produce subject groups capable of taking responsibility for their own world. To do this, he would manipulate the transversal lines that cut across the varying levels of discourse in any particular milieu, opening the coefficient of transversality in the group, and ultimately reconfiguring the power dynamics that subsisted there.

[70] Guattari, *Psychoanalysis and Transversality*, 218.
[71] Guattari, *Psychoanalysis and Transversality*, 218.
[72] Guattari, *Psychoanalysis and Transversality*, 219.
[73] Guattari, *Psychoanalysis and Transversality*, 299–300, 316, 357.
[74] Guattari, *Psychoanalysis and Transversality*, 352. This model of dissident collective writing and publication was reused by Guattari outside a strictly political setting with the research group CERFI.

Guattari's work during this period directly informed his later work with Deleuze, and it is possible to place his concept of the 'coefficient of transversality' within Deleuze and Guattari's larger philosophical task. Guattari describes the coefficient of transversality as 'a certain opening or closing of the collective acceptance' of various forms of group investments.[75] To put this another way, we could say that the coefficient of transversality of a group determines the way in which such a group relates to the outside, and to those connections that escape its internal composition. Transformation occurs at the level of group subjectivity only when this coefficient of escape is set at the correct level; too high and the group will be subjugated to an external image; too low and it will turn in on itself towards a reliance on group phantasy. Transformation is determined by the relation of a group to that which escapes it. My intention here is not to claim that Guattari invented the concept of the line of flight during his early writing on Institutional Psychotherapy without naming it as such, but to point out the way in which he was exploring the role played by 'escape' or 'flight' in transformational change. The idea that transformations rely on a particular kind of escape will, in *Anti-Oedipus* and *A Thousand Plateaus*, form the basis of one aspect of the line of flight.

Materialism contra Lacan

Guattari's relationship with Marxism and his relationship with Lacanianism were both heterodox. In one sense, however, it was his adherence to Marx's materialism that led Guattari to break from Lacanian orthodoxy over the question of structuralism. Against Lacan's Hegelian understanding of the structural and dialectical nature of change, Guattari would insist on the material nature of the Real. Briefly put, we could say that just as Marx was happy to call himself a pupil of Hegel and to hail him as a 'mighty thinker', while simultaneously criticising his master for 'mystifying' the dialectic and ignoring the material and productive basis for reality which exists independently of the structural articulations of thought,[76] Guattari remained a committed pupil of Lacan, while criticising Lacan's mystification of the Real and his refusal to deal with the material and machinic nature of the unconscious. Marx famously argued

[75] Guattari, *Psychoanalysis and Transversality*, 290.
[76] Marx, *Capital*, 103.

that Hegel's focus on thought over material nature meant that his understanding of the dialectic was 'standing on its head' and that it 'must be inverted'.[77] Borrowing this turn of phrase, we might say that Guattari aimed to invert Lacanian theory by jettisoning structural linguistics, simultaneously putting psychoanalysis on its feet by accepting, and then working with, the material and productive nature of the unconscious.

During the 1950s Lacan attempted to resolve several issues that he perceived in the received interpretation of Freud's work. Specifically, he aimed to overcome the split between Freud's psychological works, where the unconscious is treated as a kind of unthought-thought structured by a strict topography, and his metapsychological works, where the unconscious is understood as an economic machine for the material mediation of sensation.[78] To produce a theory that could account for both the socially structured nature of desire and the apparently biological and pre-social nature of the drives, Lacan prioritised Freud's psychological and structural theory of desire over his metapsychological theory, ultimately aiming to show that the drives are always already embedded within a linguistic structure. In his first two seminars, Lacan argues that 'the drives are completely embedded in language and that they are structured like a language'.[79] In Lacan's structural and linguistic reading of Freud, the drives appear as the paradoxical element, or *objet petit a*, which circulates within the structure and guarantees both the constant slippage of the signifier and the constant deferral of the fulfilment of desire.[80]

Commenting on the *objet petit a*, Miller writes that Lacan 'invented it to try to integrate drives into the structure of language', but that in doing so, 'he paid a price; for in the structure of language, you have signifiers and meanings, but he was obliged to

[77] Marx, *Capital*, 103. Exactly how this is understood is a matter of contention. For example, Althusser is insistent that it is not a simple inversion, but a complete overturning of the Hegelian dialectic (*Reading Capital*, 15, 28 n. 10).

[78] See Schuster, *The Trouble with Pleasure*, 27–47, where the author differentiates the alternative methods used by Lacan and Deleuze to overcome this perceived split.

[79] Miller, 'An Introduction to Seminars I and II', 20.

[80] In *The Seminar of Jacques Lacan, Book XI*, Lacan gives a more complex description of the relation of the subject to the drives, namely that they share the same topological space (203–9). In this text Lacan also explains that the drives are like 'headless subjects' (181–4) that circulate around the *objet a* (174–84). See Widder, *Political Theory after Deleuze*, 100–4.

invent something which is neither'.[81] It is Lacan's decision to include the drives within a linguistic structure that allows him to reverse the traditional priority of instincts over the complexes and to argue that the human psyche is social and structured by language 'all the way down'. However, as Miller adds, 'if you do that, instinct in humans appears to be dependent on structure as social'.[82] Specifically, this move allows Lacan to claim that the Oedipus complex is not simply an acquired condition, but a necessary aspect of the structure of thought. This affected Lacan's therapeutic practice, because once the apparently organic and pre-social nature of the drives has been recognised as linguistic in nature, the analyst need only deal with the analysand's use of language to cure them: '[I]n psychoanalysis proper, you do not refer anything that is said to what is ... you simply check whether his or her discourse is consistent.'[83] Despite retaining his official allegiance to Lacan, Guattari was uncomfortable with this move away from Freud's material and economic metapsychology of the unconscious.

According to Lacan's tripartite schema, that which is included in neither the Imaginary nor the Symbolic belongs to the Real. There are at least two different interpretations of Lacan's early formulation of the Real. According to the first, the Real is external and prior to the symbolic order, something 'concrete and already full, a brute, pre-symbolic reality'.[84] On the other hand, by his use of the *objet petit a* as an empty placeholder for the lost object of desire, Lacan also describes the Real as the gap in the symbolic structure of thought. It is 'a void which is not nothing, but functions to empty the *real* material of the partial drives into language'.[85] For Guattari, those followers of Lacan who concentrate solely on the latter of these two interpretations make the mistake of confusing the Real with its structural *representation*. According to Guattari, while the Real can only be represented within symbolic reality by a void, psychoanalysis must move past this mere representation and deal with the pre-symbolic nature of the Real as it exists outside of its manifestations in structural thought. If psychoanalysis restricts itself to the Symbolic register, then it can never account for the fact that our motivations

[81] Miller, 'An Introduction to Seminars I and II', 19.
[82] Miller, 'An Introduction to Seminars I and II', 20.
[83] Miller, 'An Introduction to Seminars I and II', 17.
[84] Ragland, 'An Overview of the Real', 192.
[85] Ragland, 'An Overview of the Real', 193–4.

for action lie outside social discourse. Taking anxiety as an example, Guattari writes that

> Freud reaffirms that anxiety precedes repression: the anxiety is caused by an external danger, it is real ... It is not therefore any use trying to recognize this persistence of anxiety beyond actual 'situations of danger' through some impossible dialogue between the ego ideal and the super-ego.[86]

Explaining his therapeutic reasoning for his insistence, Guattari adds: 'It is obvious that the theoretical field, while it carries with it a unique requirement of coherence, cannot be separated from the pragmatic field.'[87]

Ultimately, Guattari criticises those structuralists who refuse to deal directly with the Real as something other than a gap in the otherwise consistent symbolic field. As Watson explains, Guattari claims that the Lacanian school closes off access to the Real, 'in order to safeguard the tranquillity of the couch setting as well as the sociopolitical status quo', and '[t]o Guattari's way of thinking, both institution and revolution require access to the real, as do creativity, production, and change'.[88] At various points in his work, Guattari distinguishes Institutional Psychotherapy from traditional psychoanalysis by the fact that the former insists on a direct interpretation of the Real,[89] while also differentiating the full speech of subject groups from the empty speech of subjugated groups by the former's ability to engage with the Real.[90] Guattari rarely criticises Lacan directly on this point, but instead attacks those Lacanians who aim to take

[86] Guattari, *Psychoanalysis and Transversality*, 104–5.

[87] Guattari, *Psychoanalysis and Transversality*, 122.

[88] Watson, *Guattari's Diagrammatic Thought*, 17.

[89] '[I]nstitutional psychotherapy ... is precisely a determination never to isolate the study of mental illness from its social and institutional context, and, by the same token, to analyse institutions on the basis of interpreting the real, symbolic and imaginary effects of society upon individuals' (Guattari, *Psychoanalysis and Transversality*, 305).

[90] See Guattari's comments regarding subjugated groups: 'Their centralization works through structure, totalization, unification, replacing the conditions of a genuine collective "enunciation" with an assemblage of stereotypical utterances cut off both from the real and from subjectivity (this is when imaginary phenomena such as Oedipalization, superegofication, and group-castration take place). Group-subjects, on the other hand, are defined by coefficients of transversality that ward off totalities and hierarchies. They are agents of enunciation, environments of desire, elements of institutional creation' (*Psychoanalysis and Transversality*, 14).

his thought in a structural direction. Guattari also argues against Lacan's therapeutic method for its inability to work with patients suffering from psychosis. Despite his ambivalence to the wider anti-psychiatry movement, Guattari sides with thinkers such as Laing in their criticism of psychoanalysis's tendency to ignore the content of the psychotic's speech and to simply search its structure for clues about their underlying condition.[91]

Guattari had a further issue with the structuralist Lacanians' interpretation of the unconscious, namely that it could not account for historical change. In his essay 'Causality, Subjectivity, and History' (1965), Guattari agrees with Lacan's claim that the subject is defined by its structural location in relation to other signifiers, but he also claims that the subject is produced by an alternative, historical process, which cannot be accounted for in a purely structural account of subjectivity. According to Guattari's argument, there is an aspect of durational time that is irreducibly real. He claims that under the auspices of the structural turn in psychoanalysis: 'Reality and history have become subject to an eternal symbolic order from which they are totally isolated and which essentially nullifies them.'[92] Guattari makes the point that while the subject experiences the symbolic structure of language as pre-existing, and while the subject is thus conditioned by the structure of language, the particular nature of the language into which the subject is thrust is historically determined. This line of argument brings Guattari into dispute with Lacan over the question of the Oedipus complex. For Lacan, the subject only comes into existence when it enters the social and symbolic field of language and, as this symbolic field is structured by the Oedipus complex, all subjectivity is necessarily oedipal. However, according to Guattari's critique, while the symbolic field pre-exists the subject, we must also give a historical account of the production of the symbolic field. To put this in psychoanalytic terms, we could say that, while conscious desire is socially structured and linguistic in form, the unconscious is not structured like language and as such it is subject to historical change. This is especially important for Guattari at a political level, because 'it is primarily at that unconscious level that history is woven and that revolutions arise'.[93]

[91] For more on Guattari's relationship with Laing, and with the anti-psychiatry movement, see *Chaosophy*, 124–9.

[92] Guattari, *Psychoanalysis and Transversality*, 238.

[93] Guattari, *Psychoanalysis and Transversality*, 245.

Guattari has not yet put forward his own account of exactly how it is possible for analysts to access the Real, or how it is possible to analyse the historical progression by which the signifying structure of society is produced. At this point, Guattari is simply making a critical assertion. He is claiming that *if* we treat the Real as inaccessible and *if* we locate the unconscious drives within the structure of language, *then* we will have no way of providing an account of the progression of history. This would mean, for example, that there would be no way to explain how the oedipal structure of language came about, or why the modes of subjectivation that existed under feudalism are different to those that exist under capitalism. It is at this point that we can see Guattari's critique of linguistic structuralism as an essentially Marxist one: Guattari claims that when the signifier is regarded as a universal category, analysis is subject to 'the cleverness of a new idealism that actually betrays the linguistic discovery of the signifier'.[94] It is a mystification of the unconscious that can only be combated by a return to materialism.

In order to save Lacanian theory from this encroaching threat of idealism, Guattari argues for a move away from the linguistic categories of Ferdinand de Saussure to the semiotic theories put forward by Louis Hjelmslev.[95] This move will allow Guattari to claim that while subjectivity is necessarily embedded in the structure of signification

[94] Guattari, *Psychoanalysis and Transversality*, 238.

[95] Hjelmslev was a Danish linguist who challenged Saussurean linguistics by recasting the distinction between signifier and signified as the distinction between an *expression plane* and a *content plane*, while simultaneously making a distinction between the form and substance of each of these planes. He was thus able to distinguish between *form of content*, *form of expression*, *substance of content* and *substance of expression*, where the substances of the content and expression of speech will be the physical and psychical material in which speech is manifest (Hjelmslev, *Prolegomena to a Theory of Language*, 57–8). Guattari was drawn to Hjelmslev's work because it shows that 'structures are connected to processes' (*The Anti-Oedipus Papers*, 201), and that, rather than being inert, 'substance functions' (*The Anti-Oedipus Papers*, 203). Using Hjelmslev's model, Guattari was able to argue that linguistic processes could interact with non-linguistic semiotic systems. This gave Guattari a way of conceptualising the semiotic nature of the unconscious without falling back on the Lacanian understanding of its being structured like a language. Having said this, Guattari later criticises Hjelmslev for his 'pseudo-dualism for expression and content' (*The Anti-Oedipus Papers*, 204). He claims that Hjelmslev leads himself into a paradox when he claims that these two terms are 'absolutely reversible', and yet treats them as 'two planes: that of the signified—content—and that of the signifier—expression' (*The Anti-Oedipus Papers*, 204). In response to this, Guattari suggests to Deleuze that in their work

and is therefore incapable of accessing the Real, signification itself is not a closed totality, but is in constant conversation with other a-signifying semiotic forms which *are* in direct contact with the Real. Here Guattari makes two significant revisions to Lacan's conception of semiotics. First, he expands the symbolic field to include not only the 'signifying semiologies' of linguistic utterance but also the 'symbolic semiologies' of non-linguistic forms of meaning, such as human gesture.[96] Second, he also picks out two further semiotic categories that operate outside of human language, namely 'diagrammatic processes' and 'natural encodings', which include those semiotic practices that operate without expressing any meaning, such as those used in information technology and computer science, and the a-semiotic transmission of codes that occurs in biological and chemical processes. Working against the general turn to linguistics, popular among his contemporaries, Guattari is keen to show that there are material semiotic systems which exist independently of language and which cannot all be captured under a single signifying logic: 'Our aim is not to blur the differences among the various semiotic machines, but, on the contrary, to see as clearly as possible what is specific to each.'[97] For Guattari, the two categories of 'diagrammatic processes' and 'natural encodings' are non-linguistic and pre-signifying and are thus pre-subjective. This means that they escape the conditions of representation and consistency that are incumbent on human language. While it might be the case that the Real can only be represented in the symbolic order by a void, semiotic processes that are non-representative have no such constraint. This means that it is possible for the analyst to work directly with the Real by looking outside the analysand's speech to the material processes that produce the possibility of the entire symbolic field. Guattari 'agrees with Lacan that the signifier remains cut off from the real ... but he at the same time insists that other semiotic components, such as those at work in nature and in science, can in fact directly connect to the real'.[98]

At this point in his work, Guattari's relationship with Lacanian theory is a complex one. Guattari is using Lacan's distinction between the Symbolic and the Imaginary in his analysis of group subjectivity,

there should not be 'two planes of expression and content but one single plane of consistency' (*The Anti-Oedipus Papers*, 207).

96 Guattari, *Molecular Revolution*, 89.

97 Guattari, *Molecular Revolution*, 90.

98 Watson, *Guattari's Diagrammatic Thought*, 48.

but he is aware that to stop at this point would be to fall into a kind of psychoanalytic idealism which would nullify the effects of history and constrain psychoanalysis from ever accounting for the possibility of revolution.[99] In order to avoid this fate, psychoanalysis must look outside language to the Real in order to give a genetic account of the production of the symbolic field. To carry out such a task, Guattari claims that psychoanalysis must do two things: first, it must recognise those semiotic processes that exist externally to linguistic structure, and then it must offer an analysis of how these pre-signifying semiotic processes interact with the symbolic field. For Guattari, to carry out such a psychoanalytic revolution would be a Marxist political act, because '[t]o recognize non-linguistic semiotic modes, according to his schema, is to find ways of escaping the control of the despotic signifier, which imposes the stifling reign of representation, in collusion with capitalism'.[100] It is as part of Guattari's attempt to follow this trajectory, and to map out the interactions between the real, material basis for psychic life and the linguistic superstructure of the symbolic field, that he would begin his analysis of the role played by 'machines'.

Machine and Structure

Guattari's introduction of the concept of the 'machine' as a means for analysing the relationship between the structure of the symbolic field and the real, material basis from which it is produced occurs in two essays, 'From One Sign to the Other' (1966) and 'Machine and Structure' (1969). In both cases, Guattari explains the process by which the structural and symbolic field of language is generated, and on both occasions the majority of the discussion is given over to an exploration of the relationship between subjectivity and 'the machine'.[101] In Deleuze's introduction to *Psychoanalysis and Transversality* he picks out these essays as 'two texts in particular that seem especially important in this collection'.[102] Here I will focus

[99] Lacan's work includes several internal changes throughout his career. Guattari's disagreements with the Lacanian school do not arise during Lacan's early emphasis on the Imaginary (in the 1930s and 1940), or during his middle stage with its emphasis on the Symbolic (1950s), but over the question of how to interpret Lacan's seminars that deal with the Real (1960s and 1970s).

[100] Watson, *Guattari's Diagrammatic Thought*, 48.

[101] Guattari, *Psychoanalysis and Transversality*, 198, 318.

[102] Guattari, *Psychoanalysis and Transversality*, 21.

my analysis on 'Machine and Structure', as the language developed by Guattari in this essay, such as that of 'desiring-machines', is carried into Deleuze and Guattari's collaborative work, whereas the terminology of 'point-signs' and 'unitary traits' used in 'From One Sign to the Other' was dropped prior to *Anti-Oedipus*.[103] 'Machine and Structure' is of extra interest because of the role it played in Guattari's personal break with Lacan and in his first meeting with Deleuze. The essay was written when Lacan asked Guattari to review Deleuze's recent publications, *Difference and Repetition* and *Logic of Sense*. However, after Guattari presented his review as a paper at Lacan's Ecole Freudienne de Paris in 1969, Lacan refused to publish it. As a result of this, and via an introduction by their mutual friend Jean-Pierre Faye, Guattari sent the text directly to Deleuze, initiating the pair's first formal meeting.[104]

In 'Machine and Structure' Guattari sets out to analyse and then critique Deleuze's general use of the concept of structure in both *Difference and Repetition* and *Logic of Sense*. Paying surprisingly little attention to Deleuze's use of psychoanalytic theory, Guattari brings together what he sees as the most insightful sections of Deleuze's work to explain a distinction of his own, namely the distinction between machine and structure. Guattari's reworking of Deleuze's concepts can be summed up as follows: first, Guattari accepts Deleuze's key distinction in *Difference and Repetition* between repetition of the same, defined by the generality of particulars that are inherently exchangeable, and repetition with difference, defined by singularities that cannot be exchanged; second, Guattari maps this distinction on to Deleuze's split in *Logic of Sense* between the surface of language, which Guattari reads as a space of generality, and the depths of the body, in which Guattari sees the productive capacity of the repetition

[103] Deleuze and Guattari's decision to drop this terminology is frustrating for the reader, as Guattari's use of the concept of the 'point-sign' to designate a partial or pre-individual element involved in the differential production of signs resonates with Deleuze's discussion of partial elements in *Difference and Repetition*. Guattari continued to use this terminology in his notes for *Anti-Oedipus*, but these terms do not appear in the final work. Guattari also connects the point-sign to differential calculus (*The Anti-Oedipus Papers*, 360).

[104] For an evaluation of the different accounts of this story, see Dosse, *Gilles Deleuze and Félix Guattari: Intersecting Lives*, 268, and Watson, *Guattari's Diagrammatic Thought*, 39. For Deleuze's first ever letter to Guattari, and for his first written response to 'Machine and Structure', see Deleuze, *Lettres et autres textes*, 35–6 and 40–4 respectively.

of difference. Guattari only criticises Deleuze's work for offering a definition of 'structure' that includes both repetition and generality. He summarises this break from Deleuze in the following way: 'Of Deleuze's three minimum conditions determining structure in general, I shall retain only the first two.'[105] Deleuze's first two conditions, which Guattari accepts wholesale, state that in any structure: '(1) There must be at least two heterogeneous series, one of which is defined as the signifier and the other as the signified', and that '(2) Each of these series is made up of terms that exist only through their relationship with one another.'[106] Deleuze's third condition, which Guattari rejects, states that any structure is made up of 'two heterogenous series [converging] toward a paradoxical element, which is their "differentiator"'.[107] Guattari's point here is that while the first two criteria deal with the generality of particulars, and are therefore correctly understood as structural, the third criterion deals with the repetition with difference of singularities, which are extra-structural. To put it briefly, if repetition and generality are radically different, then they should not both be considered as aspects of the structure. It is to resolve this difficulty that Guattari introduces his distinction between machine and structure: 'The essence of the machine is precisely this function of detaching a signifier as a representative, as a "differentiator", as a causal break, different in kind from the structurally established order of things.'[108] While language is structural and defined by its generality, the material body is machinic and is defined by the repetition of difference. As Watson puts it so concisely: 'Using Deleuze's terms, Guattari posits that machines involve repetition with difference, while structures consist in repetition of the same.'[109]

It is worth clarifying here that the structuralism that Guattari finds, and critiques, in Deleuze's earlier work is not a traditional form of structuralism. Deleuze had already made his own criticisms

[105] Guattari, *Psychoanalysis and Transversality*, 381.

[106] Guattari, *Psychoanalysis and Transversality*, 381.

[107] Guattari, *Psychoanalysis and Transversality*, 381. It is unclear whether either Deleuze or Guattari distinguish between the two spellings of the 'differenciator' and the 'differentiator'. In *Différence et répétition*, Deleuze uses *différenciant* (48, 90, 154, 159, 161, 316, 355) but in *Logique du sens* he uses *différentiant* (66). Guattari seems to misquote *Logique du sens* here by using the term *différenciant* (Guattari, *Psychanalyse et transversalité*, 240). However, this is 'corrected' in the English translation (*Psychoanalysis and Transversality*, 322, 382).

[108] Guattari, *Psychoanalysis and Transversality*, 322.

[109] Watson, *Guattari's Diagrammatic Thought*, 3.

of structuralist thought based on the need to give a genetic account of the incarnation of structures. For example, in the field of linguistics, Deleuze is critical of those Saussurean forms of structuralism that 'constantly speak in negative terms and assimilate the differential relations between phonemes to relations of opposition'.[110] This is inadequate for Deleuze because 'opposition teaches us nothing about the nature of that which is thought to be opposed'.[111] Turning away from Saussure, Deleuze finds an alternative and genetic theory of language in the writing of Gustave Guillaume, whose work carries out 'the substitution of a principle of differential position for that of distinctive opposition'.[112] Following Guillaume, Deleuze will attempt to show how individual phonemes, which constitute the building blocks of the linguistic structure, must first be differentiated in speech. In brief, we could say that Deleuze had already challenged structuralist thought by showing the necessity for a virtual structuralism in which the differential relations that produce the structure are held between pre-individual, rather than individual, entities.[113] However, while Guattari appreciates Deleuze's virtual interpretation of structuralism, he argues that Deleuze is wrong to assume that the 'differenciator' which 'makes the difference' between the pre-individual elements is internal to the structure.[114] If this differenciator operates via the repetition of difference, then it should not be counted as an element of the structure, but should instead be designated as a 'machine'.

The driving force behind Guattari's criticism of Deleuze's virtual structuralism rests on a disagreement over the nature of historical change. According to Guattari, when Deleuze explains the motivating force behind structural change by positing a paradoxical element, referred to variously as the esoteric word, the phallus or even the *objet petit a*, within the structure itself,[115] he constrains the possibility of real, historical change. According to Guattari's reasoning, such an account of structure can never explain the way in which the particular form of any given structure is contingent upon its historical production. For Guattari, any given structure develops historically

110 Deleuze, *Difference and Repetition*, 255.
111 Deleuze, *Difference and Repetition*, 256.
112 Deleuze, *Difference and Repetition*, 256.
113 Deleuze is not the first to make such arguments. As well as drawing on Guillaume's work, Deleuze was influenced by Roman Jakobson's concept of the 'zero phoneme' (*Logic of Sense*, 83).
114 Deleuze, *Difference and Repetition*, 365.
115 Deleuze, *Desert Islands*, 170.

because of something alien to it, which intrudes on it. While it may be the case that this intrusion is represented within the structure by way of a paradoxical element such as the *object petit a*, the driving force behind this eruption must be located outside the structure in a material and 'machinic' process. Guattari claims that to 'identify the peculiar positions of subjectivity in relation to events and to history' it will be necessary to recognise that no given structure can ever be analysed as something distinct but must always be treated as the structural articulation of something non-structural.[116] This non-structural or extra-structural element, which is articulated by a given structure, Guattari calls the machine. Putting forward his basic claim, Guattari states that 'each contingent structure is dominated ... by a system of machines' and that conversely 'a machine is inseparable from its structural articulations'.[117]

In some ways it might be more accurate to say here that Guattari's analysis in 'Machine and Structure' does not really criticise Deleuze so much as offer a particular reading of his work that plays up the split between the structural articulation of language and the non-structural force of repetition. Guattari's comments on Deleuze's description of the voice in *Logic of Sense* give us a good example of this. Almost echoing Deleuze, he writes that '[t]he voice, as speech machine, is the basis and determinant of the structural order of language', but he is careful to warn against overtly structuralist readings of Deleuze:

> In trying to see things the other way round, starting from the general, one would be deluding oneself with the idea that it is possible to base oneself on some structural space that existed before the breakthrough by the machine.[118]

Guattari's use of the concept of 'the machine' to designate that which is external to structural thought and that which produces structural thought via the repetition of difference is not without precedent. In fact, we can see clear precursors of this concept in two of Guattari's most important influences: first in Marx's description of the relation between the material and economic base of reality

[116] Guattari, *Psychoanalysis and Transversality*, 318.

[117] Guattari, *Psychoanalysis and Transversality*, 318.

[118] Guattari, *Psychoanalysis and Transversality*, 322. Deleuze writes: 'The voice ... presents the dimensions of an organized language, without yet being able to grasp the organizing principle according to which the voice itself would be a principle' (*Logic of Sense*, 221).

and its intellectual and super-structural articulations, and second in a section of Lacan's second seminar titled 'Odd or Even? Beyond Intersubjectivity', where Lacan uses the concept of the machine to describe the interrelation of the Real and the Symbolic structure of language. In what remains of this chapter I will explore each of these references in turn, before returning to Guattari's comments in 'Machine and Structure' to clarify his use of the term 'machine' and its connection to his understanding of subjectivity, historical change and transformation.

From Base to Superstructure

One of the grounding principles of Marxist theory, which announces its radical break from Hegelian philosophy, is the distinction made between the economic base of a society and its institutional superstructure. According to Marx, each stage of history is defined by its mode of production, where the mode of production is understood as a set of material and economic relations that serve to uphold society and provide for its material needs. At different stages of history, this economic base of society has been constituted by various relations between land, labour and machinery. What is key here is that the accepted level of political and intellectual discourse is shown to operate at a remove from the historical progress of society, such that anyone interested in the progression of society must turn away from purely intellectual debates and involve themselves in the material conditions of their environment. Describing the role of economic relations, Marx writes that '[t]he totality of these relations of production constitutes the economic structure of society, the real foundation, on which arises a legal and political superstructure'. As a result of this, he claims that '[i]t is not the consciousness of men that determines their existence, but their social existence that determines their consciousness'.[119] What is crucial here is that, for Marx, the realm of human thought and understanding does not progress according to its own dialectic, as it does with Hegel, but as a result of alterations in the material constitution of society. For example, Marx explains that technological advances in agricultural and industrial techniques alter the constitution of the material basis for society, and that this leads to a secondary change at the level of the political and legal frameworks of intellectual life. This process does not

[119] Marx, 'A Contribution to a Critique of Political Economy', 263

occur smoothly, however, and as such the historical development of society involves a series of social revolutions: 'At a certain stage of development, the material productive forces of society come into conflict with the existing relations of production ... The changes in the economic foundation lead, sooner or later, to the transformation of the whole, immense, superstructure.'[120] Just as Marx claims that changes in the base can be determined with the precision of a natural science, Guattari's materialist psychoanalysis of machinic desire can be read as an attempt to develop a science capable of understanding the unconscious operation of desire.

Translating Guattari's criticisms of Deleuze's structural account of thought, as they are given above, into the terminology of Marxist theory, we might say that Guattari argues that Deleuze's explanation of the structural nature of thought can only account for the legal, political and institutional superstructure of social life, and that by locating the 'paradoxical element' within the structure of thought he is failing to recognise the way in which the whole of the structure is in fact contingent upon the historical development of the means of production. Marx and Engels are careful to clarify that the relation between the base and the superstructure of society is not a simple one-way relation, and Guattari is similarly careful to recognise the complexity of the relation between what he calls the 'machine' and the 'structure'. Marx and Engels make at least two clarifications to their general point about the way in which the material base of society affects the constitution of the superstructure; first that the different superstructural activities of human beings, such as those in the fields of art and politics, can develop at different rates in their relation to the base, and second that the relation between the base and the superstructure is a reciprocal one in which the material base only determines the superstructure in the last instance.[121] In his essay 'Nine Theses of the Left Opposition', Guattari claims that Marxist theorists have historically failed to give a proper account of the relation between the basic and superstructural elements of social life. He calls it a 'real puzzle for Marxist theorists' and one 'that revolutionary Marxism must resolve at all costs on the level of

[120] Marx, 'A Contribution to a Critique of Political Economy', 263.

[121] Marx and Engels make this point early in their work. See their comments on Feuerbach (*The German Ideology*, 61). For a full discussion of the difficult base–superstructure relation in Marx and Engels's work, see Rigby, *Marxism and History*, 177–80.

theory and on the level of practice, if it wants to move beyond the alternative between vulgar materialism and Hegelian idealism'.[122] The reason for this failure, according to Guattari's analysis, is that Marxist theorists have never successfully solved 'the problem of the subject'.[123]

Returning to Guattari's founding claim in 'Machine and Structure' that 'each contingent structure is dominated ... by a system of machines' and that conversely 'a machine is inseparable from its structural articulations',[124] we can now see this claim as a reworking of the Marxist assertion that the social superstructure is dominated by the material structure of the means of production and that the means of production is inseparable from the superstructure. With this in mind, Guattari aims to go further than Marx by using psychoanalytic theory to explain the way in which the subject emerges only in its relation with the 'machine' at this exact point of intersection between the material base of society and the intellectual superstructure. While the subject of feudalism is produced in part by its direct material relation with the scythe or the thresher, the subject of capitalism is produced by its interactions with the factory and the machinery of industrial production. Aware of the myriad difficulties that Marxist theorists have traditionally faced when trying to think through the 'problem of the subject', Guattari returns to psychoanalytic theory, by which he hopes to explain the production of subjectivity using the Lacanian terminology of the Real and the Symbolic.

Lacan's Machines

When Guattari devises this distinction between machine and structure, he is not only offering a Marxist reading of Deleuze's work, and he is not simply rejecting Lacanian theory. As is so often the case in his work, Guattari borrows from Lacanian terminology even when offering revisions to the work of his teacher. For this purpose, Guattari turns to a discussion in Lacan's second seminar which begins in the section titled 'Odd or Even? Beyond Intersubjectivity', and which continues in his 'Seminar on "The Purloined Letter"'.[125] In this bizarre lesson, Lacan devises a game by which he hopes to

[122] Guattari, *Psychoanalysis and Transversality*, 146.
[123] Guattari, *Psychoanalysis and Transversality*, 146.
[124] Guattari, *Psychoanalysis and Transversality*, 318.
[125] Lacan, *The Seminar of Jacques Lacan, Book II*, 175–90; Lacan, *Écrits*, 35–41.

explore 'what in a confused fashion is called cybernetics' in order to answer the question '*what is the subject?*'[126] By the use of this game, Lacan shows how a symbolic field can be produced by an unthinking and machinic process. The Lacanian psychoanalytic subject is a symbolic construction; it inhabits the Symbolic field, rather than that of the Imaginary or the Real, and is defined by a set of structural and symbolic laws. In this seminar, Lacan explores the nature of this symbolic subject by explaining the process by which the entire symbolic field is constituted.

The game that Lacan describes, and which his seminar audience play, is a version of 'evens and odds' in which one player flips a coin and the other player must guess the outcome. Lacan explains how it is possible for a machine, which is not conscious, to play the game, and to do so with a strategy. The game begins with a string of random coin tosses, which are written down as a string of symbols; here the plus sign is used to signify heads and the minus sign is used to signify tails. At this point it is clear that for each toss of the coin there is a 50/50 chance of the machine successfully guessing the outcome. Lacan then explains what happens if you introduce an arbitrary set of symbolic rules into the recording of the series. In Lacan's example, each consecutive group of three coin tosses is named using the following rules: any three tosses with the same result (either + + + or – – –) is called a 1; any three tosses that include two consecutive tosses of the same result (+ + –, + – –, – – + or – + +) is a 2; and finally, any three tosses that include no consecutive tosses of the same result (– + – or + – +) is a 3. Lacan is now able to transcribe a string of pluses and minuses into a string of numbers. When writing this string, each of the numbered triplets of coin tosses overlaps with the previous triplet by two. The string of tosses that results in the series + + – + – – + would contain five groupings of three tosses as follows: (+ + –) (+ – +) (– + –) (+ – –) and (– – +), which would be transcribed as 2, 3, 3, 2 and 2. What fascinates Lacan here is that while in the string of pluses and minuses there is no connection between the signs – pluses and minuses follow each other at random – in the string of numbers a set of rules emerges: 'This transformation alone gives rise to extremely precise laws. The 1s the 2s and the 3s cannot succeed each other in just any order.'[127] For example, Lacan explains

[126] Lacan, *The Seminar of Jacques Lacan, Book II*, 175.
[127] Lacan, *The Seminar of Jacques Lacan, Book II*, 193.

that a 1 will never be able to follow a 3 and that an indefinite number of 2s is always possible between a 1 and a 3.

What is important here is that an arbitrary set of rules produces a string of symbols that have a syntax. In this transcription, each symbol determines the possibilities open to the symbol that will come next, so that 'independently of any attachment to some supposedly causal bond, the symbol already plays, and produces by itself its necessities, its structures, its organisations'.[128] Lacan is interested in this non-causal but necessary connection between the symbols in the chain because it gives him the opportunity to explain the possibility of unconscious memory. According to the arbitrary rules of transcription used above, certain patterns emerge in the string of numbers that have effects on other numbers occurring at a great distance from them. For example, if a string of an even number of 2s is preceded by a 1, then it will be followed by a 1, but when an odd number of 2s is preceded by a 1, it will be followed by a 3. It is therefore possible for the chain of symbols to 'remember' what happened further back in the chain.[129] The lesson that Lacan draws from this game, and from the emergence of syntactical rules in the chain of transcribed numbers, is that it is possible to explain the emergence of the entire symbolic field of language as an effect of an unconscious process, carried out by a machine. As we move from the level of the coin tosses to the level of their transcription, 'we are no longer at all in the domain of the real, but in that of the symbolic'.[130] The lesson that Guattari draws from Lacan's seminar is that the Real and the Symbolic relate to one another via a process in which a machine gives rise to a structure. The machinic and unthinking process that produces the random string of pluses and minuses can be thought of as the productive and material base of this system, while the resulting string of transcribed numbers can be understood as a superstructure of thought, ultimately determined and inseparable from that which produces it.

[128] Lacan, *The Seminar of Jacques Lacan, Book II*, 193.

[129] Lacan uses this phenomenon to argue for the existence of unconscious memory. Fink explains that, in this example, 'rather than being remembered by the individual (in an active way, that is, with some sort of *subjective* participation), things are "remembered" for him or her by the signifying chain ... We have here a clear connection between the letter (or signifying chain) and the unconscious. The unconscious *cannot* forget, composed of "letters" working, as they do, in an autonomous, automatic way' ('The Nature of Unconscious Thought', 183).

[130] Lacan, *The Seminar of Jacques Lacan, Book II*, 182.

However, Guattari's interpretation of Lacan's 'Seminar on "The Purloined Letter"' differs significantly from that of the majority of Lacanians. For example, for Bruce Fink, while this seminar 'points to the limits of structure, suggesting there is something "above and beyond" structure, something "outside of" and radically different from or in excess of structure', the work of the seminar is ultimately seen as a way of 'extending ever further the impact of structure' by showing that whatever is 'beyond' the structure is something 'which nevertheless can be seen at work "within" structure itself'.[131] This is patently not the case for Guattari, who sees this seminar as a means for describing the Real without simply reducing it to something internal to the structure of the Symbolic. Fink and Guattari differ in their readings of Lacan by focusing on different aspects of the coin game: while Fink concentrates on the automatic and machinic production of structural rules and concludes that even the unconscious is structured like a language, Guattari concentrates on the fact that the rules which allow for the transcription of the coin tosses into a symbolic field are *arbitrary*, leading him to conclude that the structure of language is not something eternal and unconscious, but something historically located.

The result of these two different readings can also be seen in Guattari's and Fink's alternative readings of the Oedipus complex. For Fink, and also for Miller, Lacan's seminar shows that the Oedipus complex is embedded in the structure of unconscious desire. For Guattari, on the other hand, the arbitrary nature of the rules of transcription shows that not only is the unconscious not oedipal, but the subject need not be either.[132] We will see in the next chapter how important this disagreement is for *Anti-Oedipus*, where Deleuze and Guattari first clarify the operational difference between mechanism and machinism. In that text, Guattari and Deleuze sum up their ambivalence to Lacan in a direct reference to his 'Seminar on "The Purloined Letter"', where they state:

[131] Fink, 'The Nature of Unconscious Thought', 174.

[132] Guattari's break from the Lacanian school can be seen clearly in the different ways in which Lacan and Guattari use the example of the coin game to reinvestigate Freud's case of the Wolfman. Lacan argues that this game explains how the Wolfman can unconsciously remember the primal scene (*The Seminar of Jacques Lacan, Book II*, 176). Guattari, writing with Deleuze, takes the opposite tack, arguing that it is only the arbitrary nature of the symbolic field that allows Freud to oedipalise the Wolfman's schizophrenic tendencies (*A Thousand Plateaus*, 29).

> We owe to Jacques Lacan the discovery of this fertile domain of a code of the unconscious, incorporating the entire chain – or several chains – of meaning ... The chains are called 'signifying chains' because they are made up of signs, but these signs are not themselves signifying.[133]

In short, Lacan was right to think of the unconscious in terms of a machinic code, but he was wrong to have modelled this code on the signifying capacities of language.

Revolutionary Escapes

If there is a single thought that binds together all of Guattari's work prior to 1969, it is that there is something non-structural, or anti-structural, in all assemblages.[134] That which is not structural is *machinic* and it is this which *escapes* structural relations, connects an assemblage with its outside, and brings about transformation. For Guattari, all subjectivity – in the form of group subjectivity – is necessarily revolutionary in the sense that it is only produced when transversal connections cut across the hierarchical stratifications in a group and put heterogeneous discourses into communication. When Guattari claims that the human being 'is caught where the machine and the structure meet', he is pointing out that human subjectivity is only produced when machinic forces cause transformations in structural relations.[135] Guattari's early writings can therefore be understood as an attempt to rethink the relation between subjectivity, history, revolution and escape.

Initially, Guattari brings Lacan's distinction between the Real and the Symbolic together with Marx's distinction between the base and the superstructure of society. Also following Lacan, Guattari locates the subject within the symbolic field. He writes that '[t]he agent of action, whose definition here does not extend beyond this principle

[133] Deleuze and Guattari, *Anti-Oedipus*, 41.

[134] I have used the terminology of 'assemblages' here, despite the fact that it was not part of Guattari's lexicon at the time. While Guattari does discuss groups that consist of heterogeneous, non-human elements, he does not begin to use the concept of the 'assemblage' until his collaborations with Deleuze.

[135] Guattari, *Psychoanalysis and Transversality*, 322. Guattari's description of the human being is similar to that given in *A Thousand Plateaus*: 'the self is only a threshold, a door, a becoming between two multiplicities' (275); 'Every society, every individual, are thus plied by both segmentarities simultaneously: one molar, the other *molecular*' (235).

of reciprocal determination, is included in the structure'.[136] Moving away from traditional interpretations of Lacan's work, Guattari then offers his own reading of Lacan's concept of the machine. According to Guattari's interpretation, the structural field of the symbolic realm is not constituted by a set of eternal rules, but is produced by the Real, where the Real is understood to be made up of a set of productive, material, machinic relations. This alteration convinces Guattari that it is a mistake to explain the dynamics of desire using the concept of the *objet petit a*, functioning only as a representation of the drives, and instead to use the concept of the '*objet-machine petit "a"*', which is 'unable to be absorbed into the references of the structure'.[137] Once Guattari has recognised that the driving force behind desire is not a gap in the symbolic structure, but the eruption of a machine into the symbolic order, he is able to conceptualise desire as something inherently productive rather than inherently lacking. However, what is just as crucial for Guattari is the fact that by separating the machine from the structure he can give a historical account of the nature of desire.

While Guattari criticises structuralism for nullifying the effects of history by capturing it within an eternal symbolic order, the concept of the machine allows him to account for historical change. He writes that machines 'are not related in their structural determinations: only by a process of historical analysis'.[138] This claim is easy to understand if we return once again to Marx's distinction between the base and the superstructure of society. The subject exists in the legal and political framework of the superstructure in the sense that one is 'subject to the law' or 'subjected to power'. The productive capacities of the machine are not, however, constrained under any such symbolic law. For example, the development of technology that moves a society from a feudalist to a capitalist mode of production advances by a historical and non-structural progression.[139] Because it is the historical development of the Real that produces the symbolic realm, in which the subject is embedded, the subject is also historically

[136] Guattari, *Psychoanalysis and Transversality*, 318.
[137] Guattari, *Psychoanalysis and Transversality*, 324.
[138] Guattari, *Psychoanalysis and Transversality*, 319.
[139] In the case of revolutionary struggle, however, Marx claims that the development of technology provides only the conditions for social transformation by creating a contradiction in the mode of production, and that class consciousness of this contradiction is required to bring about the revolutionary transformation.

defined by the mode of production that produced it. It is only a small step from this claim to Guattari and Deleuze's later criticism of the institution of psychoanalysis. If psychoanalysis restricts itself to the symbolic realm of the political and legal subject, and if the political and legal superstructures refuse to reflect contemporary changes in the mode of production, then the model of subjectivity used by psychoanalysis will soon become regressive and anti-revolutionary.

According to his reinterpretation of the base/superstructure relation, Guattari saw an appalling mismatch developing between the accelerating pace of material change and the inertia of political and legal structures: 'With industrial capitalism, the spasmodic evolution of machinery keeps cutting across the existing hierarchy of skills.'[140] This means that workers become alienated from their society and have no way of being recognised by the legal and political frameworks that govern their lives. According to Guattari's analysis, the mismatch between the Real and the Symbolic places the human being in a double-bind. It only survives because political and legal institutions manage to 'conceal what is happening by setting up systems of equivalents, of imitations' such as the 'oppressive myth of the model worker'.[141] Guattari names this process of concealment 'anti-production'.[142] To this list of anti-productive practices we could add the way in which the institution of psychoanalysis upholds the oppressive myth of the Oedipus complex and its necessary equivalent of the lacking, neurotic subject.

All Guattari's psychoanalytic and political work prior to 1969 leads him to conclude first that revolutionary modes of subjectivity – those not conditioned by the structural determinations of the symbolic order – are possible, and secondly that such modes of subjectivity are necessary if we are to move past the political stalemates that plague contemporary life. For Guattari, political revolution is always a subjective revolution.[143] Another way to put this would be to say

[140] Guattari, *Psychoanalysis and Transversality*, 322.

[141] Guattari, *Psychoanalysis and Transversality*, 320.

[142] This term plays a similar role to that of 'ideology' for Marx; however, Guattari locates this less in the people's consciousness and more in the disciplinary functions of social institutions.

[143] As well as placing Guattari in the history of Marxist theory's attempt to think through the production of revolutionary subjectivities, this move also locates Guattari in a philosophical trajectory that runs through Nietzsche, Foucault and Deleuze.

that, for Guattari, any social transformation is always a psychic transformation.

Periods of political oppression and stagnation occur 'when the superstructures are imposed as impossible representations of machine effects', while revolutions are possible 'when the machine represents social subjectivity for the structure'.[144] The work of the politically committed psychoanalyst must be to aid in the exploration and discovery of new forms of subjectivation that are capable of *escaping* from the structural status quo. Psychoanalysts must recognise that the unconscious is not structured like a language and is not a theatre for the dramatisation of desire, but a factory of material relations.[145] The unconscious must be understood as a factory not only in the sense that it is productive, but also in the political sense that it is the site of structural subjugation. With this in mind, we can now see how closely Guattari's work at La Borde is connected to his political project. His attempts to aid in the production of group subjectivity should not only be understood as a therapeutic means for treating psychosis, but also as an attempt to deal with the cause of psychosis, namely the double-bind created by the incompatibility of the material unconscious and the structural forms of consciousness currently available. Ultimately, Guattari would claim that the theoretical tools available to psychoanalysts were incapable of the task at hand because of the way that they are restricted to a single discourse. After having defined revolution as a moment at which the machine is able to fully determine the form of the structure, Guattari explains that 'no such permanent grasp of machine effects upon the structures could really be achieved on the basis of only one "theoretical practice"'. Instead, such a task 'presupposes the development of a specific analytical praxis at every level of organization of the struggle'.[146] This, as we will see in the next chapter, is what Guattari will try to achieve in his schizoanalytic work with Deleuze.

[144] Guattari, *Psychoanalysis and Transversality*, 237.

[145] Guattari describes the unconscious as a factory early on: 'Grabbing psychoanalysts by the collar and putting them in an asylum is like putting a medieval priest in a factory, or a pool! They would both try to escape by exorcisms and excommunications' (*Psychoanalysis and Transversality*, 73).

[146] Guattari, *Psychoanalysis and Transversality*, 329.

3

Anti-Oedipus and Desiring-Machines

Transformative Desire

Anti-Oedipus is a book about transformations. Specifically, Deleuze and Guattari's first collaborative work is a book which offers a new conceptualisation of desire as the transformative force that drives historical change. The book initially uses this concept of desire to offer an account of the historical transformations of power that constitute our political history, and that have led us into our contemporary, capitalist way of life. With this historical analysis in hand, the book then goes on to tackle the pressing political question of how desire's transformative capabilities can be turned to the production of a post-capitalist future.

The concept of the line of flight is first introduced by Deleuze and Guattari in *Anti-Oedipus*. It arrives in this work with little introduction and yet it plays a central and organising role in the conceptual architecture that they develop in the book. Simply put, Deleuze and Guattari use the concept of the line of flight to define the way that desire operates when it is not inhibited, captured or turned against itself by the structuring forces of social reality. The concept is an important one, in this sense, because it connects Deleuze and Guattari's theory of desire with their theory of political change. The fact that the concept emerges here is also telling because, unlike many of the other concepts deployed in *Anti-Oedipus*, the line of flight is a novel creation that does not appear directly in the lexicon of either of the authors' previous works. In this chapter, and in the one that follows, I will argue for a particular interpretation of the role that the concept of the line of flight plays in *Anti-Oedipus*. Specifically, I will argue that the concept is used in at least four distinct senses in the text, all of which are necessary to define the political project of schizoanalysis. To do this, in this chapter I will first concentrate on Deleuze and Guattari's novel conception of the unconscious. I will show how the pair use several insights from Guattari's earlier, materialist and anti-structural confrontations with Lacan to reformulate the metaphysical framework offered by Deleuze in his earlier works. This will allow me to explain what Deleuze and Guattari mean when they write that, in the unconscious, 'it is not the lines of pressure that matter, but on the contrary the lines of escape (*lignes de fuite*)'.[1] In the subsequent chapter, I will continue my analysis of the role of the line of flight in *Anti-Oedipus* by considering Deleuze and Guattari's historical and political analysis of capitalism.

Up to this point, I have offered my account of what we might call the pre-individual field of the concept of the line of flight by locating the conceptual moves in both Deleuze's and Guattari's separate works before 1969 that prefigure their later use of the concept. In this chapter I will tackle the individuation of the concept directly. However, the fertile domain of individuation created by the collision of these two thinkers has its own historical context. Deleuze and Guattari first met in 1969, with the civil unrest, student protests and massive general strikes of May '68 still fresh in their minds. Besides the grand scale of the protests, what marked out the uprisings of 1968 was the fact that they were relatively spontaneous and were directed by a dislocated assembly of students and workers' groups. The protests also manifested in an enormous outpouring of desire, with the writing of slogans, songs and graffiti demonstrating the drive and passion that animated the students and the workers alike. What is more, the events were not predicted by the political scholars of the time, by the government, or by the French Communist Party, and they received little institutional support.[2] These circumstances fuelled Guattari's scepticism about the revolutionary power of the official French Communist Party, which he had already criticised for its role in restoring the bourgeoisie to power after the end of the Second World War,[3] and whose politics he declared 'totally determined by the state of the economic and social relations of State monopoly capitalism'.[4] Deleuze had also retained his distance from

1 Deleuze and Guattari, *Anti-Oedipus*, 371. As mentioned previously, accepted English translations of *Anti-Oedipus* render *ligne de fuite* as 'line of escape'. In order to find some consistency with Deleuze and Guattari's later work, and with the majority of the secondary literature, I will include the French phrase *ligne de fuite* in brackets whenever it is rendered other than as 'line of flight' in the translations.

2 For more on the role of the PCF in the events of May 1968, see Bell and Criddle, *The French Communist Party in the Fifth Republic*, 90–3.

3 Guattari, *Psychoanalysis and Transversality*, 158.

4 Guattari, *Psychoanalysis and Transversality*, 247–8.

the Communist Party, making him an exception among French intellectuals of the time. Despite this, he was a vocal supporter of the student protests and was the only professor in the philosophy department at Lyon to publicly declare his support and attend the student-organised events.[5] Thus, before their meeting, both Guattari and Deleuze were aware that a new theory of desire and a new theory of political revolution were required, one that did not rely on party political power and that could account for the supposed unpredictability of May '68.

Their first meeting was organised after Guattari had sent Deleuze a copy of his essay 'Machine and Structure'. These first meetings were highly productive, with each forced to rethink their previous work in a mutual attempt to develop a theory of desire that could account for May '68 and overcome the failures of traditional Freudianism and traditional Marxism. Only three years later, the result of these conversations emerged as *Anti-Oedipus*, a veritable explosion of novel ideas combining philosophical moves from Kant, Spinoza and Nietzsche, insights from the writings of D. H. Lawrence, Samuel Butler and Antonin Artaud, as well as the anthropological studies carried out by Pierre Clastres, Marcel Griaule and Germaine Dieterlen (along with the ontologies of the different societies they studied such as the Dogon, Guayaki and nomads from Mongolia), the psychoanalytic work of Freud, Reich, Klein and Lacan, and of course the theories of political economy advanced by Marx and Engels, Adam Smith and David Ricardo. The book is an attempt to offer an account of universal history that incorporates a theory of desire and of the unconscious, which can explain the drivers of political change and political revolution, as well as the ways that these revolutions go sour or morph into self-destructive fascisms.[6] It is in the context of this psychoanalytic and politically motivated text that the concept of the line of flight is born.

[5] Dosse, *Gilles Deleuze and Félix Guattari: Intersecting Lives*, 177.

[6] While this might sound like a direct continuation of Guattari's work and a change of direction for Deleuze, many of the conceptual innovations of Deleuze's previous metaphysical work involved reworkings of both Marxist and Freudian concepts. Deleuze's earliest academic interests also concerned the relationship between desire and the existence of societal norms. See Deleuze's edited selection of texts in *Instincts et institutions* (1953), the introduction of which is translated in *Desert Islands*, 19–21.

Negative Psychoanalytic Task: Dealing with the Oedipus Complex

One of the central aims of *Anti-Oedipus* is to provide a theory of the unconscious that challenges both the Freudian convention of interpreting the unconscious as a kind of theatre, where the narrative of desire is played out, and the Lacanian convention of interpreting the unconscious as an inaccessible and impossible 'Real' defined by its structural role, namely as the gap, cut or lacuna within the Symbolic.[7] Perhaps the clearest reason for Deleuze and Guattari's rejection of these approaches is that they both, in their own way, subordinate the activity of unconscious desire to some form of social convention. In both cases this subordination of the unconscious is carried out by a championing of the Oedipus complex. Criticising Freud's insistence on the universality of the Oedipus complex, Deleuze and Guattari question what it means to say that Freud 'discovered Oedipus in his own self-analysis'.[8] According to their reading, it would be more accurate to say that what Freud 'discovered' was only that the familial situation in which he was raised shared certain traits with those of the patients he treated because of the common family form that conditioned them. Freud's decision to draw on the myth of Oedipus is then simply one way of explaining a societal norm by utilising a familiar trope from his own 'Goethian classical culture'.[9]

Unfortunately, according to Deleuze and Guattari's reading, Freud reverses the order of determination by which the social convention of the nuclear family creates oedipal subjects, instead claiming that the familial romance is a 'mere dependence on Oedipus'.[10] Starting from this error, Freud then 'neuroticizes everything in the unconscious at the same time as he oedipalizes, and closes the familial triangle over the entire unconscious'.[11] The reason that this generalised use of the Oedipus complex is so disastrous in the eyes of Deleuze and Guattari

[7] Lacan does not strictly define the unconscious as inaccessible as he does offer a route to the unconscious via the structure of language. It would be more accurate to say that Lacanian theory treats desire as necessarily barred, and therefore the unconscious is only readable in the effects produced by the repression of social reality. Deleuze and Guattari will attempt, however, to analyse desire directly, without any reliance on its repression.

[8] Deleuze and Guattari, *Anti-Oedipus*, 62.

[9] Deleuze and Guattari, *Anti-Oedipus*, 62.

[10] Deleuze and Guattari, *Anti-Oedipus*, 62.

[11] Deleuze and Guattari, *Anti-Oedipus*, 62.

is that, by elevating the Oedipus complex to the level of the necessary form of desire, Freud also made desire inherently representative or signifying, rather than productive. It is in this move that Deleuze and Guattari claim that 'the unconscious ceases to be what it is – a factory, a work-shop – to become a theatre, a scene and its staging'.[12]

To clarify, Deleuze and Guattari do not attempt to dismantle the entire Freudian edifice, but instead attempt to extract those Freudian insights that capture the active, productive and pre-personal aspects of unconscious desire from those that reduce the unconscious to a theatre for the eternal staging of the oedipal drama. Specifically, they credit Freud with the discovery of the unconscious and with the discovery of the abstract category of desire, praising in particular his 1915 paper 'The Unconscious', where he brought together his dynamic, topographical and economic models of the unconscious. Much to the satisfaction of Deleuze and Guattari, here Freud also shows that unconscious desire is 'exempt from mutual contradiction', so that 'there are in this system no negation, no doubt, no degrees of certainty', and finally that the impulses in this system 'are not ordered temporally, are not altered by the passage of time; they have no reference to time at all'.[13]

On top of this, Deleuze and Guattari are particularly enamoured by Freud's work in 'Beyond the Pleasure Principle' (1920), where Freud moves past his earlier theories of an unconscious desire motivated by the pleasure principle to more critical and metaphysical questions concerning the necessary existence of a more complex relationship with reality, especially in the context of the apparent tendency of life towards death.[14] Among many other arguments, it is here that Freud elaborates on the ways in which the unconscious is not necessarily ordered by the categories of space and time, and offers a direct challenge to Kantian metaphysics:

> As a result of certain insights afforded to us by psychoanalysis, Kant's dictum that time and space are necessary forms of human thought is today very much open to debate. We have come to appreciate that unconscious psychic processes are in themselves 'timeless'.[15]

[12] Deleuze and Guattari, *Anti-Oedipus*, 62.

[13] Freud, 'The Unconscious', 186–7. See also Freud's comments on 'the quantitative distribution of the libido' ('An Outline of Psychoanalysis', 11).

[14] This essay also plays a significant role in Deleuze's previous account of the three syntheses (*Difference and Repetition*, 120–40).

[15] Freud, 'Beyond the Pleasure Principle', 155.

While Deleuze and Guattari are more cautious in their analysis of Kant, they praise these works of Freud because it is here that he explicates the abstract concept of desire, without tarnishing this discovery with the apparent necessity of sexual repression.

In the case of Lacan, Deleuze and Guattari also attempt to split those insights they deem useful from those that confirm the psychoanalytic structuring of unconscious desire. Both of these sides of Lacan's work can be seen in his treatment of the Oedipus complex. For Deleuze and Guattari, Lacan's most influential impact on the interpretation of the Oedipus complex was his claim that it was purely imaginary. Where Freud had claimed that all desire related back to the first feeling of lack experienced by the child when he/she was removed from the mother by the imposition of the father, Lacan 'shows on the contrary that Oedipus is imaginary, nothing but an image, a myth'.[16] This means that instead of thinking about the Oedipus complex as something which comes into existence at a particular point in the development of subjectivity, Lacan sees it as a myth that is used to explain the fact that in order to enter the Symbolic realm of social interaction, the subject must necessarily be lacking, barred or castrated.

Interestingly, Lacan's argument against Freud's mythical version of the Oedipus complex is given most explicitly in the two seminars, *The Other Side of Psychoanalysis* and *On a Discourse that Might not be a Semblance*, which he delivered from 1969 to 1971, at exactly the same time that Deleuze and Guattari were writing *Anti-Oedipus*.[17] During these two seminars, Lacan continually refers to the Oedipus complex as a myth and as a dream of Freud.[18] He offers a close reading of the Oedipus myth that Freud borrows from Sophocles, and the alternative Oedipus story that Freud articulated in *Totem and Taboo*, and shows how they contradict each other. Using Barthes' analysis of the structure of myth, Lacan argues that both versions of the Oedipus myth are an attempt to deal with the unanswerable question of origin, and that both ultimately grapple with the difficulty of an individual's conception through the sexual relationship of the parents. However, according to Lacan, the role that the father plays in these two stories is dramatically different. In Sophocles' Oedipus, neither the father nor the child is allowed to

16 Deleuze and Guattari, *Anti-Oedipus*, 340.

17 Lacan, *The Seminars, Book XVII*; and *Le séminaire, livre XVIII*.

18 Lacan, *The Seminars, Book XVII*, 128.

fulfil their desire for the mother. The curse laid upon Oedipus is the result of a previous injunction put upon the father, which forbade him from consummating his marriage. It is when the father breaks this rule that he sets in motion the narrative that will ultimately lead to his own death and the repetition of the transgression by his son. In this story, the father and the son are ultimately 'castrated' by the impossibility of enjoyment.

The oedipal story in *Totem and Taboo*, on the other hand, does not place the same restriction on the primal father. According to this story, the father initially had free access to all women, but when he is killed by the horde of brothers the remaining image of the dead father constitutes a rule against the fulfilment of desire by incest. It is the second version of the Oedipus story that Lacan refuses to accept. He calls it a 'cock-and-bull story' and refers to Freud's 'blessed story of the father of the horde' as a kind of 'Darwinian buffoonery'.[19] Speaking of the power of the father, Lacan writes that 'the mystagogy that makes him into a tyrant is obviously lodged ... at the level of the real father as a construction of language', and adds '[t]he real father is nothing other than an effect of language'.[20] Crucial for Deleuze and Guattari in this interpretation is the fact that if the Oedipus complex is a myth, then it does not necessarily tell us anything about the nature of desire, but only about a particular way in which that desire has been repressed.

However, the error that Deleuze and Guattari claim to locate in Lacanian psychoanalysis can be seen creeping in just as soon as Lacan first dismisses Freud's version of the Oedipus myth as imaginary. Immediately after Lacan's critique of Freud's Oedipus myth in seminar XVII, he writes that, despite it being a myth, in analysis 'the myth of Oedipus is necessary to designate the real'.[21] By defining the Oedipus complex as necessary for the interpretation of desire, Lacan is able to develop a structural account of desire, supposedly abstracted from its social, cultural and historical context. It is precisely at this point – the point at which the imaginary Oedipus complex is defined as necessary – that Deleuze and Guattari depart from the Lacanian reading of desire. In *Anti-Oedipus*, Deleuze and Guattari identify the structural development in Lacanian analysis as a missed opportunity in which the discovery of the imaginary nature of

[19] Lacan, *The Seminars, Book XVII*, 114, 112.
[20] Lacan, *The Seminars, Book XVII*, 127.
[21] Lacan, *Le séminaire, livre XVIII*, 48.

the Oedipus complex was followed by a reimposition of the oedipal system in structuralist terms. They write that 'it was inopportune to tighten the nuts and bolts where Lacan had just loosened them', and even joke about how perfectly the logic of the Oedipus myth is reintroduced in Lacan's structuralist account, claiming that 'it is like the story of the Resistance fighters who, wanting to destroy a pylon, balanced the plastic charges so well that the pylon blew up and fell back into its hole'.[22]

In Deleuze and Guattari's eyes, Lacan had managed to destroy the mythical Oedipus only by creating a structural one, and in this way had reintroduced all of the misconceptions about desire inherited from Freud. Regardless of whether it is used as a mythical reference point or a structural law, if unconscious desire is captured by the yoke of Oedipus, then it will appear as an a-historical mirror of human nature. For Deleuze and Guattari, this interpretation of desire involves an illusion that reverses the true order of determination: unconscious desire is not produced by our lived, socially constructed reality, but is the productive force that gives rise to such a reality. It cannot, therefore, be the case that unconscious desire represents or mirrors the social convention of the nuclear family; on the contrary, it must be the case that desire is inherently an-oedipal and is only captured by the structure of the Oedipus complex under certain historical conditions.

Positive Psychoanalytic Task: Defining Desiring-production

Deleuze and Guattari's engagements with psychoanalysis are not merely critical in *Anti-Oedipus*, and it is their stated aim to provide a positive theory of the unconscious that does not reduce it to either a theatre for the shadow play of desire or a structural void necessary for the process of analysis. Given the fact that the previous two chapters offered readings of earlier works by both Deleuze and Guattari, perhaps the most direct way to give a clear account of the positive and productive theory of the unconscious that they develop in *Anti-Oedipus* is to show how it differs from the equivalent theories offered in the pair's work prior to their collaboration.

We saw in the last chapter how Guattari's essay 'Machine and Structure' challenged the form of structuralism found in both *Difference and Repetition* and *Logic of Sense* because of the fact that

[22] Deleuze and Guattari, *Anti-Oedipus*, 84, 268.

Deleuze was forced to include a non-structural element – variously called the object = x, or the differentiator – into his definition of the structure itself. In opposition to this, Guattari opened up a distinction between the category of the *structure*, which requires nothing more than two heterogeneous series, the terms of which are defined mutually by their reference to one another, and the category of the *machine*, which functions outside the structure and plays a role in its genesis via a process of incessant repetition. With Guattari's insistence on the separation of the structure and the machine in mind, in *Anti-Oedipus* Deleuze and Guattari are able to explain exactly where Lacan's oedipal theory of desire goes wrong, namely in that it does not recognise the a-structural and machinic nature of desire, which, far from being structured like a language, or necessarily structured by the Oedipus complex, is a machine that has logical priority over the structure.

When this challenge to the foundations of structuralism is incorporated into *Anti-Oedipus*, we find that the ontological categories offered in *Difference and Repetition* are considerably altered. In *Difference and Repetition*, Deleuze had claimed that the genesis of any actual experience required both a field of individuation and a virtual Idea. The former was intensive and dynamic and served to drive the individuation and the dramatisation of spatio-temporal dynamisms, while the latter was differential and provided the structuring template by which the actualisation of experience could be given form. To put it briefly, in *Anti-Oedipus*, the main alteration to this process is that the virtual Idea is no longer considered necessary for the process of actualisation, and the intensive field of individuation is considered capable of directing its own actualisation. The intensive field is renamed as the multiplicity of desiring-production, and the spatio-temporal dynamisms, which are now considered as machinic and self-directed, are renamed as desiring-machines. Desiring-production differs from the intensive field defined in *Difference and Repetition*, and from the 'depths' as they are defined in *Logic of Sense*, because of the fact that they do not require any structuring from the heights of the virtual Idea in order to be productive. This is why Deleuze and Guattari claim that 'desiring-production is production of production'.[23] Desiring-machines, on the other hand, differ from the spatio-temporal dynamisms of *Difference and Repetition* because of the fact that they operate according to three immanent syntheses of

[23] Deleuze and Guattari, *Anti-Oedipus*, 6.

production, which require no interaction with the virtual. Summarising their position, Deleuze and Guattari state that the real decision to be made in analysis is not between Lacan's structural Oedipus and Freud's mythical one, but 'between Oedipus, structural as well as imaginary, and something else that all the Oedipuses crush and repress: desiring-production'.[24]

Where Deleuze and Guattari do retain the category of the virtual in *Anti-Oedipus*, it is no longer used to designate a differential structure that dominates the actualisation of reality, but is instead considered as a secondary effect of the machinic process of desiring-production. Take the example of the Oedipus complex again: Deleuze and Guattari show that, while it is the case that a particular, tripartite structure of desire is regularly found in the family unit, this structure is an effect of desiring-production and not its cause. To follow this logic is not to question the 'vital importance' of the love attachments formed in the family, but it is a question of knowing 'what the place and the function of parents are within desiring-production', rather than doing the reverse and 'forcing the entire interplay of desiring-machines to fit within the restricted code of Oedipus'.[25] Following from this reasoning, Deleuze and Guattari state that '*it is Oedipus that depends on desiring-production ... And it is the Oedipus complex that is virtual.*'[26] Oedipus is virtual in the sense that while it is made real in any number of human relationships, it has no actual existence, no spatio-temporal location and no necessity.

This reorientation of the virtual is crucial for Deleuze and Guattari's theory of unconscious desire because it opens the possibility of defining desire as distinct from the forces that dominate and repress it. For Lacan, and perhaps for the early Deleuze too, desire can never be considered apart from its repression, and hence the Real unconscious remains constantly blocked and always impossible; however, Deleuze and Guattari's theory makes space for a direct analysis of desiring-production. More specifically, while Lacanian structuralism can only consider desire as it is captured in the oedipal net, Deleuze and Guattari aim to analyse those flows of desire that escape the virtual Oedipus. From this perspective, these *escapes* are not anomalies, but are indicative of the very foundation of desire itself. Much of the psychoanalytic project of *Anti-Oedipus* is given

[24] Deleuze and Guattari, *Anti-Oedipus*, 59.
[25] Deleuze and Guattari, *Anti-Oedipus*, 51.
[26] Deleuze and Guattari, *Anti-Oedipus*, 140.

over to explaining how desiring-machines function, and how they generate our lived experience without the input of virtual Ideas.[27] Central to this task is Deleuze and Guattari's account of the nature of machinic processes and of the three syntheses of the unconscious that define the operations of desire. Here I will first give a brief account of the role of machinic processes, before introducing each of the three syntheses in turn.

In *Anti-Oedipus*, Deleuze and Guattari do not simply borrow the concept of the machine from Guattari's work in 'Machine and Structure' but develop it further. Here, they explain their use of the category of the machinic in contradistinction to theories of both mechanism and vitalism, and their aim is to produce the category of the machinic by splitting the difference between these two traditional categories.[28] Deleuze and Guattari take mechanistic theories as those that explain the real as a series of combinations and collisions of inert material elements, such as atoms, whereas traditional vitalisms assume a teleological force that runs through matter and orientates it. The problem that they see with this binary is that while mechanistic theories are capable of explaining how systems – be they composed of bodies or other structures – maintain themselves over time, they cannot explain how these systems arise. On the other hand, theories of vitalism can explain the genesis of form, but rely on an otherwise consistent and inert matter.

Deleuze and Guattari overcome this distinction by recognising the intensive nature of matter. While theories of mechanism and vitalism each take the extended nature of space and of time for granted, in *Anti-Oedipus* 'matter' is not something already distributed in space and made up of distinct units; instead it is nothing other than a field of intensities. Intensities always cancel themselves out in extensity and drive the individuation and dramatisation of what in *Difference and Repetition* Deleuze had called spatio-temporal dynamisms, which compose their own space and time as they unfold. Crucially then, desiring-machines do not operate within the structures of time and

[27] The category of the machinic is perhaps the most complex and widely misunderstood innovation of *Anti-Oedipus*. In later editions of the French publication, Deleuze and Guattari added an appendix to correct some of the major misconceptions surrounding their concept of desiring-machines, published in English as 'Balance-Sheet for "Desiring-Machines"' (Guattari, *Chaosophy*, 90–117).

[28] For a clear account of Deleuze and Guattari's attempts to collapse the mechanist/vitalist divide, see Colebrook, *Deleuze and History*, 1–32. Colebrook also explores Deleuze and Guattari's conception of death and its relation to history.

space, but produce these structural effects. The tendency of intensive matter that is always oriented outside of itself is what Deleuze and Guattari call desire, and it is the drive of this material desire that produces the actual relations of bodies in space and time. Deleuze and Guattari explain that their theory of desiring-machines 'shatters the vitalist argument by calling into question the specific or personal unity of the organism, and the mechanist argument ... by calling in question the structural unity of the machine'.[29] Following from this, the pair note that once the structural unity of the machine has been undone, 'a direct link is perceived between the machine and desire, the machine passes to the heart of desire, the machine is desiring and desire, machined'.[30]

In 'Machine and Structure', Guattari first defined the machine using Deleuze's category of repetition, in which what is repeated is never the same, but something different. This insistence is carried over into *Anti-Oedipus* via the fact that desiring-machines are said to have no structural consistency of their own; they do not function by simply maintaining a structure, but instead by continually breaking down.[31] To put this another way, the driving force of desire is nothing other than the drive towards difference; it is that which continually differs from itself. One important effect of this intensive driving force that distinguishes the theory of desiring-machines from both mechanism and vitalism is that it is capable of generating a *history*. Vitalism traditionally requires a particular form of life, such as that of human beings, to orientate its development and is thus, in a certain sense, anti-historicist, while mechanistic theories traditionally assume that temporal moments are nothing other than reversible or exchangeable states of matter. In contrast to this, desiring-machines emerge historically because the bodies that they compose can only be understood via a historical analysis of the intensive relations that give rise to them. By defining machinic processes, and therefore the activity of desiring-machines, in this way, Deleuze and Guattari give an intensive, materialist and historical account of the unconscious.

29 Deleuze and Guattari, *Anti-Oedipus*, 313. Deleuze and Guattari are referring to Samuel Butler, who they credit with first collapsing the distinction between mechanism and vitalism.

30 Deleuze and Guattari, *Anti-Oedipus*, 314.

31 Opposing them to mechanistic processes, Deleuze and Guattari write: 'Desiring-machines, on the contrary, continually break down as they run, and in fact run only when they are not functioning properly' (*Anti-Oedipus*, 33–4).

Another way to characterise Deleuze and Guattari's machinism, and its challenge to mechanism, would be to say that while mechanistic accounts of reality always separate a force from the mechanism that transmits it, machinic accounts conceive of things solely in terms of the interrelation of forces. It is for this reason that Deleuze and Guattari define machines in general, and desiring-machines in particular, as systems of flows and breaks in which 'every machine functions as a break in the flow in relation to the machine to which it is connected, but at the same time is also a flow itself, or the production of a flow, in relation to the machine connected to it'.[32] Flows are only cut by other flows, and there is no external mechanism that moderates their behaviour. If we were to ask what it is that is flowing, then the answer for Deleuze and Guattari could only be 'unconscious desire', understood as a material and intensive force.

To explain how this material and intensive unconscious functions, Deleuze and Guattari offer a transcendental account of unconscious desire. Just as Kant had developed his own critical philosophy of reason, not by considering the external factors that limit reason but by considering it immanently and noting the illusions that reason creates by its own mode of functioning, in *Anti-Oedipus* Deleuze and Guattari give an immanent account of the machinic processes of desire. In place of Kant's immanent and critical account of reason, Deleuze and Guattari define what they call the three syntheses of the unconscious, noting the ways in which each of these syntheses can lead to a specific transcendental illusion. When turning to the three syntheses of the unconscious as they are given in *Anti-Oedipus*, it is worth noting that even in 'Machine and Structure', while Guattari was first differentiating the two concepts in question, he was also careful to note that 'a machine is inseparable from its structural articulations and, conversely, that each contingent structure is dominated ... by a system of machines'.[33] The theory of desiring-machines in *Anti-Oedipus* is consistent with this early intuition, and when Deleuze and Guattari describe the three syntheses of the unconscious that determine the operation of desiring-machines, these operations are inextricable from the structural articulations of the body that they serve to organise. In *Anti-Oedipus* there is a continuum between machine and structure, which is filled with the becoming of a body. Bodies can either become more or less organised, depending on the

[32] Deleuze and Guattari, *Anti-Oedipus*, 39.
[33] Guattari, *Psychoanalysis and Transversality*, 318.

activities of the desiring-machines, and can thus tend towards one of two poles; becoming an organised and structured body that takes the form of an organism, or becoming a Body without Organs (BwO). Specifically, the desiring-machines operate according to three syntheses, called the connective synthesis of production, the disjunctive synthesis of recording and the conjunctive synthesis of consumption-consummation.[34] These syntheses describe the self-organising capabilities of intensive matter. They are driven by the tendency within matter to differentiate itself, a tendency which Deleuze and Guattari name *desire*.[35]

The first, connective synthesis is the operation by which desiring-machines connect to one another. If the field of desiring-production is understood as a kind of distribution of energetic indeterminacy, then the first synthesis of the unconscious is the process by which different areas in this field attract one another and form connections. It builds on Freud's notion of libidinal investment and the nature of the drives and is just that process by which desire, understood as the tendency inherent in intensive states, constantly reaches outside of itself. As we have already noted, desiring-production is a multiplicity, and desiring-machines can therefore never be understood as individual. There is never just one machine, but always 'machines driving other machines, machines being driven by other machines, with all the necessary couplings and connections'.[36] Borrowing from the psychoanalytic tradition, especially that of Melanie Klein, Deleuze and Guattari take the case of the child's mouth, understood as a sucking machine, coupled to the breast, understood as a machine producing milk, as their primary example of the connective synthesis. In line with their critical project, Deleuze and Guattari aim to differentiate between legitimate and illegitimate interpretations of this primary synthesis. According to their analysis, interpretations of this synthesis fail to be legitimate when they do not recognise the fact that the connections made here are always *transverse* connections between *heterogeneous* and *partial* elements. They argue that any interpretation of this synthesis that takes the elements that are connected in

[34] An analysis of how this presentation of the three syntheses differs from Deleuze's earlier account will follow later in this chapter.

[35] Deleuze and Guattari's comments echo Simondon's critique of hylomorphic accounts of the relation between matter and form, and his development of the concept of 'information' in *L'individu et sa genèse physico-biologique*.

[36] Deleuze and Guattari, *Anti-Oedipus*, 1.

the synthesis as logically preceding the connections made between them involves a logical fallacy. To treat the connective synthesis as a process occurring between pre-given homogeneous elements produces a transcendental illusion in the following way: that which creates a linear series of connections in a homogeneous field must be different in kind from that which it produces; the process of the first synthesis cannot therefore take for granted the pre-existence of the elements that it connects, or of the homogeneity of the field in which it connects them; the first synthesis must therefore connect only *partial* elements, drawn from *heterogeneous* fields. It is important to note here that the transversal nature of the first synthesis results in a series of connections between machines that is constant and additive, not just an 'and', but always 'and…' 'and then…'[37]

It is in this first synthesis that the BwO is created. Borrowing the term from Artaud, Deleuze and Guattari use the concept of the BwO to designate the unformed and unorganised state of the body, which desiring-machines must work against in the first synthesis to form connections.[38] Most generally, the BwO stands for matter without a form of content or expression. The genesis of desiring-machines and the BwO are concurrent because they each articulate a force that opposes the other. They both rely on the tension produced in 'the opposition of the process of production of the desiring-machines and the nonproductive stasis of the body without organs'.[39] At this point, the BwO is understood as nothing other than that force of inertia against which the connective tendency of desire must work. The first synthesis, by which matter constantly creates new transversal connections between heterogeneous partial elements, begins to construct regularities in matter, understood as primitive chains of code, and these regularities are defined against the threat of absolute indeterminacy in which difference is equally distributed. The BwO is just that name for the even distribution of indeterminate difference. As connections are constantly formed and reformed by desiring-machines, desiring-production takes on different levels of organisation. The BwO is therefore one pole towards

[37] Deleuze and Guattari, *Anti-Oedipus*, 5.

[38] The BwO was first introduced by Deleuze in *Logic of Sense*, where it played a slightly different role (223). For a clear articulation of the concept, and its relation to structure, see Young, Genosko and Watson, *The Deleuze and Guattari Dictionary*, 51–5.

[39] Deleuze and Guattari, *Anti-Oedipus*, 10.

which the desiring-machines can tend, namely the pole of absolute disorganisation.

The second synthesis of the unconscious is the disjunctive synthesis of recording. This describes the way in which desiring-machines detach themselves from one another in order to make new connections: for the mouth to move from the breast to the hand, to the hair, to a stone etc., it must also break each connection in turn. Here Deleuze and Guattari develop some of Freud's thoughts concerning memory and the role of signs in the psyche. They intend to show that by the process of constant disconnection–connection, the desiring-machines 'attach themselves to the body without organs as so many points of disjunction, between which an entire network of new syntheses is now woven, marking the surface off into co-ordinates, like a grid'.[40] The processes of disconnection and disjunction are said to 'record' desire because they leave traces on the BwO, like scars, where connections have been continually reopened and reclosed.[41] Once again, Deleuze and Guattari differentiate between the legitimate and illegitimate uses of this synthesis. Here, legitimate interpretations recognise the inclusive nature of the disjunctions, while illegitimate uses treat disjunctions as exclusive. I will come back to the distinction between inclusive and exclusive disjunctions later in this chapter; however, put briefly, Deleuze and Guattari's argument is that because of the transversal nature of the connections being made, the disjunctions of desiring-machines cannot be binary, but instead must be seen as affirming alternatives. To assume that disjunctions are exclusive is based on a transcendental illusion because it involves projecting back the possibility of opposition (which only holds between individuals) to a pre-individual process. According to the legitimate use of the second synthesis, disjunctions do not involve opposition or negation, but positive difference. This means that the aforementioned 'grid' produced on the BwO, which allows for the recording of the process of desire, is not yet a structure in the normal sense of the word. The inclusive nature of the disjunctions means that the process of the second synthesis operates

[40] Deleuze and Guattari, *Anti-Oedipus*, 13. Deleuze and Guattari speak of both attaching and detaching in relation to the second synthesis (13, 43). Just as Deleuze and Guattari's machinism conceptualises desire as a flow and a break simultaneously, in the second synthesis each apparent detachment is simply an attachment to something else.

[41] Deleuze and Guattari, *Anti-Oedipus*, 360.

not by the binary of 'either or', but by the constant extension of an 'either or ... or ... or'.[42]

The third synthesis of the unconscious is that of the conjunction of consumption–consummation, and it describes the way that the first two syntheses give way to the production of a subject, who exists alongside the desiring-machines and who experiences the intensities produced on the BwO. Deleuze and Guattari write that in the third synthesis, 'the subject is produced as a mere residuum alongside the desiring-machines'.[43] According to this analysis, the first two syntheses produce a series of 'intensive quantities', which could otherwise be thought of as pure sensations. These intensive quantities must be 'consumed' by 'personages' who are not yet individuals.[44] In fact, the subject is an effect of these states, rather than being their owner. In his analysis of the third synthesis of the unconscious, Nathan Widder explains the relationship between the subject and the intensive states produced in the first two syntheses when he writes that '[t]hese states are in no way chosen by the subject; rather, the subject is *driven* to them, and is constituted by being so driven'.[45] The difference between the legitimate and the illegitimate uses of the third synthesis depends on whether the subject recognises itself as a product of these sensations or projects its own image back into the process as the producer of these states.

With this in mind, Deleuze and Guattari can now offer their account of the Oedipus complex as an example of the illegitimate use of the three syntheses. The recognition of this illusion is central to their anti-psychoanalytic project in *Anti-Oedipus*, in which they attempt to show that the traditional insistence on the necessity of the oedipalisation of the child relies on exactly this kind of illusion. The illegitimate use of the third synthesis occurs when the subject produced there 'confuses himself with this third productive machine and with the residual reconciliation that it brings about: a conjunctive synthesis of consummation in the form of a wonderstruck "So *that's* what it was!"'[46] This misapprehension occurs when the subject

42 Deleuze first describes the difference between inclusive and exclusive disjunctions in *Logic of Sense*, 194–201. The distinction is important in *Anti-Oedipus* where it marks the difference between the legitimate and the illegitimate use of the second synthesis.

43 Deleuze and Guattari, *Anti-Oedipus*, 19.

44 Deleuze and Guattari, *Anti-Oedipus*, 92–5.

45 Widder, *Political Theory after Deleuze*, 109.

46 Deleuze and Guattari, *Anti-Oedipus*, 19.

places itself, as an individual, before the process of individuation that produces it. It is a retrospective appropriation of the processes of desiring-machines by the subject, who is produced only as an after-effect of the three syntheses. Specifically, the illegitimate use of the third synthesis follows from an illegitimate use of the second synthesis in the following way: while a legitimate and inclusive use of the disjunctive synthesis produces a schizophrenic subject, who experiences only intensive quantities (as delusions and hallucinations), an illegitimate and exclusive use of the disjunctive synthesis produces a neurotic subject who experiences desire as a relation between extended quantities.

The way in which the third synthesis of the unconscious relates to the BwO is also dependent on whether it is applied legitimately or illegitimately. According to the former, the body is produced as a site of becoming on which desire remains productive and active, while according to the latter the body becomes an organised, structured and stratified body across which desire can no longer flow. Thus, while it is possible for the unconscious to produce a productive BwO, the systematic misrepresentation of the three syntheses by psychoanalysis instead produces an organism in which each organ plays a specific role in desire and for which genuine change, outside of an oedipal structure, becomes impossible.

There are at least two key differences that should be highlighted here between the three syntheses of the unconscious given in *Anti-Oedipus* and the three syntheses of the production of sense given in *Logic of Sense*, and to a certain extent the three passive syntheses given in *Difference and Repetition*. First, the order of the three syntheses has been altered. In *Logic of Sense*, Deleuze describes the production of the surface of sense, which separated the primary depths of bodies from the secondary organisation of language, via the three syntheses of connection, conjunction and disjunction. Deleuze worked on the assumption that it was necessary for a certain kind of subject to be produced in the second synthesis before the disjunction of signifiers could be possible; however, in *Anti-Oedipus*, partly due to a new conception of a-signifying semiotics drawn from Guattari's work on Hjelmslev, Deleuze and Guattari can now explain the disjunction of recording on the BwO without reference to a subject of any kind. This is important for Deleuze and Guattari because while the Oedipus complex plays a central role in Deleuze's dynamic account of genesis in *Logic of Sense*, in *Anti-Oedipus* the complex is recognised as nothing other than a misapplication of the syntheses.

Consequently, the synthesis of conjunction is placed after, rather than before, the synthesis of disjunction.

Second, while the three syntheses of sense in *Logic of Sense* were placed *between* the primary order of bodies and the tertiary structure of language, in *Anti-Oedipus* the three syntheses operate in the depths of desiring-production. In *Logic of Sense* the primary order of bodies could not be given a semiotic articulation as it was pre-signifying, but in *Anti-Oedipus* this is no longer the case, and it is possible for Deleuze and Guattari to claim that the three syntheses are located directly in the unconscious and material real.[47] We could say that the theory of signification available to Deleuze at the point of writing *Logic of Sense* only allowed him to give an account of the three syntheses of sense using Carroll's menagerie of esoteric words, but that at the point of writing *Anti-Oedipus* Deleuze and Guattari can draw on the functioning of a-signifying semiotics to locate the three syntheses directly within the schizophrenic order of language glimpsed in Artaud's use of the breath-word.[48] To compare this move with the categories of *Difference and Repetition*, we can simply say that the three syntheses of the unconscious are not virtual or abstract in relation to the unconscious, but are actually present there. They define the way in which the intensive field of desiring-production is able to explicate itself without the direction of the virtual Idea.

This material, intensive and historical definition of the unconscious, and this explication of the immanent regulation of the three syntheses, allows Deleuze and Guattari to describe unconscious desire separately from the various ways in which it is repressed.

[47] This resonates with Dan W. Smith's argument that the major difference between *Logic of Sense* and *Anti-Oedipus* is that it is only in the latter that Deleuze 'unhesitatingly attempts to write about the "depths" in a straightforward manner'. See Smith, 'From the Surface to the Depths', 146. While Smith is correct to make this assertion, it is Guattari's reformulation of Deleuze's structuralism and his introduction of a machinic conception of semiotics that allows Deleuze to write about the depths in this manner. See Thornton, 'The Rise of the Machines'.

[48] Deleuze had a robust critique of Saussurean linguistics before he began his collaborations with Guattari. However, while Deleuze uses the work of Gustave Guillaume to challenge the notion of difference utilised by Saussure, he does this in order to give a genetic account of signification, while maintaining signification as the model for language. Deleuze's analysis of Lewis Carroll is telling: esoteric words help us to explore the realm of non-sense and challenge the ground of sense, but what makes them nonsensical is specifically their failure to signify anything. The breath-words and howl-words of Artaud challenge the grounds of sense in another way, namely by exposing the bodily dimension of sound.

The machinic unconscious is not understood as a kind of Real or brute force, which requires external articulation, but as an unconscious in possession of its own mode of articulation. It is the machinic character of the unconscious, on top of its intensive nature, that allows Deleuze and Guattari to write that in the unconscious, 'it is not the lines of pressure that matter, but on the contrary the lines of escape (*lignes de fuite*)'.[49] This is to say that the unconscious is not only an intensive field consisting of areas of pressure, which can only be understood by way of its repression, but a machinic entity capable of following its own line of articulation, which is not conditioned by any social structure but flees and escapes in a direction defined immanently by the legitimate use of its three syntheses. This discovery entails a major reworking of the process of analysis. While psychoanalysis can only point towards the underlying lines of pressure in the unconscious by considering the processes of psychic repression, 'schizoanalysis follows the lines of escape (*lignes de fuite*) and the machinic indices all the way to the desiring-machines'.[50] Before we move on to see how Deleuze and Guattari connect their analysis of these lines of flight to the project of revolutionary political change, it is important to recognise why they also claim that the activity of lines of flight renders the unconscious schizophrenic.

Multiplicity of Code and the Schizophrenic Unconscious

A number of questions still remain concerning Deleuze and Guattari's new model of the unconscious. Specifically, how is it possible for an intensive field to contain its own conditions of articulation? The answer provided in *Anti-Oedipus* is that 'every machine has a sort of code built into it, stored up inside it'.[51] Rather than following the direction of virtual Ideas, the intensive field of desiring-production explicates itself according to the chains of code that are contained within desiring-machines. In order to explain this use of 'coding' it will be necessary to look again at how Deleuze and Guattari attempt to overturn Lacanian linguistic structuralism. In their resolutely ambivalent fashion, Deleuze and Guattari at once praise Lacan for his 'discovery of this fertile domain of a code of the unconscious' while criticising his decision to treat this code as if it were a single

[49] Deleuze and Guattari, *Anti-Oedipus*, 371.
[50] Deleuze and Guattari, *Anti-Oedipus*, 372.
[51] Deleuze and Guattari, *Anti-Oedipus*, 41.

language, when it is 'a multiplicity so complex that we can scarcely speak of *one* chain or even *one* code of desire'.[52] To put it briefly, Deleuze and Guattari agree with Lacan that the explication of unconscious desire necessarily goes by way of a semiotics, but they refuse Lacan's claim that this semiotics is signifying, or that it is structured like a language.[53]

For Lacan, reality is made up of the two realms of the Symbolic and the Imaginary, which constitute the lived reality of social experience of the psychoanalytic subject. Reality, according to this reading, is made up of a structure of linguistic and social signifying relations and is related to conscious life. The Real, Lacan's third category, is that which cannot be captured by either the Symbolic or the Imaginary and which sits outside them.[54] The Real is the site of trauma, of *jouissance* and of unconscious desire. According to this account, the subject is only produced at the moment that it enters the Symbolic; however, as the laws governing the linguistic structure of the Symbolic pre-exist the subject, the subject is never able to fully constitute itself there, while real, unconscious desire always remains 'impossible' for the subject, who can only ever experience it as that which was necessarily repressed in order to enter the Symbolic.

According to this psychoanalytic structuralism, the functioning of desire is analogous to the functioning of signification. While any one signifier gains its meaning not by its relation to an external signified, but by the way that it refers to other signifiers, in the same way desire is not defined by that which it desires, but by the way it relates to other desires. Similarly, just as the Symbolic realm is constituted by a constant slippage of meaning from one signifier to the next, desire is constituted by a constant deferral. The subject thinks it desires an object, but upon attaining the object it realises that this was just a stand-in for something else and thus goes on to desire another object. To designate the real object of desire, which is constantly lost and always retreating from the subject, Lacan uses the term *objet petit a*.

52 Deleuze and Guattari, *Anti-Oedipus*, 41.

53 While it could be argued that the virtual Ideas in *Difference and Repetition* were a-signifying, the important innovation of *Anti-Oedipus* is the ability to analyse processes that are a-signifying and yet semiotic in nature.

54 Lacan's theory of the three registers is not formally introduced during his seminars as a complete theory, but develops throughout his career. References to these three registers begin at least as early as his first seminar, *Freud's Papers on Technique*, and continue throughout the rest. For more, see the accompanying sections in Evans, *An Introductory Dictionary of Lacanian Psychoanalysis*.

The impossibility of ever reaching this object, and of fulfilling desire, is constituted by the law of the father and the threat of castration. Thus, in Lacanian terminology, we can say that the subject of desire is a barred subject, the object of desire is the *objet petit a*, and the role of the law is played by the phallus. The barred subject is always in the process of reaching for a desired object and yet always failing to attain it; the *objet petit a* is the name for this desired object, which always retreats and is never attainable; and the phallus is the abstract third term that signifies the constant failure of the desiring subject to attain the desired object.[55]

This structural account of unconscious desire operates by using linguistics to universalise the Oedipus complex. The account is oedipal in the sense that it takes desire to be always unfulfilled, always lacking, and always castrated by the paternal injunction of law. However, as we have already seen, Deleuze and Guattari argue that the logic of the Oedipus complex is based on a kind of transcendental illusion by which the contemporary, capitalist forms of social repression are assumed to be the logical foundation of desire, rather than its effect. For Deleuze and Guattari, desire is not necessarily lacking but is inherently productive, while the real of the unconscious is not impossible or inaccessible, but material and intensive.

While Deleuze and Guattari agree that the unconscious must involve a process of recording by which unconscious memory is created, the semiotics of this system are not signifying and hence the logic of desire is not oedipal. They write that the chains of the unconscious 'are called "signifying chains" because they are made up of signs, but these signs are not themselves signifying'.[56] In a challenge to Lacan, and drawing on Guattari's work in 'Machine and Structure' and on his interest in the semiotic theories of Hjelmslev, Deleuze and Guattari are claiming here that the unconscious process of recording functions by use of a semiotics that is a-signifying. Such semiotic processes function without referring to anything outside themselves and without the need to express any content. For example, both genetic code and computer code operate by the use of signs, but they do not

[55] Lacan's theory of desire does not remain constant throughout his work, and the relationship between these three elements alters during his career. For his most nuanced description of the desiring relationship of the subject, see 'The Subversion of the Subject and the Dialectic of Desire in the Freudian Unconscious', in *Écrits*, 671–700.

[56] Deleuze and Guattari, *Anti-Oedipus*, 41.

express any sense that exists outside themselves.[57] Perhaps the most important aspect of such semiotic systems for Deleuze and Guattari is their ability to refuse the binary, exclusive disjunctions offered by Saussurean signification, in favour of a form of inclusive disjunction. A brief analysis of the difference between exclusive and inclusive disjunctions will be useful here in order to show how Deleuze and Guattari claim that the coding of desiring-machines functions.

Well before the publication of *Anti-Oedipus*, at the time of writing *Logic of Sense*, Deleuze made a distinction between those forms of judgement that are based on binary and exclusive disjunctions, in which two different options are set up against each other and one must be selected in preference to the other, and the form of inclusive disjunction, in which two options differ from one another without being opposed, and can thus be affirmed together. An inclusive disjunction is defined as 'an operation according to which two things or two determinations are affirmed *through* their difference, that is to say, that they are objects of simultaneous affirmation only insofar as their difference is itself affirmed and is itself affirmative'.[58] In this case, 'we are no longer faced with an identity of contraries, which would still be inseparable as such from a movement of the negative and of exclusion'.[59] However, while Deleuze makes this distinction in *Logic of Sense*, he also claims there that this 'positive difference' of inclusive disjunctions 'belongs to topology and to the surface'.[60] This is because, given the understanding of signification utilised by Deleuze at this point, the organisation of the voice bears only exclusive disjunctions of opposition, while the primary depths lack the necessary organisation all together. At the point of writing *Anti-Oedipus*, on the other hand, Deleuze and Guattari speak of a form of semiotic encoding produced by the second synthesis of desiring-machines. Here, the constant disjunction and reconnection of desiring-machines to the BwO creates a web of code that is neither signifying nor exclusive.[61] The upshot of this is that when it comes to

[57] Watson, *Guattari's Diagrammatic Thought*, 47.
[58] Deleuze, *Logic of Sense*, 197.
[59] Deleuze, *Logic of Sense*, 197.
[60] Deleuze, *Logic of Sense*, 197.
[61] The first thing that Deleuze and Guattari ever co-published was a paper titled 'The Disjunctive Synthesis', which reworks Deleuze's earlier reading of disjunction from *Logic of Sense* and points towards their use of disjunction in the immanent critique of desire in *Anti-Oedipus*. See Deleuze and Guattari, 'La Synthèse disjonctive', 54–62.

desiring-machines, 'the breaks in the process are productive, and are reassemblies in and of themselves', which means that '[d]isjunctions, by the very fact that they are disjunctions, are inclusive'.[62] Given the form of positive difference used here, we can say that the semiotic encodings that direct the operation of desiring-machines rely on an immanent conception of disjunction, and thus determine the operation of desiring-machines without being external to them.

Once again, it is interesting to note here how Deleuze and Guattari's conceptual innovations are turned against the Oedipus complex. While they claim that the recording function of the unconscious is carried out immanently by a series of inclusive disjunctions, they also claim that an illegitimate reading of the disjunctive synthesis, which considers it from a transcendent point of view, is at the core of the oedipal understanding of desire. They claim that the disjunctive synthesis 'is capable of two uses, the one immanent, the other transcendent', and ask 'why does psychoanalysis reinforce the transcendent use that introduces exclusions and restrictions everywhere in the disjunctive network, and that makes the unconscious swing over into Oedipus?'[63] Their point here is that, under a certain reading favoured by Lacanians, there are two options open to the child: either accept the pre-given laws of the Symbolic structure and constitute yourself as a barred subject within a community of speakers where you will remain castrated; or foreclose the Symbolic, fail to develop a subject position at all and become psychotic. In this case, the child must either pass through oedipalisation and become a neurotic, or fail to pass through oedipalisation and become a psychotic.

Deleuze and Guattari's critique of this reading is subtle; they do not simply claim that it is better to refuse oedipalisation and become psychotic, but instead that we can refuse the binary decision, or exclusive disjunction, that the whole of the Oedipus complex presents us with. They claim that 'the exclusive relation introduced by Oedipus comes into play not only between the various disjunctions conceived as differentiations, *but between the whole of the differentiations that it imposes and an undifferentiated [un indifferencie] that it presupposes*'.[64] The result of this analysis is that the binary options of the oedipalised neurotic and the foreclosed psychotic result from a

[62] Deleuze and Guattari, *Anti-Oedipus*, 45.
[63] Deleuze and Guattari, *Anti-Oedipus*, 86–7.
[64] Deleuze and Guattari, *Anti-Oedipus*, 87.

transcendent misapprehension of the recording process of the unconscious in which 'there is Oedipus on either side'.[65]

The schizophrenic mode that Deleuze and Guattari champion in *Anti-Oedipus* is not based on the model of the schizophrenic patient who is foreclosed to the Symbolic and has thus become catatonic. Instead, what Deleuze and Guattari seek out is the immanent mode of functioning of the unconscious, where all disjunctions are inclusive and where the question of Oedipus does not arise. This move is important because it gives a positive and productive role to schizophrenia. They claim that in the case of those catatonics given a diagnosis of schizophrenia, it is the case that their 'loss of reality is not the effect of the schizophrenic process, but the effect of its forced oedipalization'.[66] For Deleuze and Guattari, the binary choice offered by Oedipus relies on a misunderstanding of the semiotic nature of the unconscious. The choice need not be between a completely a-signifying and chaotic abyss and a signifying linguistic structure. Instead, it is possible to recognise that the unconscious is a semiotic system that is neither an undifferentiated chaos nor a fully differentiated structure, but an encoded machinic process that resists this binary. From a transcendent interpretation of unconscious recording, it would follow that the intensive field of desiring-production required some kind of external direction; however, the immanent interpretation of unconscious recording as a series of inclusive disjunctions requires no such thing.

The Schizophrenic Line of Flight

Given this analysis of the way in which the intensive field of desiring-production contains its own conditions of articulation, we are now closing in on Deleuze and Guattari's first uses of the concept of the line of flight. In *Anti-Oedipus*, Deleuze and Guattari use the concept of the line of flight to designate a 'schizoid breakthrough' which is always 'schizophrenic, machinic, and dispersed'.[67] They say that the line of flight is 'extra-oedipal', that lines of flight have 'the capacity for causing the flows of desire to circulate', and that they resist the 'familial position' of the Oedipus complex.[68] In this

[65] Deleuze and Guattari, *Anti-Oedipus*, 87.
[66] Deleuze and Guattari, *Anti-Oedipus*, 134.
[67] Deleuze and Guattari, *Anti-Oedipus*, 311, 373.
[68] Deleuze and Guattari, *Anti-Oedipus*, 136, 381, 311.

sense, the concept of the line of flight holds an important position in the book. It is central to the anti-oedipal project of showing that the unconscious is not structural, in either a strictly linguistic or oedipal sense, and that unconscious desire is never lacking, but is positive, creative and productive. However, in order to give a technical definition of the line of flight, as it appears in this section of the book, it is important to show how it operates in relation to the coded, machinic and a-signifying nature of the unconscious.

As we have seen, according to Deleuze and Guattari, the unconscious does not represent anything. It is a factory made of desiring-machines and not a theatre for the dramatisation of desire. It is constituted by 'flows and partial objects' that form semiotic chains that are constantly being decoded and recoded.[69] Much like the genetic code, it is an open-ended series of coded chains that constantly rewrite themselves. As we have also seen, the processes by which this code is constantly rewritten are defined by the constant connection, disjunction and conjunction of desiring-machines. However, the resulting encodings never remain static because the three syntheses just mentioned are of a special kind; namely they are 'transverse connections, inclusive disjunctions, and polyvocal conjunctions'.[70] What this means is that rather than connections being formed only between part-signs of the same chain of code, the connections are transversal and so they cut across multiple chains of code. Connections are made when a partial element escapes (*fuite*) one chain to connect with another. Then, because the disjunctions formed are inclusive and not exclusive, the processes of connection and disjunction are never arrested, but continue fleeing (*fuite*) unceasingly, such that the chains 'all intersect, following the endlessly ramified paths of the great disjunctive synthesis'.[71] In this way, we can see that there are certain processes within the unconscious that resist the possibility of the codes becoming engrained and that ensure that desire continues to differ from itself. These processes are transformations or mutations that ward off the possibility of stagnation. In his introduction to *Anti-Oedipus*, Mark Seem calls them 'the schizzes-flows—forces that escape coding, scramble the codes, and flee in all directions'.[72] When a part-sign makes a connection that

[69] Deleuze and Guattari, *Anti-Oedipus*, 308.
[70] Deleuze and Guattari, *Anti-Oedipus*, 315.
[71] Deleuze and Guattari, *Anti-Oedipus*, 42.
[72] Deleuze and Guattari, *Anti-Oedipus*, xxiii.

is transversal, and when the disjunction from the previous chain is inclusive, 'the chain no longer has any other function than that of deterritorializing the flows and causing them to pass through the signifying wall, thereby undoing the codes', and it is thereby called 'a chain of escape (*fuite*), and no longer a code'.[73] With the chain of escape, 'the signifying chain has become a chain of decoding and deterritorialization, which must be apprehended—and can only be apprehended—as the reverse of the codes and the territorialities'.[74] Subsequently, these decoding processes of the unconscious are named as 'the lines of flight (*fuite*)', and their activity is to 'follow the decoded and deterritorialized flows' of the unconscious.[75] Lines of escape, or lines of flight, are simply those schizophrenic processes of the unconscious that create mutations in the code by making transversal links between codes, in an open and inclusive series of disjunctions. The first sense of the word *fuite*, when it appears in the phrase *ligne de fuite*, is therefore the fleeing or escaping of partial elements from one code to another.[76]

There is, however, a second sense in which the line of flight 'escapes' or 'flees'; namely, it designates that which resists capture by signification. While Deleuze and Guattari aim to show that the unconscious is not structural but machinic, it remains the case that the unconscious can only be *represented as structural*. This is to say that, due to the persistent illusion of individual being in representation, the unconscious appears as structural, or is given to us as such. This makes the practice of schizoanalysis more difficult: 'What complicates everything is that there is indeed a necessity for desiring-production to be induced from representation, to be discovered through its lines of escape (*lignes de fuite*).' To put this another way, as an a-signifying machine the unconscious cannot be given directly within the signifying web of consciousness; however, by starting from the point of view of the structure, the analyst can work back to the machinic unconscious by following those lines that constantly fail to be adequately captured by the structure. The primary example of

73 Deleuze and Guattari, *Anti-Oedipus*, 360–1.

74 Deleuze and Guattari, *Anti-Oedipus*, 360.

75 Deleuze and Guattari, *Anti-Oedipus*, 401.

76 Speaking of the genetic code of the wasp and the orchid, an example Deleuze and Guattari will use again in *A Thousand Plateaus*, they write that in the unconscious: 'Each chain captures fragments of other chains from which it "extracts" a surplus value, just as the orchid code "attracts" the figure of the wasp: both phenomena demonstrate the surplus value of a code' (*Anti-Oedipus*, 42).

how the schizoanalyst must complete this task is presented in cases of schizophrenia. Rather than interpreting schizophrenia as a failure to enter the structure of the Symbolic, or as a lack of subjective consistency, schizophrenic processes must be understood as excessive and creative forces that actively resist the oedipal structure and escape from it at all costs. Deleuze and Guattari state that in order to reach the unconscious, 'schizoanalysis follows the lines of escape (*lignes de fuite*) and the machinic indices all the way to the desiring-machines'.[77]

When we see that, despite its illusions, the structural interpretation of the unconscious can still be a useful tool for discovering the machinic unconscious, it becomes clear why Deleuze and Guattari hold such an ambivalent relationship to Lacan. By breaking with Freud, by showing that the Oedipus complex is imaginary, and by setting up a structural interpretation of the unconscious, Lacan had developed a rigorous method for locating all of the ways in which the unconscious resists the structure of oedipal desire that is imposed on it. Speaking of Lacan, Deleuze and Guattari write that '[t]o trace back from images to the structure would have little significance and would not rescue us from representation, if the structure did not have a reverse side that is like the real production of desire'.[78] While the structure is a mere representation of the unconscious, this 'reverse side' is made up of 'pure positive multiplicities where everything is possible, without exclusiveness or negation, syntheses operating without a plan, where the connections are transverse, the disjunctions included, the conjunctions polyvocal'.[79] The signs that compose the signifying structure might follow the rules of signification, but the 'signs of desire' on the side of the machine have 'no other statutory condition than that of being dispersed elements of desiring-machines that are themselves dispersed'.[80] Given this practical restriction on schizoanalysis, which necessitates an engagement with the structural representation of the unconscious, the importance of the lines of flight are doubled. Not only do they have a functional role in the unconscious, namely to constantly ward off the possibility of the codes becoming engrained by creating constant transformations and mutations of the code, but they also have a practical significance for

[77] Deleuze and Guattari, *Anti-Oedipus*, 372.
[78] Deleuze and Guattari, *Anti-Oedipus*, 339.
[79] Deleuze and Guattari, *Anti-Oedipus*, 339.
[80] Deleuze and Guattari, *Anti-Oedipus*, 339.

the schizoanalyst. The semiotic encodings of desiring-machines can only be partially captured by the signifying structure of Oedipus, of which they are the reverse side.[81] What escapes this capture are those processes of decoding that cannot be integrated into the sociolinguistic structure. These are the lines of escape, or the lines of flight, that the schizoanalyst must follow.

In order to clarify how the line of flight functions in this second sense it will be useful to briefly explore the way in which Deleuze and Guattari draw on Deleuze's earlier reading of Riemann's concept of the multiplicity to describe the relationship between the structural representation of the unconscious, which Lacan's analysis made possible, and the machinic unconscious that is its reverse side. This will lead us back to the critique of linear perspective and the question of intensive depth that Deleuze discussed in *Difference and Repetition.* To put it briefly, Deleuze and Guattari equate the structured representation of the unconscious with the discrete multiplicity of Riemannian geometry and with the structured space of linear perspective. Here, depth is produced in representation by means of discrete elements, in this case linguistic signifiers, that relate to one another on a flattened plane. The machinic unconscious, on the other hand, is analysed using the Riemannian understanding of the continuous multiplicity in which the endless transversal connections of part-signs create an unconscious of intensive depth.

While Deleuze and Guattari do not mention Riemann by name in *Anti-Oedipus*, they are clearly drawing on his work when they describe the process by which the unconscious envelops 'distances within intensive quantities' such that 'it does not divide without changing its nature or form'.[82] They also draw on the language of differential calculus to name the 'flows and partial objects' of the machinic unconscious as 'infinitesimal lines of escape (*lignes de fuite*)'.[83] It is also claimed repeatedly that desiring-production,

[81] When referring to the machinic unconscious as the 'reverse side' of the structure, Deleuze and Guattari include a footnote on Leclaire's interpretation of Lacan (*Anti-Oedipus*, 340). However, it is also likely that the 'reverse side' (*l'envers*) is a reference to Lacan himself, whose seminar of 1969–70 was titled 'L'envers de la psychanalyse' or 'The Reverse Side of Psychoanalysis'. Following this chain of reference once more, Lacan seemingly alights on this title for his seminar as an allusion to Balzac's final novel *L'Envers de l'histoire contemporaine*, published in English as *The Wrong Side of Paris.*

[82] Deleuze and Guattari, *Anti-Oedipus*, 95–6.

[83] Deleuze and Guattari, *Anti-Oedipus*, 308.

understood as the basic material of the unconscious, is a continuous multiplicity:

> It is only the category of multiplicity, used as a substantive and going beyond both the One and the many, beyond the predicative relation of the One and the many, that can account for desiring-production: desiring-production is pure multiplicity, that is to say, an affirmation that is irreducible to any sort of unity.[84]

By describing the difference between the structural representation of the unconscious and the machinic unconscious itself in these terms, Deleuze and Guattari are also able to explain how the two relate to each other. As we saw in the first chapter of this book, an n-dimensional curved space can be represented within a flat space of n + 1 dimensions. For example, it is possible to represent a two-dimensional space of regular positive curvature as the surface of a three-dimensional sphere. However, in order for this representation to be given, a regular measurement is required, taken outside the space in question, by which to measure the relative distances within the curved space. In contrast to this method, which relies on the ability to transcend the multiplicity in question in order to measure and order it, by the use of differential calculus it is possible to give an immanent account of spaces of fixed or variable curvature without embedding them in a higher-dimensional space.

Using this terminology, we can say that Deleuze and Guattari take the Lacanian structuralist account of the unconscious as a *representation* of the unconscious, which functions by taking the oedipal relation between the mother and the child as the transcendent measuring rod against which to judge all other relations. The problem with this method is that it relies on an external measure that can never be immanently justified, and that by the use of this measure the infinite variation of the multiplicity in question is reduced to a single, ordered expression. What Deleuze and Guattari attempt to do in *Anti-Oedipus* is to start with the representation of the unconscious that is handed down to them, but then to carry out a kind of differential calculus of the unconscious in order to move past this representation and towards an immanent account.

Interestingly, in a small number of comments, Deleuze and Guattari return to the example of linear perspective, which Deleuze discussed in *Difference and Repetition* as one example of the way

[84] Deleuze and Guattari, *Anti-Oedipus*, 45.

in which a representation of space can fail to capture the intensity of the dimension of depth. In the previous analysis, we saw how Deleuze showed that linear perspective creates an organised and regular space of perception at the cost of burying the intensive nature of space under the representation of extensity. This was most evident in the fact that linear perspective gives priority to the two dimensions of height and breadth, which are said to generate the dimension of depth, rather than the other way around. This critique of linear perspective, as it is given in *Difference and Repetition*, acts as a model for the analysis of psychoanalytic structuralism in *Anti-Oedipus*. For example, talking of the way in which Lacan's work points towards the intensive and machinic unconscious as the 'reverse side' that is hidden under the face of the structure, Deleuze and Guattari write: 'It is this entire reverse side of the structure that Lacan discovers, with the "a" as machine.'[85]

However, in an interview given in 1973 in which Deleuze and Guattari defended some of their concepts from *Anti-Oedipus*, Guattari offers more insight into just how the lost object of desire, or the *objet petit a*, points to the real machinic unconscious: 'I'm not at all sure that the concept of the "a" object in Lacan is anything but a vanishing point, an escape, precisely, from the despotic character of signifying chains.'[86] The vanishing point in a painting of linear perspective is the point at which depth is represented by making it disappear at an infinite distance, beyond the picture plane. According to this analysis, while linear perspective gives only the illusion of depth, the vanishing point, where parallel lines escape the plane to meet at infinity, offers the viewer a point at which to escape from this frame. What Deleuze and Guattari seem to be saying here is that instead of seeing the object of desire as a kind of cut, a gap, or a vanishing point (*point de fuite*) in the structural organisation of desire, we must recognise that this structural organisation is only a representation, and that by treating desire as an intensive excess rather than a lack in extensity it is possible to follow the line drawn by this desire (*ligne de fuite*) to reach the real unconscious.

[85] Deleuze and Guattari, *Anti-Oedipus*, 339. The little 'a' here refers to the French word *autre* and so is often translated as 'o' for 'other'. I have retained the 'a' in order to conform with the quote from *Chaosophy* below.

[86] Guattari, *Chaosophy*, 69. The 'vanishing point' referred to here is written in French as *point de fuite*.

This way of speaking about psychoanalytic structuralism in *Anti-Oedipus* is of particular interest to us here because of the way it combines insights from both Deleuze and Guattari's work prior to their collaboration. According to the interpretation of structuralism given by Deleuze in *Difference and Repetition* and *Logic of Sense*, both the vanishing point in linear perspective and the *objet petit a* in Lacanian psychoanalysis can be read as second order differences, much like the 'empty square' or 'object = x' required in any structure to allow for the circulation of elements between series. However, after Guattari's reworking of Deleuzian structuralism in his essay 'Machine and Structure', the pair can recognise that this element should not be considered as part of the structure at all, but as a machinic element that exists outside the structure and is not contained by its rules. In 'Machine and Structure' Guattari had already named the lost object of desire the '*objet-machine petit "a"*'.[87] Later, in *Anti-Oedipus*, Deleuze and Guattari develop this idea further to show that, rather than being a mere vanishing point (*point de fuite*) in the extended structure of desire, the unconscious is a machine that operates by drawing lines of flight (*lignes de fuite*) that create the extended structure as a secondary effect. The 'beyond' indicated by the vanishing point of structural psychoanalysis is not an undifferentiated abyss, but a heterogeneous interconnection of part-signs in intensive relations: not an oedipal theatre, but a productive machine.[88]

At the beginning of this chapter the line of flight was given a provisional role as the concept used by Deleuze and Guattari to define the way that desire operates when it is not inhibited, captured or turned against itself by the structuring forces of social reality. Given the subsequent analysis of Deleuze and Guattari's critique of the Oedipus complex, their immanent account of the three syntheses of unconscious, and their positive, machinic, material and intensive account of the unconscious of desiring-production, it is now possible

[87] Guattari, *Psychoanalysis and Transversality*, 323–4.

[88] Returning to the question of linear perspective, Deleuze and Guattari elaborate this point through an analysis of the later works of J. M. W. Turner, where the structured space of linear perspective gives way to a space of pure colour, a 'transverse organization of the canvas is born, with lines of escape (*lignes de fuite*) or breakthrough' (*Anti-Oedipus*, 403). They call this move a 'decoding of the flows of painting' via a use of 'schizoid lines of escape (*lignes de fuite*)' which they contrast with 'a properly pictorial axiomatic that chokes off the escapes (*fuites*), closes the whole constellation to the transversal relations between lines and colors, and reduces it to archaic or new territorialities (perspective, for example)' (403).

to add some nuance to this definition. Lines of flight are drawn in the unconscious when the code embedded in desiring-machines undoes itself by extracting elements from one code and making transversal connections between heterogeneous chains of code. These lines are endlessly ramified by the inclusive disjunctions of the second synthesis to create ever new forms of desiring activity. This procedure is central to the schizophrenic process of desire, which constitutes the unconscious as a continuous, intensive and a-signifying multiplicity. From the point of view of representation, these lines of flight appear only as processes that escape the capture of signification. Rather than following the Lacanian psychoanalytic tendency of treating these escapes as empty placeholders for the structural invariant of lack, Deleuze and Guattari advocate a new form of schizoanalysis in which these lines of flight are treated as positive and creative and are followed in order to reach the real nature of the machinic unconscious.[89]

According to *Anti-Oedipus*, desire is the driving force of difference; it is that which continually differs from itself and in doing so drives processes of transformation. While psychoanalysis has investigated desire, it has always represented it in a way that obfuscates its transformative nature, seeing it as repetition-of-the-same, eternally captured by the structural triangulations of the family. *Anti-Oedipus* offers a positive and transformative image of desire, and it is the concept of the line of flight that allows it to do so.

[89] Lacanian theory does not simply define desire as a lack in the Symbolic, but also as an excess in the Real. However, when Deleuze and Guattari were publishing *Anti-Oedipus* in 1972, Lacan's work gave precedence to the former articulation. For more on the opposing methodologies of Lacan and Deleuze, see Schuster, *The Trouble with Pleasure*, 98–100.

4

Anti-Oedipus and Social Machines

Political Transformations

Following the discussion of Deleuze and Guattari's reformulation of desire, in this chapter I will explore the theory of history and of political change put forward in *Anti-Oedipus*. We have seen how Deleuze and Guattari rethink the concept of the unconscious to highlight the role played by schizophrenic processes and by lines of flight, but what we have yet to cover is the way that such a theory opens on to broader political questions concerning the production of reality and its historical transformation. To complete our analysis of the role played by the concept of the line of flight in *Anti-Oedipus*, here I will show how Deleuze and Guattari use insights from Nietzsche, Freud, Marx and others to offer a new account of the world-historical position of capitalism. This analysis will introduce us to the distinction between the molecular and the molar registers of political activity, and to the different historical stages of Deleuze and Guattari's account of political economy. Finally, by bringing together Deleuze and Guattari's theory of the unconscious with their theory of political change, I will explain why the pair claim that it is only via the revolutionary practice in which the schizoanalyst 'follows lines of escape (*lignes de fuite*)' that the social structure of capitalist relations will be overcome.[1] This chapter concludes with a review of the various ways in which Deleuze and Guattari utilise the concept of the line of flight in *Anti-Oedipus*. Here I will pick out four distinct uses of the concept and explain how each of these uses relates to the others. Before reaching this point, however, it will be necessary to get a handle on the mode of political analysis that Deleuze and Guattari are engaging in.

[1] Deleuze and Guattari, *Anti-Oedipus*, 372.

Molecular Processes and Molar Histories

Far from being a one-dimensional polemic against structural psychoanalysis, *Anti-Oedipus* is a kind of political manifesto that incorporates an analysis of the history of political power. In this respect, Deleuze and Guattari are as indebted to Nietzsche as they are to either Freud or Marx.[2] By drawing on Nietzsche's analysis of debt and guilt in the second essay of *On the Genealogy of Morality*, and the continuation of these themes in *The Anti-Christ*, Deleuze and Guattari attempt to use Freudian and Marxist theory to bring about what Nietzsche called a transvaluation or 'revaluation of all values'.[3] In order to give an account of the concept of the line of flight in its full theoretical context, in this section I will explore the place of schizoanalytic concepts in Deleuze and Guattari's political thought. Schizoanalysis is not intended to simply replace psychoanalysis as a method of cure, but is designed as a mode of historical-materialist criticism, capable of producing revolutionary modes of subjectivity. Deleuze and Guattari argue in *Anti-Oedipus* that Marxism must be reworked in order to account for the problem of subjectivity, and that this can be done by analysing the history of political economy in terms of desire. Contra Marx, and drawing on insights from Reich, Spinoza and Nietzsche, Deleuze and Guattari claim that it is not ideology that tricks people into working against their own self-interest, but that people become enslaved when their desire is captured by an organisation of force that they cannot resist.[4] Deleuze and Guattari's attempts to combine a theory of desire and a theory of political economy can be seen clearly in their use of the previously discussed concepts of desiring-production and desiring-machines, which each attempt to combine the category of labour-power, first analysed by Adam Smith and David Ricardo and later utilised so effectively by Marx, and the category of libido, first analysed by Freud.

Yet another way to characterise the political project of *Anti-Oedipus* is to focus on Deleuze and Guattari's responses to traditional

2 For an account of Deleuze and Guattari's theory of social machines that does justice to the influence of Nietzsche, see Widder, *Political Theory after Deleuze*, 113–22.

3 Nietzsche, *The Anti-Christ*, 11. It is not by chance that the title of *Anti-Oedipus* reflects Nietzsche's *Anti-Christ*.

4 For an overview of Deleuze and Guattari's Freudo-Marxism, and the place of Nietzsche, Spinoza and others within it, see Holland, *Deleuze and Guattari's Anti-Oedipus*, 16–19, 106.

Marxist accounts of historical change. As we will see, Deleuze and Guattari's schizoanalytic focus on processes of transformation allows them to offer an alternative to the apparent dichotomy between revisionary and revolutionary accounts of historical change.[5] Before moving on to explore the historical account given in *Anti-Oedipus* of the development of different modes of desiring-production, it will therefore be useful to consider Deleuze and Guattari's use the concept of history in a little more detail. First, the form of historical materialism put forward by Deleuze and Guattari is a subtle one that leads them to claim that the separate discoveries of the category of labour-power and the category of desire were made possible by a specific set of historical conditions. This historical analysis of the discovery of labour-power and of desire serves to cement Deleuze and Guattari's historical critique of the Oedipus complex. Simply put, they claim that it is only with the rise of capitalism, and the separation of the public life of the factory from the private life of the family, that the processes of social reproduction and human reproduction become distinct. Here, 'the elements of production and antiproduction are not reproduced in the same way as humans themselves, but find in them a simple material that the form of economic reproduction preorganizes in a mode that is entirely distinct from the form this material has as human reproduction'.[6] Only once the two domains of work and family have been divided, and thus the two processes of social reproduction and human reproduction have become distinct, is it possible for Smith and Ricardo to set up a science of the former, and for Freud to set up a science of the latter. What makes Deleuze and Guattari's concept of history so interesting here is their claim that while the concepts of labour-power and libido only arise historically, our ability to think this moment in terms of its place in universal or world history relies on the prior existence of a particular form of libidinal economy. Here Deleuze and Guattari follow Marx directly, when he writes: 'World history has not always existed; history as world history [is] a result.'[7] In order to understand how Deleuze and Guattari can simultaneously hold what seem to be

[5] In this respect, it would be interesting to read *Anti-Oedipus* alongside Nathan Coombs's book *History and Event*. While it does not cover the work of Deleuze and Guattari, this book offers an otherwise comprehensive account of recent French attempts to think the continuous changes of history alongside the revolutionary breaks that punctuate it.

[6] Deleuze and Guattari, *Anti-Oedipus*, 286.

[7] Marx, *Grundrisse*, 110.

two contrary positions, namely that the categories of labour-power and libido only arise historically and that history only arises due to a particular combination of libido and labour-power, it will be necessary to introduce the distinction that they make between the two regimes of the molar and the molecular. This distinction will allow us to see how Deleuze and Guattari's account of the unconscious interacts with their political claims, and to see where the concept of history fits within them.

The distinction that Deleuze and Guattari make between the two regimes of the molar and the molecular explains why, from within the perspective of capitalism, social reproduction and desiring-production appear to us as separate, and why the Marxist category of labour-power seems distinct from the Freudian category of libido. In effect, what Deleuze and Guattari argue is that while 'there is never any difference in nature between the desiring-machines and the technical social machines', there is 'a certain distinction between them, but it is merely a distinction of *regime*, depending on their relationships of size'.[8] To distinguish between the two regimes of desiring-production and social production, Deleuze and Guattari borrow the concepts of the *molecular* and the *molar* from the physical sciences. The authors call these 'the two directions in *physics*—the molar direction that goes toward the large numbers and the mass phenomena, and the molecular direction that on the contrary penetrates into singularities, their interactions and connections at a distance or between different orders'.[9] While a physical object might be constituted at one level by a collection of *molecular* elements that obey particular physical laws (such as attraction and repulsion), certain qualities, such as temperature and pressure, are only defined by the interaction of a large number of molecules and so can only be attributed to *molar* formations. To take a mundane example, while the table in front of me appears to be solid, dark in colour and warm to the touch, at the molecular level the table is mostly made up of empty space, and the molecules that constitute the table have neither a colour nor a temperature. Rigidity, colour and temperature are nothing other than effects produced by statistical aggregates of a large number of molecules that themselves possess neither rigidity, colour nor temperature. As there is only one table, there is no material distinction between the molecular and the molar constitutions

[8] Deleuze and Guattari, *Anti-Oedipus*, 33.
[9] Deleuze and Guattari, *Anti-Oedipus*, 308.

of the table, and yet there are different regimes of rules governing these two aspects. Similarly, Deleuze and Guattari want to claim, while desiring-production is the 'production of production' and is therefore constitutive of all matter, this unconscious formulation gives rise to a social reality that follows a different set of rules.[10] Just as we must look past the molar formations of physical bodies to discover the molecular processes that produce them, Deleuze and Guattari argue that we must look past social formations of desire to the unconscious processes that produce these effects. For Deleuze and Guattari, 'desiring-machines are precisely that: the microphysics of the unconscious, the elements of the microunconscious'.[11]

One of the factors that differentiates Deleuze and Guattari's use of this terminology from its application in contemporary physics, and that also separates them from the traditional empiricist logics of corporeal substance utilised by figures such as Locke and Berkeley, is their relative use of these terms. For Deleuze and Guattari, the molar and the molecular are not absolutely distinct, but simply offer two different angles from which any phenomenon can be analysed. Thus, while it might seem that the personal realm of desire forms the molecular ground for the molar aggregate of the state, it is also the case that the individual desiring subject is itself a molar aggregate. When examining any particular desiring phenomenon, two routes of analysis are available; you can either analyse the molecular forces that produce the phenomenon, or you can analyse the statistical effects produced at the level of molar aggregates.[12]

For Deleuze and Guattari, the distinction between the molar and the molecular regimes of organisation explains the genesis of history as an emergent quality of molar formations of desire. According to twentieth-century developments in the physical sciences, the unidirectional flow of time is explained by the entropic tendency of heat to dissipate. However, this phenomenon is based on a statistical tendency of the interaction of a large number of molecules and relies on a theory of probability rather than a relation of strict causation. It follows from this that the ordering of time is unidirectional only

[10] Deleuze and Guattari, *Anti-Oedipus*, 4–6.

[11] Deleuze and Guattari, *Anti-Oedipus*, 200.

[12] The relative nature of the molar and molecular registers is transformed in *A Thousand Plateaus*, where any assemblage is said to open itself on to both a plane of organisation that stratifies it and a plane of consistency that destratifies it (77–81).

according to a molar regime of organisation, while at the level of the molecular regime this is not the case.[13] Taking once again our prior example of the table, the physical laws that govern the molecules that produce the table are time-symmetrical, while the laws of thermodynamics that govern the emergent qualities of the table, such as its temperature, are time-asymmetrical. In *Anti-Oedipus*, the authors attempt to show that the social forms of political economy analysed by Marx, such as feudalism and capitalism, are the molar, statistical effects of large aggregates of desire and that under this perspective they are ordered by a 'universal history'.[14] However, they also aim to show that the unconscious processes that produce these statistical aggregates are not ordered historically.[15] To put this another way, for Deleuze and Guattari, the distinct forms of political economy analysed by Marx are a series of group fantasies and their historical progression is only an effect of the way they are fantasised.

Anti-production and the Ironic History of Capitalism

The molecular functioning of desire, governed as it is by the three syntheses of the unconscious discussed in the previous chapter, constitutes a pre-individual realm in which part-signs circulate in an open process of coding and decoding, but the effects that these processes create when taken as a large group form a series of molar aggregates with a fixed historical order. Somewhat counterintuitively, this does not mean that historical analyses of political change can be set to one side, but instead it requires a new technique by which schizoanalysis can reconstruct the way in which history has been fantasised. This is because the molar effects of desire act back on desiring-production and capture it in organisations that work against the very interests of desire. While Deleuze and Guattari describe the relation between the molecular and the molar organisations of desire as a broad 'parallelism between social production

[13] For a simple overview of this interpretation of molecular physics, see Rovelli, *Seven Brief Lessons on Physics*, 60. For a more in-depth look at the role of statistical probabilities in determining the directionality of time, see Halliwell, Pérez-Mercader and Zurek, *Physical Origins of Time Asymmetry*, 108–15.

[14] Deleuze and Guattari, *Anti-Oedipus*, 153–4.

[15] Deleuze and Guattari give a more schematic account of this distinction in *A Thousand Plateaus* when they clearly distinguish the category of 'becoming' from that of 'history'.

and desiring-production', they also say that 'this parallelism was in no way meant as an exhaustive description of the relationship between the two systems of production' because 'there is a strong tendency on the part of the forces of antiproduction to operate retroactively on (*se rabattre sur*) productive forms and appropriate them'.[16] Large social formations such as feudalism and capitalism are thus not treated as modes of production in their own right. Instead, they are understood as representational or phantasmatic effects, produced by the productive capacity of desiring-production, which then act back on these productive forces to capture and contain them under a certain image.[17] The historical narrative that Deleuze and Guattari offer in *Anti-Oedipus* of the development of capitalism is thus an ironic account of the way that production has been fantasised through the categories of 'Savages, Barbarians, [and] Civilised Men'.[18]

There are two things to note here concerning the relation between social machines and desiring-machines. First, the representation of production in the molar aggregates is not a good guide to the real functioning of desiring-machines. This is mostly because 'every time that production, rather than being apprehended in its originality, in its reality, becomes reduced (*rabattue*) in this manner to a representational space, it can no longer have value except by its own absence, and it appears as a lack within this space'.[19] This is the reason why desire, which is manifestly productive according to an immanent mode of analysis, appears as a lack in social formations. Structural forms of analysis constantly fail to recognise the productive capacity of desire, always casting it back into the net of Oedipus, because when 'a structural unity is imposed on the desiring-machines' it 'joins them together in a molar aggregate', in which 'the partial objects are referred to a totality that can appear only as that which the partial

[16] Deleuze and Guattari, *Anti-Oedipus*, 33.

[17] Perhaps the best example of this is the *Urstaat*. The *Urstaat* is a name for the original formation of the state, but rather than being taken as naming a particular historical moment, the concept captures the mythical status of the origin and the ways in which any particular state relies on a fantasised origin. The concept of the *Urstaat* plays on Freud's concept of the *Urszene*, normally translated as the 'primal scene'. This is the subject's fantasy of his/her own conception, an act that by definition must have occurred before the individual was born, but that remains in the unconscious memory as a fantasy that regulates desire in the subject.

[18] Deleuze and Guattari, *Anti-Oedipus*, 153.

[19] Deleuze and Guattari, *Anti-Oedipus*, 337.

objects lack, and as that which is lacking unto itself while being lacking in them'.[20]

Second, while a structural analysis of the molar formations of social machines might seem to follow a necessary and linear path, the apparently necessary relations between each of the molar formations are illusory. In direct contrast to those structuralist Marxists, such as Althusser, who attempt to give a rigorous scientific account of historical materialist history, Deleuze and Guattari argue that 'universal history is the history of contingencies, and not the history of necessity'.[21] Through an analysis of the molecular forces that produce molar formations, they show that in order for capitalism to have been produced, 'great accidents were necessary, and amazing encounters that could have happened elsewhere, or before, or might never have happened'.[22] Deleuze and Guattari are careful in *Anti-Oedipus* to distance themselves from the traditional Marxist practice of analysing the material conditions of historical progression, and stress that in order to understand the history of capitalism, it is important to recognise the ways in which the apparent historical development of forms of production is an effect of group fantasy that must be treated as such. They clarify this point succinctly when they write: 'In a word, universal history is not only retrospective, it is also contingent, singular, ironic, and critical.'[23]

The three stages of historical progression that Deleuze and Guattari name as part of their ironic analysis include primitive societies of savages, despotic societies of barbarians and capitalist societies of civilised men. Each of these three stages is not primarily defined by its mode of production, but by the mode of anti-production used to organise the socius. In his introduction to *Anti-Oedipus*, Eugene Holland defines anti-production as 'the conversion of a portion of the superabundant forces of production into a counter-force that

[20] Deleuze and Guattari, *Anti-Oedipus*, 337.

[21] Deleuze and Guattari, *Anti-Oedipus*, 154. As with Lacan, Deleuze and Guattari's relationship with Althusser is double-sided. By taking a Spinozist reading of Marx over a Hegelian one, Deleuze and Guattari praise Althusser for opening the possibility of an analysis of historical materialism that does not rely on the negative. However, Deleuze and Guattari break from Althusser over the possibility of producing a scientific reading of this process and its structural consistency.

[22] Deleuze and Guattari, *Anti-Oedipus*, 154. See also Lundy 'Why Wasn't Capitalism Born in China?'.

[23] Deleuze and Guattari, *Anti-Oedipus*, 154.

absorbs, distributes, or consumes already-produced products'.[24] While desiring-production is a creative and productive force, it appears differently under each of these molar formations because of the different ways in which it is captured by a structure that represents it as a lack. Each molar formation of anti-production is understood 'as the controlled expenditure of excess', and for Deleuze and Guattari it is therefore 'co-terminous with the process of organizing social relations in systems of debt of various kinds'.[25] In parallel with their decision to treat the unconscious as a site of coding, rather than a site of signification, in *Anti-Oedipus* the three different social formations are considered through the different ways in which they encode society. According to Deleuze and Guattari's analysis, primitive societies organise the socius through a process of coding in which the material flows in society are differentiated and kept separate from one another. Here the 'primitive territorial machine' is 'already a social machine, a megamachine, that codes the flows of production, the flows of means of production, of producers and consumers'.[26] Without strict social hierarchies, the danger facing primitive societies is that certain individuals might take up positions of control by hoarding a surplus of goods. To resist this possibility, so-called primitive societies destroy any excess that is produced in rituals of sacrifice or of celebration, and organise the remaining flows of goods in areas of life that are qualitatively distinct from one another. In order to ward off the possibility of a social hierarchy forming, it is important that the different areas of social life are coded separately. In these societies, '[f]lows of women and children, flows of herds and of seed, sperm flows, flows of shit, menstrual flows: nothing must escape coding'.[27]

Primitive societies do not transform into barbarian societies via any kind of necessary progression, in which the internal contradictions of their mode of production cause collapse. On the contrary, primitive societies are only transformed due to a contingent set of circumstances by which something arrives from the outside to disrupt their mode of anti-production. Specifically, primitive societies

[24] Holland, *Deleuze and Guattari's Anti-Oedipus*, 64.

[25] Holland, *Deleuze and Guattari's Anti-Oedipus*, 64.

[26] Deleuze and Guattari, *Anti-Oedipus*, 156.

[27] Deleuze and Guattari, *Anti-Oedipus*, 156. This might be a useful point to note an unexplored masculinist tendency in Deleuze and Guattari's philosophical anthropology. For more on this problem, see Thornton, 'Deleuze and Guattari's Absent Analysis of Patriarchy'.

are colonised by despotic regimes that come over the horizon and capture them. Here, the whole organisation of production and anti-production is altered according to the desire of the despot. Rather than destroying their surplus products in ritual celebrations and offerings, when primitive societies are colonised by external powers the surplus is collected by the despot in the form of taxes. This requires a vast machinery of overcoding by which value is extracted from the previous codes and transferred to the despot. The process by which a despotic society captures a primitive society initiates the formation of a state. In this way, '[o]vercoding is the operation that constitutes the essence of the State', while the role of the state is nothing other than 'to overcode all the existing flows, and to ensure that no intrinsic code, no underlying flow escapes the overcoding of the despotic machine'.[28]

The precise mode by which despotic regimes manage to overcode the previously coded flows of primitive societies is of great interest to Deleuze and Guattari, because these same methods will be utilised later by the capitalist mode of anti-production. Of primary importance here is the emergence of writing in the form of the written decree or law, which must be translated from one language to another. For, while 'language itself does not presuppose conquest', it is the case that 'the levelling operations (*les operations de rabattement*) that constitute written language indeed presuppose two inscriptions that do not speak the same language: two languages (*langages*), one of masters, the other of slaves'.[29] The requirement for the colonised people to be able to decode the written decrees issued by the despot means that the act of translation cuts across all of the coded flows that were previously kept separate. Deleuze and Guattari write that the 'imperial inscription countersects all the alliances and filiations', and in this way all the 'coded flows of the primitive machine are now forced into a bottleneck, where the despotic machine overcodes them'.[30] According to this analysis, the whole operation of signification is recast as a kind of imperial capture, in which the centrality of a master signifier allows a fixed set of signifiers to dominate that which they signify. Speaking of the defining points of any system of signification, Deleuze and Guattari write that the 'arbitrary nature of the thing designated, the subordination of the signified,

28 Deleuze and Guattari, *Anti-Oedipus*, 217–19.
29 Deleuze and Guattari, *Anti-Oedipus*, 226.
30 Deleuze and Guattari, *Anti-Oedipus*, 217.

the transcendence of the despotic signifier' all point to the fact that 'writing belongs to imperial despotic representation'.[31]

The central example of how the despot overcodes the previously coded flows of primitive societies concerns the emergence of the incest taboo, which will later form the basis of the Oedipus complex under capitalism.[32] According to Deleuze and Guattari's analysis, in primitive societies the incest taboo does not function as a constraint or a limitation on desire, but only as a 'a prescription to form or strengthen family alliances, to share or distribute wealth, to knit social ties, by insisting that the young find their spouses exogamously, outside of their own family group or clan'.[33] However, under the form of the state, colonised peoples are considered as being infinitely indebted to the despot, who has a symbolic right to procreate with all women in the society, regardless of the pre-existing codes of lineage and affiliation. Taking on the symbolic position of the father, the despot must reissue the prescription of the incest taboo as a law in which incest, 'which had appeared as a mere after-image of positive marriage-inducements under savagery, now becomes in a sense ubiquitous and inevitable, if only symbolically, with the new-alliance and direct-filiation relations of despotism'.[34] This act of overcoding on the part of the despot, inscribed in a written law, forms the basis of the Oedipus complex because it is the first moment when the productive capacity of desire is misrepresented as a lack within a generalised system of signification. As Deleuze and Guattari put it in *Anti-Oedipus*, it is only with the Oedipus complex that 'desire gets *displaced* onto an erroneous signified belonging to the prohibitive system of representation rather than to desire itself'.[35] It follows from this that, '[f]ar from being repressed by the incest prohibition, Oedipal desire is in fact produced by it'.[36] Through this historical analysis of the modes of capture used by despotic regimes, Deleuze and Guattari equate the state form with a process of overcoding and

[31] Deleuze and Guattari, *Anti-Oedipus*, 260.

[32] Instead of relying on Freud's account of incest in *Totem and Taboo*, Deleuze and Guattari draw on Nietzsche's analysis of the transformation of debt into guilt in the second essay of *On the Genealogy of Morality*. See sections 21 and 22 of this essay, where Nietzsche comments on the relation between Christian morality and guilt (*On the Genealogy of Morality*, 62–4).

[33] Holland, *Deleuze and Guattari's Anti-Oedipus*, 70.

[34] Holland, *Deleuze and Guattari's Anti-Oedipus*, 75.

[35] Deleuze and Guattari, *Anti-Oedipus*, 37.

[36] Deleuze and Guattari, *Anti-Oedipus*, 37.

aim to show that both writing and the incest taboo are inherently linked with despotism.

Before moving on to an analysis of capitalism, we must consider the way that *escape* functions in both primitive and despotic regimes of production and anti-production. As we saw previously, the main form of anti-production operative in primitive societies is the use of rituals to encode each of the material flows that pass through society in order to keep them separate from one another. It is of primary importance here that 'nothing must escape coding'.[37] Despite the many differences between the primitive and the despotic processes of coding and overcoding, the possibility of escape is also a principal threat to the dissolution of despotic regimes. Put in material terms, the possibility that anyone might appropriate the full products of their labour, and thus build up a personal surplus, is as much a threat to the despot as it is to the primitive society. What makes things worse is the fact that the process of overcoding carried out by the state disrupts the previous system of coding and opens up new possibilities for desiring-production to evade capture by the social machinery. Guillaume Sibertine-Blanc, in his analysis of Deleuze and Guattari's political philosophy, emphasises this point, quoting a key passage from *A Thousand Plateaus*: '*The archaic State does not overcode without also freeing a large quantity of decoded flows that escape from it.*'[38] This puts the colonisation of barbarian societies in a constant state of unrest, in which the process of overcoding social practices always releases the possibility of a breakdown. It is for this reason that Deleuze and Guattari write that, by definition, '[t]he despot is the paranoiac'.[39]

This process is important for our analysis of the concept of the line of flight because, while Deleuze and Guattari use this term to designate one thing in their analysis of the unconscious, they also use the concept in their historical analysis of political economy. For example, social repression functions in part by 'choking off the flows' lines of escape (*lignes de fuite*)'.[40] For both primitive and despotic regimes of power, which organise the socius via a process of coding or overcoding, any routes by which the flows might become decoded and might escape from the body of the socius must be blocked off.

37 Deleuze and Guattari, *Anti-Oedipus*, 156.
38 Deleuze and Guattari, *A Thousand Plateaus*, 495.
39 Deleuze and Guattari, *Anti-Oedipus*, 210.
40 Deleuze and Guattari, *Anti-Oedipus*, 396.

Defined as they are by their respective practices for coding social flows, and for resisting the possibility of decoding and escape, we can now say that the lines of escape, or the lines of flight, act as the external limit of both primitive and despotic societies.

For Deleuze and Guattari, the emergence of capitalism, like the emergence of despotism, relies on a series of contingent factors.[41] Using a similar method here as with their analysis of both savagery and despotism, capitalism is seen first and foremost as a mode of representation which captures the productive forces of desire within a particular image, rather than being productive itself. What sets capitalism apart from the previous modes of social organisation is the fact that rather than operating by a process of coding or overcoding, in which the decoding of flows presents an external limit to the socius, capitalism operates precisely by and through the process of *decoding*. Specifically, Deleuze and Guattari aim to show how a number of factors, including the increased circulation of money in the merchant class and the resulting disarticulation of feudal power, produce a situation in which the underlying codes of primitive societies and the overcoded practices of despotism are usurped by a vast and generalised process of decoding. Drawing directly from Marx's work in *Capital*, Deleuze and Guattari see the emergence of capitalism as involving the coming together of two distinct processes: 'on one side, the deterritorialized worker who has become free and naked, having to sell his labor capacity; and on the other, decoded money that has become capital and is capable of buying it'.[42] While the twin processes of coding and overcoding resisted the possibility of an accumulation of power via strict social conventions that ensured the circulation of goods, the process of decoding carried out by capital achieves the same effect by the reverse means. The accumulation of capital is not forbidden, but the constant displacement of social codes resists the possibility of any one hierarchy becoming static and ensures that goods continue to circulate. The decoding carried out by capitalism is not a single process, but the convergence of a number of related processes, including 'the deterritorialization of wealth through monetary abstraction; the decoding of the flows of production through merchant capital; the decoding of States through financial capital and public debts; the decoding of the means of

[41] In *Anti-Oedipus*, Deleuze and Guattari show why, despite adequate formal conditions, capitalism did not emerge during the Roman Empire (243).

[42] Deleuze and Guattari, *Anti-Oedipus*, 245.

production through the formation of industrial capital'.[43] This convergence leads Deleuze and Guattari to define capitalism primarily as 'the generalized decoding of flows', which is not restricted to a particular field but becomes universal by constantly reaching outside itself and decoding the processes it finds there.

While savagery and barbarism both rely on making *qualitative* distinctions between flows, capitalism is different because it relates the flows to one another and decodes them via a series of *quantitative* equivalences. In this sense, capitalism is the first form of social organisation that can properly be called an economy. As Holland puts it: 'Savagery and despotism are organized symbolically, via codes and over-codes, while capitalism is organized economically, via axioms.'[44] In opposition to the symbolic nature of both primitive and despotic methods of organisation, which use qualitative distinctions to discover differences in kind between the various functions in society, the *axiomatisation* carried out by capital conjoins these heterogeneous flows and extracts the excess that is produced there by quantifying them: 'Quantified flows under capitalism get conjoined solely on the estimation that this or that conjunction will produce surplus-value; such estimation involves economic calculation rather than belief: symbolic meaning has nothing to do with it.'[45]

In order to continue functioning, capitalism must never fully erase the social formations that preceded it, but must incorporate them into its machinery. Generalised processes of decoding are thus kept in balance with massive projects of social recoding carried out by the primitive, and especially the despotic, tendencies that exist within capitalism. In the wake of every process of decoding, these latent forces of despotism are given the space to use the despotic machinery of the state, namely the written word and the Oedipus complex, to recode the socius. In this way, capitalist processes play both sides in a global tug-of-war of decoding and recoding. In the hands of capitalism, nation-states work to 'recode with all their might, with world-wide dictatorship, local dictators, and an all-powerful police, while decoding—or allowing the decoding of—the fluent quantities of their capital and their populations'.[46] As a quantitative axiomatic, the 'co-opting power of capitalism can be explained by the

43 Deleuze and Guattari, *Anti-Oedipus*, 245.
44 Holland, *Deleuze and Guattari's Anti-Oedipus*, 64.
45 Holland, *Deleuze and Guattari's Anti-Oedipus*, 66.
46 Deleuze and Guattari, *Anti-Oedipus*, 242.

fact that its axiomatic is not more flexible, but wider and more englobing', so that here, 'no one escapes participation in the activity of antiproduction that drives the entire productive system'.[47] The quantitative nature of the axiomatic of capital means that the socius no longer experiences decoding as an external limit to be warded off, but as something internal to capitalism to be constantly surpassed. Sibertine-Blanc explains that while non-capitalist formations 'encountered decoded flows as an extrinsic, accidental, "real limit," capitalist formations made it their internal limit, a structural limit that they continuously destroy to rediscover on a new scale'.[48]

The decoding power of lines of flight plays a specific role within the anti-productive capacity of capitalist societies. For this reason, Deleuze and Guattari see schizophrenia as having a different strategic and revolutionary potential under capitalist regimes. In both primitive and despotic societies, the decoding of flows was synonymous with the problem of over-production; the productive processes of society had to be coded in ritual or overcoded by taxes in order to ward off the possibility of a constant surplus. In the case of capitalism, because the extraction of surplus value from the productive work of the working class through the commodity form leaves the workers unable to buy back the fruits of their labour in sufficient quantities, crises of over-production still occur and still form the external limit of capitalism.[49] However, here they are separated from the process of decoding, which has become the internal or *real* limit of capitalism. While the despot was defined as inherently paranoiac and seen as constantly warding off the possibility of decoding that would lead to schizophrenia, the processes of capitalism are paranoid-schizoid, switching incessantly between processes of decoding and recoding. Capitalism therefore relies on schizophrenia as much as it does on paranoia, while it carries out each of these two functions in turn.

The Revolutionary Line of Flight

In *Anti-Oedipus*, the concept of the line of flight is used in a clinical sense to designate a particular function of the unconscious, but it is

[47] Deleuze and Guattari, *Anti-Oedipus*, 257.

[48] Sibertin-Blanc, *State and Politics: Deleuze and Guattari on Marx*, 46.

[49] For Deleuze and Guattari's analysis of the problem of over-production in capitalism, see *Anti-Oedipus*, 252, and Holland, *Deleuze and Guattari's Anti-Oedipus*, 138.

also used in a political sense to designate the possibility of revolution. To understand this use of the concept we must analyse the place of schizophrenia within capitalism. Given the claim that social machines are defined as much by their processes of anti-production as by their productive capacities, Deleuze and Guattari write that 'there is no social formation that does not foresee, or experience a foreboding of, the real form in which the limit threatens to arrive, and which it wards off with all the strength it can command'.[50] In the case of primitive and despotic regimes of power, this foreboding explains 'the obstinacy with which the formations preceding capitalism encaste the merchant and the technician, preventing flows of money and flows of production from assuming an autonomy that would destroy their codes'.[51] As we have seen, for capitalism, '[s]chizophrenia is the absolute limit'.[52] This means that we should be able to see the capitalist processes of anti-production closing off the possibility of schizophrenia. This is why Deleuze and Guattari take such a strong political stance against the institutions of psychoanalysis, even while they hold on to some of its conceptual innovations. For Deleuze and Guattari, the institution of psychoanalysis, and its obsession with the Oedipus complex, is a key implement in capitalism's toolbox of anti-production. Whenever desire threatens to escape the structuring forces of capital, and whenever the worker no longer desires his own subjugation – in short, whenever the desire of the individual is no longer aligned with the circulation of capital – the priests of psychoanalysis are on hand to re-oedipalise the subject.

For Deleuze and Guattari, the schizophrenic process is revolutionary, and the schizophrenic subject should be seen as 'demonstrating for our benefit an eminently psychotic and revolutionary means of escape (*point de fuite*)'.[53] Schizophrenia is seen as a revolutionary force for Deleuze and Guattari because it draws lines of flight that point the way to an escape from capitalist regimes of power. Capitalism would rather have 'a society of neurotics than one successful schizophrenic who has not been made autistic', and in order to achieve this aim, psychoanalysis acts as a counter-revolutionary force that closes off these lines of flight and covers them over with

[50] Deleuze and Guattari, *Anti-Oedipus*, 192.
[51] Deleuze and Guattari, *Anti-Oedipus*, 192.
[52] Deleuze and Guattari, *Anti-Oedipus*, 192.
[53] Deleuze and Guattari, *Anti-Oedipus*, 145.

the image of Oedipus.[54] To clarify, Deleuze and Guattari claim that capitalism will only come to an end if people stop desiring their own subjugation, and that this will only happen when people are no longer oedipalised. Because schizophrenia is a process that resists oedipalisation, the institutions of psychiatry and psychoanalysis are used under capitalism to capture schizophrenics and to block their development.

Some caution is advised here. While Deleuze and Guattari pick out schizophrenia as the absolute limit of capitalism, they do not claim that to become schizophrenic is to become revolutionary. As we have seen, unlike both primitive and despotic societies, capitalism does not rely on a process of qualitative coding, but on a quantitative axiomatic of continuous decoding and recoding. This means that, in a certain sense, capitalism relies as much on a constant production of schizophrenia, on the side of the decoding of flows, as it does on the production of neurotics, on the side of recoding. While it is one of the cornerstones of Deleuze and Guattari's analysis that the 'oedipal alliance is capitalism's molar unit', it is also the case that schizophrenia plays the role of the molecular unit, constantly working to decode flows, to connect heterogeneous flows together, and thus to open up new arenas for the extraction of surplus value.[55] It is for this reason that Deleuze and Guattari write that capitalism 'produces schizos the same way it produces Prell shampoo or Ford cars, the only difference being that the schizos are not saleable'.[56] Capitalism requires schizophrenia as one of its two poles, but it also requires that the decoded flows released in schizophrenia are constantly recaptured. The power of the capitalist order comes from the function of 'binding the schizophrenic charges and energies into a world axiomatic that always opposes the revolutionary potential of decoded flows with new interior limits'.[57] According to this analysis, capitalism is constantly walking the fine line between the production of schizophrenia, and the huge deterritorialisations of the social field that come with it, and the oedipal production of neurotics via the regressive forces of the family, the state and the psychoanalytic institution. This is why, despite constantly creating schizophrenics, 'capitalist production is constantly arresting the schizophrenic process and transforming the

[54] Deleuze and Guattari, *Anti-Oedipus*, 112.
[55] Guattari, *The Anti-Oedipus Papers*, 36.
[56] Deleuze and Guattari, *Anti-Oedipus*, 266.
[57] Deleuze and Guattari, *Anti-Oedipus*, 267.

subject of the process into a confined clinical entity, as though it saw in this process the image of its own death coming from within'.[58]

The revolutionary claim made by Deleuze and Guattari relies on the possibility that the decoded flows produced by the capitalist axiomatic might resist, or escape, the regressive forces of recoding that continually block the lines of flight and recapture them in the net of Oedipus. What makes this possibility difficult to see is the fact that the schizophrenic process is constantly confused with the clinical schizophrenic. Here Deleuze and Guattari bemoan the fact that we have 'the same word, schizo, to designate both the process insofar as it goes beyond the limit, and the result of the process insofar as it runs up against the limit'.[59] Much of the confusion surrounding the apparent revolutionary force of schizophrenia is based on a misapprehension of this distinction. For Deleuze and Guattari, there is a revolutionary schizophrenic *process* of the unconscious, which is decoding, and which has the potential to undo capitalist relations, and then there is the schizo as a clinical *entity*, who has been captured by the recoding side of the capitalist axiomatic.

In our earlier analysis of the concept of the line of flight as it related to desiring-machines, we found that there were two different senses in which the concept was used. First, the concept of the line of flight was used from the perspective of the machine, where it designated those processes of transversal connection and inclusive disjunction in which partial elements escape from one chain of code to connect with another chain in an infinite series of open disjunctions. Second, the concept of the line of flight was used from the perspective of the structure, where it pointed to the excess of desire that could never be fully captured by the structural articulation of desire. In this second sense, lines of flight acted as a kind of signpost which the schizoanalyst could follow 'all the way to the desiring-machines'.[60] Given the fact that desiring-machines and social machines are both articulations of the same reality but under different regimes, it is not surprising that we will also find two senses of the concept of the line of flight at play in the latter.[61] In the case of our analysis of

[58] Deleuze and Guattari, *Anti-Oedipus*, 266.

[59] Deleuze and Guattari, *Anti-Oedipus*, 147.

[60] Deleuze and Guattari, *Anti-Oedipus*, 372.

[61] The parallels between Deleuze and Guattari's analysis of desiring-machines and social machines are remarkable: direct connections are made between the concept of the BwO and what Deleuze and Guattari call 'the socius'; and the three syntheses of connection, disjunction and conjunction relate to the three stages

social machines, and of the history of capitalism, the first sense of the line of flight relates to the decoding of the flows that act as the external limit of primitive and despotic regimes and that capitalism internalises as the limit that it must always transgress. The second sense of the concept of the line of flight, on the other hand, relates to the schizophrenic process as the absolute limit of capitalism, which escapes the recoding of the Oedipus and is charged with revolutionary potential.

An appreciation of this distinction leads to a number of important points for Deleuze and Guattari, especially concerning the distinction between the schizophrenic and the revolutionary. In *Anti-Oedipus*, they write that the 'schizo is not revolutionary, but the schizophrenic process—in terms of which the schizo is merely the interruption, or the continuation in the void—is the potential for revolution'.[62] The role of the schizoanalyst is thus to follow the schizophrenic process without being blocked. There is consequently 'a whole world of difference between the schizo and the revolutionary: the difference between the one who escapes, and the one who knows how to make what he is escaping escape'.[63] To put it simply, the imperative of *Anti-Oedipus* is not to follow the line of flight into madness, but to follow the line of flight without being captured and thus to refuse the capitalist axiomatic while avoiding the danger of becoming mad. When Deleuze and Guattari use the concept of the line of flight as a means for describing a way of escaping the social machinery of capitalism, they present two distinct options: 'the paranoiac counterescape (*contre-fuite*) that motivates all the conformist, reactionary, and fascisizing investments, and the schizophrenic escape (*fuite*) convertible into a revolutionary investment'.[64] While the first case relates to desire's ability to escape the axiomatic of capital, the latter 'has the capacity for causing the flows of desire to circulate following their positive lines of escape (*lignes de fuite*), and for breaking them again following breaks of productive breaks'.[65] The question of revolutionary potential is thus not only a question of how to produce lines of flight, but how to follow them. With this

of savages, barbarians and civilised men, with the illegitimate use of the three syntheses mapping on to the primitive, despotic and capitalist modes of anti-production. See Holland, *Deleuze and Guattari's Anti-Oedipus*, 61.

62 Deleuze and Guattari, *Anti-Oedipus*, 374.

63 Deleuze and Guattari, *Anti-Oedipus*, 374.

64 Deleuze and Guattari, *Anti-Oedipus*, 374.

65 Deleuze and Guattari, *Anti-Oedipus*, 381.

in mind, we can reframe Deleuze and Guattari's problem in terms of the production of transformation. Capitalism, with its constant process of decoding and recoding desire, is defined by a limited and controlled form of internal transformation. However, what Deleuze and Guattari want to uncover is the process of the transformation of capitalism itself.

The practice of schizoanalysis becomes a necessary tool for revolutionary action in precisely this regard. While desire is constantly finding leaks or cracks through which it can escape the net of Oedipus, and by which it momentarily escapes the social machinery of capitalism, these escapes are not sustained. Under capitalism, transformation itself is co-opted by a form of repetition in which nothing changes. In order for the many schizophrenic escapes to produce 'the world of transverse communications' that Deleuze and Guattari refer to as a 'new earth where desire functions according to its molecular elements and flows', the various lines of flight must meet one another in such a way that they cannot be recaptured by the recoding aspects of the capitalist machinery.[66] In order to actively work towards this outcome, the schizoanalyst must analyse the molecular functioning of desire, and distinguish the legitimate from the illegitimate uses of the syntheses of the unconscious. For this reason, Deleuze and Guattari write that 'it is not enough to construct a new socius as full body; one must also pass to the other side of this social full body, where the molecular formations of desire that must master the new molar aggregate operate and are inscribed'.[67] The first way in which the revolutionary schizoanalyst must relate to lines of flight is therefore by working with the molecular flows of desire. The best way to do this is to work on the project of transforming subjugated groups into subject groups, as they were previously defined by Guattari's work in Institutional Psychotherapy. In the final pages of *Anti-Oedipus*, Deleuze and Guattari return to this distinction, writing that '[i]n the subjugated-groups, desire is still defined by an order of causes and aims', however '[s]ubject-groups on the other hand have as their sole cause a rupture with causality, a revolutionary line of escape (*ligne de fuite*)'.[68] Once these subject groups have been created, and once they have produced their individual lines of flight, the revolutionary task consists in following each of these lines of flight, which cut across or

66 Deleuze and Guattari, *Anti-Oedipus*, 350.
67 Deleuze and Guattari, *Anti-Oedipus*, 412.
68 Deleuze and Guattari, *Anti-Oedipus*, 412.

transect social relations, to make them form connections with one another.

Deleuze and Guattari's aim is therefore to construct a molecular revolution by connecting heterogeneous lines of flight together in a non-representational continuous multiplicity of desire. This revolution will not resemble a unified revolution of molar formations, but a multiplicity of schizophrenic lines of flight, all initially opened up by the decoding process of capitalism, but ultimately escaping both the recoding of the state and the recoding of Oedipus. Deleuze and Guattari claim that if you push the different processes of decoding so far that they cannot be recaptured, then 'the movement of deterritorialization creates of necessity and by itself a new earth'.[69] Only in this case will the flows of desire 'cross the threshold of deterritorialization and produce the new land' in which 'the person who escapes (*fuit*) causes other escapes (*faire fuir*), and marks out the land while deterritorializing himself'.[70] The relationship of the revolutionary schizoanalyst to the concept of the line of flight is thus quite subtle. The aim of schizoanalysis is not simply to produce lines of flight, as it is definitely not the aim to simply become schizophrenic, but to work on the molecular side of desire to form transverse connections between a number of lines of flight. Through the convergence of these lines of

[69] Deleuze and Guattari, *Anti-Oedipus*, 353. Contemporary iterations of 'accelerationism' often refer to Deleuze and Guattari's work, and to their comment in *Anti-Oedipus* that 'the flows are not yet deterritorialized enough, not decoded enough, from the viewpoint of a theory and a practice of a highly schizophrenic character', and their apparent command '[n]ot to withdraw from the process, but to go further, to "accelerate the process"' (260). Nick Land's reference to this passage is especially notable in this regard (*Fanged Noumena*, 449). A careful analysis of Deleuze and Guattari's work shows, however, that they never simply advocate an intensification of capitalist forces. On the contrary, they continually call for an intensification of only the decoding aspects of capital to the cost of its regressive practice of recoding. This practice does not involve a bolstering of market forces, for example, but an alternative use of the many mechanisms employed by capital. The example that Deleuze and Guattari take in *Anti-Oedipus* is telling: 'Psychoanalysis is especially satisfying in this regard: its entire perverted practice of the cure consists in transforming familial neurosis into artificial neurosis (of transference), and in exalting the couch, a little island with its commander, the psychoanalyst, as an autonomous territoriality of the ultimate artifice. A little additional effort is enough to overturn everything, and to lead us finally toward other far-off places' (353). The point here is not simply to push psychoanalysis so far that it breaks, but to select those aspects of the process capable of transforming psychoanalysis from within.

[70] Deleuze and Guattari, *Anti-Oedipus*, 354.

flight the schizoanalyst can construct an 'active point of escape (*point de fuite*)' in which a number of desiring-machines, including 'the revolutionary machine, the artistic machine, the scientific machine, and the (schizo) analytic machine', can become 'parts and pieces of one another' in a multiplicity of desiring-production freed from the anti-productive forces of primitive codings, despotic overcodings and the capitalist axiomatic of constant decoding and recoding.[71]

We are now in a position to define four distinct uses of the concept of the line of flight in *Anti-Oedipus*, and to explain how each of these uses correlates with the political project that Deleuze and Guattari articulate in the book. Of the four uses of the concept of the line of flight, the first two relate to an analysis of desiring-machines and the latter two relate to an analysis of social machines. The four senses of the line of flight are as follows: 1) those processes of desire witnessed by the psychoanalyst that refuse to be captured by Oedipus; 2) the lines traced by the legitimate uses of the syntheses of the unconscious, namely the transverse connections and inclusive disjunctions between heterogeneous chains of code that form the multiplicity of desiring-production; 3) the decoded social flows that threaten primitive and despotic regimes of power as an external limit and that are internalised by capitalism; and 4) the absolute limit of capitalism that can be reached when the decoded flows released by capital cannot be recaptured and reterritorialised by it. Taking these four senses of the concept of the line of flight in turn, the schizoanalytic project can be described by the way that it relates to each of them. The aim of the schizoanalyst is to work with those aspects of desire that escape from the traditional psychoanalytic domain of Oedipus (the first sense), in order to reach a direct analysis of the processes of desiring-machines as they function in the schizophrenic unconscious (the second sense). This understanding of the molecular regime of desire will allow the schizoanalyst to conduct an analysis of the way in which formations of desire are decoded in society (the third sense) and to understand how these decoded flows of desire can be made to escape the recoding processes of capitalism (the fourth sense) in order to bring about a post-capitalist future. Taken this way, the concept of the line of flight is a complex one which runs through the many aspects of *Anti-Oedipus*, both psychoanalytic and revolutionary, and connects them together in a political programme for the construction of a molecular revolution.

71 Deleuze and Guattari, *Anti-Oedipus*, 354.

In closing this chapter, it is important to note that *Anti-Oedipus* is not an attempt to provide a general philosophy of transformation. On the contrary, the book is a relatively focused study of the specific role that desire plays in the historical transformation of human society. By considering the conceptual architecture of this book in some detail, what I hope to have shown is that Deleuze and Guattari's invention of the concept of the line of flight is part and parcel of their attempt to explicate the transformative force of desiring-production. In the two chapters that remain, we will see how Deleuze and Guattari's specific concern in *Anti-Oedipus* with the role of desire in the transformation of capitalism into a post-capitalist future morphs, in *A Thousand Plateaus*, into a more general and more experimental concern with transformation as such.

5

A Thousand Plateaus and the Metaphysics of Transformation

Transformation Generalised

A Thousand Plateaus, published as the companion volume to *Anti-Oedipus* in 1980, is Deleuze and Guattari's most substantial work. It is also in this text that they offer their most highly developed philosophy of transformation. As we will see, the comments on transformative processes contained here are made possible by the way in which Deleuze and Guattari take the individuation of the concept of the line of flight to a new degree of abstraction. As we have seen, in *Anti-Oedipus* Deleuze and Guattari marshal a wide variety of historical theories, developed by an array of philosophical, political, anthropological and psychoanalytic thinkers, in an attack on structuralism and on structural psychoanalysis in particular. They do this for practical and political purposes, and their aim is to produce a new activity – *schizoanalysis* – that will be able to work directly with the unconscious in order to transform the machinery of oedipal desire and thus bring about a political transformation in the capitalist mode of production. In doing this, the pair also begin to use the phrase 'line of flight' in at least four different ways. While each of these four uses of the concept of the line of flight relates to the specific transformations just mentioned, in *A Thousand Plateaus* Deleuze and Guattari liberate the concept of the line of flight from this specific transformational objective and put it to use in a variety of new ways.

In *A Thousand Plateaus*, the targets of Deleuze and Guattari's analysis are remarkably broad. Not only do they aim to combat the binarising, structuralist, molar tendencies within the discipline of psychoanalysis, but they also aim to dismantle these tendencies in almost every other arena of thought. Here, any dealings with psychoanalysis proper are relegated to a single chapter, while other sections are given over to bringing about transformations in linguistics, literature, music and religion, as well as the more strictly philosophical domains of metaphysics, ontology and ethics. In this chapter, I will show

how, as the aperture of Deleuze and Guattari's machinery of analysis continues to widen, and as more and more disciplinary discussions are enveloped by their discourse, their philosophical concepts take on a higher and higher level of coherence. Specifically, I will show how, across its many uses in the book, Deleuze and Guattari take the individuation of the concept of the line of flight to its dénouement.

My analysis of the concept of the line of flight as it appears in *A Thousand Plateaus* is split across this chapter and the one that follows. To begin, this chapter covers much of the philosophical terminology of the book, taking in the distinctions between the tree and the rhizome, the plane of organisation and the plane of consistency, and content and expression, as well as Deleuze and Guattari's theory of the stratification of matter. Here I will show why Deleuze and Guattari articulate their thought in terms of 'lines' and not 'points', and offer a new characterisation of the line of flight as a philosophical concept. The model of political analysis that they develop alongside and within this philosophical discourse, with its focus on the analysis of regimes of signs and the abstract machines that effectuate them, will be covered in the following chapter. There I will show how the philosophical concept of the line of flight is deployed in Deleuze and Guattari's updated political analysis of the state, and how it accompanies a pragmatic approach that is somewhat more cautious than the schizoanalytic practices outlined in *Anti-Oedipus*. I have organised these two chapters in this way in order to emphasise the generality of Deleuze and Guattari's philosophy of transformation, as it appears in this text: in *A Thousand Plateaus*, unlike in *Anti-Oedipus*, Deleuze and Guattari's metaphysics of transformation is not tied to a specific political practice, and the political analysis that does appear should be seen as but one possible application of this philosophy.

Before moving on to discuss the concept of the line of flight as it appears in *A Thousand Plateaus*, it will be worth pausing to briefly restate what it means to say that Deleuze and Guattari create the *concept* of the line of flight. In *What is Philosophy?* Deleuze and Guattari famously claim that 'philosophy is the art of forming, inventing, and fabricating concepts'.[1] Philosophy proceeds by way of problems, which it articulates by producing new concepts that respond to them. Under this interpretation, a philosophical concept does not represent the world, nor does it define an abstract

[1] Deleuze and Guattari, *What is Philosophy?*, 2.

component of the world; instead it responds to the world by expressing a problem. Instead of following Plato's model of concepts as universal forms, Kant's *a priori* ideas, or Nietzsche's understanding of the concept as a captured and sedimented metaphor, Deleuze and Guattari treat concepts as complex bodies made up of components that cohere around a particular problem. Concepts, as they are defined at this point in Deleuze and Guattari's work, are not the same as Ideas, as defined in *Difference and Repetition.* It would be most accurate to say that, at the point of writing the earlier text, Ideas were understood as virtual and problematic multiplicities, whereas at the point of writing *A Thousand Plateaus*, concepts are understood as multiplicities that respond to a problem.

As we saw in Chapter 2, if concepts are multiplicities, then they must be composed of pre-individual singularities. A concept comes into existence when a set of singularities combine in a specific way, so that a concept can be understood strictly as nothing other than 'the point of coincidence, condensation, or accumulation of its own components'.[2] When asked in an interview in 1991 what concepts they had created, Deleuze and Guattari picked out the concept of the refrain or the *ritornello*. This concept is nothing other than a response to the problem of the grounding, or ungrounding, of thought and is composed by a condensation or coincidence of a series of singularities, including 'a' tune, 'a' territory and 'a' home. To say that Deleuze and Guattari create the concept of the line of flight is to say that this concept responds to, or expresses, a problem, and that it does so by combining a series of singularities in a novel way. In what follows, we will see that the problem Deleuze and Guattari are responding to concerns the possibility of transformation. The singularities that compose the concept include, among others, 'an' assemblage, 'an' escape and 'a' regime of signs.

The Vegetal Image of Thought

In the first chapter of this book I showed how Deleuze's work in *Difference and Repetition* challenged the very core of traditional philosophical thinking by arguing for the logical priority of difference over identity. The consequence of this challenge was a new mode of philosophical analysis that took neither identity nor negation as its ground, but actively took part in the ungrounding of thought via

[2] Deleuze and Guattari, *What is Philosophy?*, 20.

an analysis of the way that experience is produced by the interplay between difference-in-itself and repetition-for-itself. In that text, Deleuze is explicitly concerned with overturning the 'dogmatic image of thought' that plagues philosophy, one based not only on identity, but on its corollaries, especially the false goals of representation and resemblance. Deleuze argues in *Difference and Repetition* that this image of thought supports itself with 'psychologically puerile and socially reactionary examples' that can only deal with the relatively simple cases of 'recognition, error, simple propositions and solutions or responses', and can never do justice to 'what should be the most valued in regard to thought – namely, the genesis of the act of thinking and the sense of truth and falsehood'.[3] At the point of writing *Difference and Repetition*, Deleuze takes this image of thought to be a kind of illusory surface effect, which appears in experience due to the individual thinker's inability to think his or her own pre-individual and pre-representational production. As Somers-Hall puts it, the dogmatic image of thought is 'a paralogism created by the reflection of thinking on itself that is at the heart of philosophy's inability to think depth appropriately'.[4]

What separates *A Thousand Plateaus* from *Difference and Repetition*, and arguably from all of Deleuze's work with and without Guattari up until this point, is its move away from the somewhat detached and cerebral activity of attempting to produce a thought-without-image and a move towards the creative and active process of producing an alternative image of thought. In Deleuze's preface for the English translation of *Difference and Repetition*, he suggests that the third chapter, concerning the image of thought, can be read as an introduction to *A Thousand Plateaus*. While the former tackles the dogmatism of the traditional image of thought, it is in the latter that Deleuze and Guattari develop the concept of the rhizome and inaugurate a new 'vegetal model of thought'.[5]

The vegetal and rhizomatic image of thought elaborated in *A Thousand Plateaus* is contrasted with an arborescent or tree-like image of thought. This arborescent image is a structural model that gives determinate identities to things by using predicates to relate

3 Deleuze, *Difference and Repetition*, 197.

4 Somers-Hall, Bell and Williams (eds), *A Thousand Plateaus and Philosophy*, 4.

5 Deleuze, *Difference and Repetition*, xvii. For more on Deleuze and Guattari's shift in approach to the question of the image of thought, see Thornton, 'The Kantian Image of Thought'.

them negatively to one another, by extracting essential properties that determine essences of things, and by organising all things into a hierarchy of genera and species based on these essences. This arborescent model of thought can be traced back to Aristotle's logic of definitions and can be seen in the many forms of classification that run through the social and natural sciences, most obviously in genealogical family trees and in phylogenetic trees. As we might expect from their critiques of structural psychoanalysis, Deleuze and Guattari criticise this model for relying on a binary logic of exclusive disjunction that creates nothing but a series of identities. They write: 'Binary logic is the spiritual reality of the root-tree ... this system of thought has never reached an understanding of multiplicity.'[6] If the concepts 'predicate', 'subject', 'object', 'genus' and 'species' all define an image of thought that is fundamentally unable to think about the dynamics of transformation, then Deleuze and Guattari aim to do away with these concepts and replace them with a selection of new concepts. Consequently, all of these concepts are dismissed in the introduction to the book, where they write:

> All we talk about are multiplicities, lines, strata and segmentarities, lines of flight and intensities, machinic assemblages and their various types, bodies without organs and their construction and selection, the plane of consistency, and in each case the units of measure.[7]

This alternative list of concepts should be understood as the toolbox required to produce and then utilise the vegetal image of thought.

In the first plateau, Deleuze and Guattari introduce the rhizome by way of six principles. These principles do not offer a definition, in the sense of picking out essential and stable traits of the rhizome, but instead outline the different ways in which it is possible to interact with the rhizomatic image of thought. The first two principles concern the connectivity and heterogeneity of the rhizome and come with the following practical directive: 'any point of a rhizome can be connected to anything other, and must be'.[8] These two principles state that rhizomatic thought operates not only by making connections, but by connecting heterogeneous elements of different orders and kinds. In fact, it is the connections that constitute the rhizome and not the other way around. As we have already noted,

[6] Deleuze and Guattari, *A Thousand Plateaus*, 5.
[7] Deleuze and Guattari, *A Thousand Plateaus*, 5.
[8] Deleuze and Guattari, *A Thousand Plateaus*, 7.

these two principles recall the transversal connections and inclusive disjunctions of the schizophrenic unconscious as it was discussed in *Anti-Oedipus*, and in many ways the act of schizophrenising psychoanalysis can be understood as Deleuze and Guattari's first undertaking in rhizomatic analysis. The third principle of the rhizomatic image of thought concerns the category of the multiplicity and recalls Deleuze's earlier attempts via Riemann to dismantle the binary between the Many and the One. According to this principle, when 'the multiple is effectively treated as a substantive', then thought becomes rhizomatic and 'ceases to have any relation to the One as subject or object'.[9] The fourth principle concerns what Deleuze and Guattari call 'a-signifying ruptures'. Here they develop the analysis of Hjelmslev's semiotics that they began in *Anti-Oedipus* and claim that because the rhizomatic image of thought does not rely on the biunivocal relations of signification, it has neither a master signifier nor a centre of meaning. Consequently it might 'be broken, shattered at a given spot, but it will start up again on one of its old lines, or on new lines'.[10] According to the fifth and sixth principles, the rhizomatic model operates by 'cartography and decalcomania' so that it is 'not amenable to any structural or generative model'.[11] This means that, due to the rhizomatic model's ability to pick out transformations over identities, it is not possible to use it to create a representation of the world. Instead, rhizomatics operates by mapping connections that co-create the world via their organisation. These final principles are perhaps the most difficult to comprehend, and I will return to them shortly. For now, we can summarise by stating that the arborescent model of thought relies on the attribution of predicates to things and the subsequent split of subjects from objects, but with the vegetal model the basis of determinations 'are not predicates of the thing but dimensions of multiplicities', and these multiplicities entertain 'neither object nor subject ... [but] variously formed matters, and very different dates and speeds'.[12]

9 Deleuze and Guattari, *A Thousand Plateaus*, 8.
10 Deleuze and Guattari, *A Thousand Plateaus*, 10.
11 Deleuze and Guattari, *A Thousand Plateaus*, 13. Decalcomania can refer to either the process of transferring a pattern on to glass or porcelain by using a design on paper as a template, or the process of creating images on paper by pressing paint between two sheets. It seems likely that Deleuze and Guattari are referring to the latter process, in which there is neither a model nor a copy, but only the mutual production of two images.
12 Deleuze and Guattari, *A Thousand Plateaus*, 290, 4.

In order to understand the role that the concept of the line of flight plays in the rhizomatic image of thought, we must first explore the way that Deleuze and Guattari explain the differing perspectives that arborescent and rhizomatic models take on the relation between points and lines. Deleuze and Guattari write: 'There are no points or positions in a rhizome, such as those found in a structure, tree, or root. There are only lines.'[13] To understand how the image of the tree operates, it will be instructive to turn to Aristotle's *Categories*. Here Aristotle argues that the essence of any species consists in its genus, together with the differentia that define the species. Some species can also become genera, when they can be further differentiated into additional species, while an individual is simply a species that cannot be further differentiated, as the requisite differentia only pick out a single particular. Consequently, Aristotle writes that 'the individual man belongs in a species, man, and animal is a genus of the species'.[14] The tradition of representing these definitions using the image of a tree begins with Porphyry's introduction to Aristotle's *Categories*. According to this method, we can define 'man' by starting with a general category such as 'substance'. We then differentiate this category into its different kinds; here they are 'thinking substance' and 'extended substance'. Taking the differentia 'extended substance' as the genus 'body', we can then differentiate this genus into 'inanimate bodies' and 'animate bodies'. Continuing this procedure of binary distinction, we can name 'animate bodies' as 'animal' and then differentiate this genus into the differentiae 'rational animal' and 'irrational animal'. Finally, the differentia of 'rational animal' can be named as the genus 'man'.[15] As an *image* of thought, this model for definition sets up a number of points, namely the genera 'substance', 'body', 'animal' and 'man', and shows the connections between these terms by using a series of lines to designate the relations between them.

The rhizomatic model does away with these points altogether, relying on the lines alone to determine the image. This means that the rhizomatic model allows for the analysis of connections without

[13] Deleuze and Guattari, *A Thousand Plateaus*, 9

[14] *Categories*, 2a13. Aristotle comments on the implications of this schema in Book III of his *Metaphysics* (998b). Deleuze offers his own analysis of the metaphysical problems generated by Aristotle's theory in *Difference and Repetition*, 40.

[15] For more on Aristotle's logic and the use of Porphyrian trees, see Eco, *Semiotics and the Philosophy of Language*, 57–67.

the use of the subjects and objects that would otherwise act as nodal points in the tree of definition. Deleuze and Guattari describe this in the following way: 'Unlike a structure, which is defined by a set of points and positions, with binary relations between the points and biunivocal relationships between the positions, the rhizome is made only of lines.'[16] The lines that make up the rhizome are not all alike, and Deleuze and Guattari list at least two kinds. Any rhizome has 'lines of segmentarity and stratification as its dimensions' on the one hand, 'and the line of flight or deterritorialization as the maximum dimension after which the multiplicity undergoes metamorphosis' on the other.[17] The role of these different lines will become more apparent when, in the next chapter, we take up the example of political formations and their transformations. At this point it is sufficient to say that any rhizome is constituted by transversal connections between heterogeneous elements, and that there are at least two kinds of connections; there are those connections that are *internal* to the rhizome and that serve to give it some consistency, and there are those connections that *escape* the bounds of the rhizome and connect it to something else. The former can be said to stratify or segment the rhizome, whereas the latter, which we can call lines of flight, serve to destratify it.

It is important to clarify at this point that Deleuze and Guattari do not claim that the world is made of rhizomes, or that there are some things that are rhizomatic and others that are not.[18] Instead, their substantive use of the concept of the multiplicity allows them to show that the world is populated by assemblages. Assemblages have tendencies towards both relative stasis and relative change, and while the arborescent or dogmatic image of thought is only capable of seeing the stratified and relatively static aspects of these assemblages, the rhizomatic image of thought allows the assemblage's tendencies towards transformation to be analysed and exploited. Brent Adkins picks up on the fact that the concept of the rhizome is used as an image and a directive for thinking rather than as a substantive

[16] Deleuze and Guattari, *A Thousand Plateaus*, 23.

[17] Deleuze and Guattari, *A Thousand Plateaus*, 23.

[18] Claims that the internet is a rhizome, or that the brain is a rhizome, miss the point that, as a model for thought, the rhizome does not define the nature of things, but only a methodology for thinking. See Young, Genosko and Watson, *The Deleuze and Guattari Dictionary*, 262–3. Many critiques of Deleuze and Guattari fail to differentiate between the rhizome as a pragmatic model and the rhizome as substantive entity. See, for example, Badiou, 'The Fascism of the Potato'.

when he argues for the central role of 'perceptual semiotics' in *A Thousand Plateaus*.[19] The point to stress here is that the rhizome – and therefore the concept of the line of flight that serves to explain the threshold of transformation for the rhizome – is directly related to a process of *thought*. As de Beistegui notes, for Deleuze and Guattari, 'thought consists not in applying universal concepts to a given situation, but in a pragmatics that will identify and exploit its rhizomatic resources'.[20] The concept of the line of flight is one part of the vegetal image of thought that allows for such a pragmatics.

Assembling the Line of Flight

If the line of flight is the maximum number of dimensions of the multiplicity after which a transformation occurs, then what is undergoing transformation here? To put this question another way, what is rhizomatic thought thinking about when connections are made that constitute lines of flight? The short answer it that rhizomatic thought engages directly with material reality, including physical and organic matter, as well as semiotic systems. However, it is important to remember that, according to a rhizomatic mode of thought, matter does not compose objects with a pre-given identity, but what Deleuze and Guattari call assemblages. To take one of their examples, an orchid is not formed by the imposition of the form of an orchid on to inert matter in order to create an individual object that possesses predicates and on which a thinking subject can pass judgement. Instead, an orchid is nothing other than a series of connections and relations that maintain a sufficient level of stability. There are the spatial relations between its parts, such as its petals and its stamen. There are the connections it forms with the insects that pollinate it. There are the connections it makes with other plants and with oceans and seas through the global cycle of water and nitrogen. To say that rhizomatic thought engages with matter is not to say that it takes inert matter as its object, on to which it imposes a form. On the contrary, rhizomatic thought is a method for mapping the connections that constitute material assemblages. In this case, it would be more accurate to say that rhizomatic thought thinks *with* matter,

19 Adkins, *Deleuze and Guattari's A Thousand Plateaus*, 13. See also Deleuze and Guattari, *A Thousand Plateaus*, 25, 215.

20 De Beistegui, '"A book? What book?" or Deleuze and Guattari on the Rhizome', 25.

rather than saying that it thinks *about* matter. As Holland clarifies, this thinking *with* has two senses: we think with the material world in the sense that we use matter as a 'tool to think', but we also think with the material world in the sense that we think 'along with the world the way it itself thinks'.[21]

By setting up *A Thousand Plateaus* as an exercise in rhizomatic thinking, Deleuze and Guattari claim to have written a book that overcomes the dogmatic tendency for thought to impose itself on the world from the outside. They write that, with the rhizomatic image, there is 'no longer a tripartite division between a field of reality (the world) and a field of representation (the book) and a field of subjectivity (the author)', but that instead 'an assemblage establishes connections between certain multiplicities drawn from each of these orders'.[22] So, rhizomatic thought thinks *with* matter by mapping the connections or the lines that constitute an assemblage. These assemblages are material, and by mapping the lines of flight, which escape the bounds of the assemblage in order to connect it to its outside, rhizomatic analysis is able bring about transformations that take place in between a field of reality, a field of representation and a field of subjectivity.[23]

While Deleuze and Guattari's decision to conceptualise this form of thinking as rhizomatic only arrives fully formed in *A Thousand Plateaus*, it is clear that the relation they articulate between matter and thought is a continuation of many of the ideas in *Anti-Oedipus*. Specifically, they develop the idea of matter as a 'matter-movement, matter-energy, and matter-flow' from Hjelmslev's semiotic concept

[21] Holland, *Deleuze and Guattari's 'A Thousand Plateaus'*, 37.

[22] Deleuze and Guattari, *A Thousand Plateaus*, 25.

[23] Deleuze and Guattari distinguish between the processes of tracing and mapping, where the former is representational and the latter is vegetal. Rhizomatic thought operates by mapping the multiple exits and entryways that connect an assemblage to its outside, rather than by tracing an outline of its form (Deleuze and Guattari, *A Thousand Plateaus*, 13). The two practices are not simply opposed as good and bad, with Deleuze and Guattari stating that 'it is a question of method: *the tracing should always be put back on the map*' (*A Thousand Plateaus*, 14). Deleuze and Guattari connect this idea to Deligny's therapeutic practice of mapping (*A Thousand Plateaus*, 224; Deligny, *The Arachnean and Other Texts*; De Toledo (ed.), *Maps And Wander Lines – Fernand Deligny*). I have described the methodology of this book as an attempt to map the individuation of the concept of the line of flight. This means that I have attempted to carry out a machinic analysis of the forces that cross into and escape from the concept, rather than attempting to trace its outline.

of *matière*.[24] As in *Anti-Oedipus*, this allows them to describe material systems that are neither vitalist nor mechanist, but that operate by machinic processes. A rhizomatic analysis of assemblages relies on a philosophy that 'is not animism, any more than it is mechanism; rather it is universal machinism'.[25] Another way in which Deleuze and Guattari's understanding of the assemblage follows from *Anti-Oedipus* concerns its relation to desire. They write that 'assemblages are passional, they are compositions of desire', and that there are 'no internal drives in desire, only assemblages'.[26] Speaking of these 'drives of desire', they also comment that 'the assemblage that draws lines of flight is on the same level as they are'.[27]

The reason for highlighting these points here is to clarify how Deleuze and Guattari conceptualise the line of flight from the point of view of ontology. When we try to ascertain whether lines of flight are movements of thought alone, or whether they are movements about which one can think, we quickly realise that they do not sit comfortably in either of these camps. Assemblages are described as material in *A Thousand Plateaus* in the same sense that the unconscious was understood as material in *Anti-Oedipus*, namely they are both machinic.[28] This materiality is neither inside nor outside thought. Assemblages are not contained in a field of reality, a field of representation or a field of subjectivity, but produce these different fields by drawing transversal connections between them. By thinking with material assemblages, rhizomatics can think the concept of the line of flight so that it occupies neither side of a traditional mind/body dualism. Lines of flight are not just in your head, but they are not simply pre-given in the world and waiting to be found by thought. The transformations that they bring about can

24 Bogue, 'Who the Earth Thinks It Is', 47.

25 Deleuze and Guattari, *A Thousand Plateaus*, 283.

26 Deleuze and Guattari, *A Thousand Plateaus*, 234, 440.

27 Deleuze and Guattari, *A Thousand Plateaus*, 234.

28 The two points made here – namely that assemblages are material only by way of being machinic and desiring, and that lines of flight operate at this primary level of the assemblage – are important because they show how Deleuze and Guattari's way of thinking about the assemblage separates them from Foucault. In a footnote to the fifth plateau, Deleuze and Guattari write that their 'only points of disagreement with Foucault' are that 'assemblages seem fundamentally to be assemblages not of power but of desire (desire is always assembled)' and that within these assemblages there are 'lines of flight that are primary, which are not phenomena of resistance or counterattack in an assemblage, but cutting edges of creation' (*A Thousand Plateaus*, 585).

thus be deemed 'incorporeal', in the sense that a transformation is brought about in a state of affairs not through the transformation of bodies, but through a transformation of the relations that constitute bodies.[29]

Refrains and Lines of Flight

Like many of the conceptual innovations of *Anti-Oedipus*, the language of territorialisation returns in *A Thousand Plateaus* with renewed specificity. In the eleventh plateau, '1837: Of The Refrain', Deleuze and Guattari introduce the novel concept of the refrain, or the *ritournelle*, to explain how territories are constituted and how they effectively produce assemblages.[30] To understand the importance of the concept of the line of flight, we must give a brief account of the role of the refrain and of the different kinds of territorial effects that it produces. To first introduce the concept in the language of *Difference and Repetition*, we could say that the refrain is the pure repetition of difference, and that it is what provides the ground (or unground) for experience by giving it an orientation. Speaking of the context of experience as a 'milieu', Deleuze and Guattari write that experience is produced by virtue of 'a periodic repetition, but one whose only effect is to produce a difference by which the milieu passes into another milieu'.[31] For the concept of the refrain, it is key that it is 'the difference that is rhythmic, not the repetition'.[32]

[29] Deleuze and Guattari discuss incorporeal transformations at length in the 'Postulates of Linguistics' plateau (*A Thousand Plateaus*, 83–121). Their analysis follows from Deleuze's *Logic of Sense*, and conceptualises performative linguistic acts as a kind of 'event' that both connects bodies with language and divides them from one another (*Logic of Sense*, 108–25). Incorporeal transformations play an important role throughout *A Thousand Plateaus* and the dates preceding each plateau denote an incorporeal transformation around which the chapter is organised. I will return to the topic of incorporeal transformations in the section titled 'Linguistic Pragmatics' in the next chapter.

[30] Throughout this chapter I have retained Massumi's translation of the French *ritournelle* as the 'refrain'. Others have argued for the use of the original Italian word *ritornello*. See Deleuze, *Two Regimes of Madness*, 377–80. While *ritornello* retains some of Deleuze and Guattari's allusion to the French for Nietzsche's eternal return, namely the *retour éternel*, I have kept Massumi's translation because it provides consistency with the English translations of Guattari's writings on the concept (Guattari, *The Machinic Unconscious*, 107).

[31] Deleuze and Guattari, *A Thousand Plateaus*, 346.

[32] Deleuze and Guattari, *A Thousand Plateaus*, 346.

The plateau on the refrain begins with the example of a child lost in the dark and examines the way that such a child can make a home for themselves and orientate themselves in an otherwise undifferentiated chaos by 'singing under [their] breath'.[33] The process by which the child guards against the disorientating darkness is given in three stages: first the child uses the sound of its own voice to make itself feel at home and to find a 'calm and stable, centre in the heart of chaos'; next the child effectively uses the refrain, and its relations with other points in the slowly appearing landscape, to draw a circle around the centre and to 'organise a limited space' where the 'forces of chaos are kept outside' so that 'the interior space protects the germinal forces of a task to fulfil'; finally, the child 'opens the circle a crack, opens it all the way, lets someone in, calls someone, or else goes out oneself, launches forth'.[34] This three-stage process – of creating a centre, determining an inside and an outside, and using this orientation to explore the world – creates what Deleuze and Guattari call a territory. Territories are the assemblages that we inhabit. It is via the refrain's repetition of difference that a determinable territory can be produced in the chaos, and this territory is the first assemblage with which one can think: 'The territory is the first assemblage, the first thing to constitute an assemblage; the assemblage is fundamentally territorial.'[35] To put this another way, we can say that it is only via the territorialisation of chaos that thought is able to find its object. Thought requires an assemblage with which to think, and 'the territory makes the assemblage'.[36]

The concept of the refrain is central to *A Thousand Plateaus* because it is what accounts for the possibility of 'consistency' without relying on any form of externally imposed order or 'organisation'.

[33] Deleuze and Guattari, *A Thousand Plateaus*, 343. Deleuze and Guattari's discussion of the refrain contrasts with the Freudian example of the Fort–Da game. In both cases the child repeats an action in order to overcome a fear; however, in the Freudian example this repetition only comes after the loss of the mother and is designed to overcome the loss felt for the presence of the mother; it is an allegory for Freud's basic understanding of repetition as a symptom. For Deleuze and Guattari on the other hand, the repetitive act of the child is originary, does not refer to any pre-existing lack, and is inherently creative. The concept of the refrain thus extends Deleuze and Guattari's positive account of desiring-production offered in *Anti-Oedipus*.

[34] Deleuze and Guattari, *A Thousand Plateaus*, 343.

[35] Deleuze and Guattari, *A Thousand Plateaus*, 356.

[36] Deleuze and Guattari, *A Thousand Plateaus*, 555.

According to Eugene Holland, the task of 'maintaining or creating consistency without imposing unity, identity, or organization ... might be said to constitute the holy grail of all of Deleuze and Guattari's work'.[37] Here, we see that Deleuze and Guattari account for such consistency in terms of the relation between processes of deterritorialisation and reterritorialisation: the relative level of consistency of an assemblage is determined by the processes of deterritorialisation and reterritorialisation that cross it. The rhizomatic image of thought that we explored at the beginning of this chapter now comes into its own. It is only via rhizomatic thinking that it is possible to map the different kinds of connections and processes that create territorial assemblages and those that cut across them. Simply put, it is possible to define three different kinds of lines in an assemblage that relate to the three stages of the refrain outlined above. First, we go 'from chaos to the threshold of a territorial assemblage' by way of lines that run between pure repetitions of difference. These lines are called 'infra-assemblage' lines because they exist 'below' the assemblage. Then one 'organizes the assemblage' via the use of 'intra-assemblage' lines, which determine an interior and separate it from an exterior. Finally, 'one leaves the territorial assemblage for other assemblages' by way of 'inter-assemblage' lines, which are passages of 'escape'.[38] This final set of lines that escape the assemblage are what Deleuze and Guattari will call *lines of flight*.

Lines of Flight and Absolute Deterritorialisations

There are two important points to make here concerning the line of flight's relation to territorial assemblages. First, despite the order in which the three stages of the refrain are presented, the lines that escape the territorial assemblage do not come after the lines that constitute it. Second, lines of flight do not simply refer to those lines that bring about processes of deterritorialisation, but specifically those that lead to *absolute* deterritorialisation. The reasoning behind the first point becomes clear when we recognise that assemblages are never individual, but are always in constant interaction with other assemblages. While the problem of consistency was just discussed in terms of a single assemblage, Deleuze and Guattari also write that this problem 'concerns the manner in which different assemblages hold together,

[37] Holland, *Deleuze and Guattari's 'A Thousand Plateaus'*, 9.
[38] Deleuze and Guattari, *A Thousand Plateaus*, 344–5.

with components of passage and relay', and that 'consistency finds the totality of its conditions only on a properly cosmic plane, where all the disparate and heterogeneous elements are convoked'.[39] This constant interaction and presupposition of assemblages explains why Deleuze and Guattari shift towards a language of deterritorialisation and reterritorialisation without maintaining a place for an originary territorialisation. All territorial processes must take a territorial context for granted, so that infra-assemblage lines, intra-assemblage lines and inter-assemblage lines are not progressions in a series, but 'all confront each other and converge in the territorial refrain'.[40] To put this another way, in the case of the child's refrain, the apparently originary chaos that surrounds the child must have been produced by a previous process of deterritorialisation. This means that, in cases of the refrain and the construction of territorial assemblages, it is the line of absolute deterritorialisation that must be taken as primary. Deleuze and Guattari explicitly warn that 'under no circumstances must it be thought that absolute deterritorialization comes suddenly, as an excess, afterward, or beyond ... In fact, what is primary is an absolute deterritorialization an absolute line of flight.'[41]

This comment, however, leads us to a discussion of the relationship between relative and absolute deterritorialisations. What does it mean to say that the line of flight brings about deterritorialisations that are absolute? In what sense is it the case that these absolute deterritorialisations are primary? The important distinction here is between those inter-assemblage lines whose connections serve to modify one assemblage so that it can maintain homeostatic relations with other assemblages, and those inter-assemblage lines whose connections with the outside bring about a complete transformation of the assemblage. The former connections can be called relative deterritorialisations because in these cases the assemblage only changes its territorialisation in relation to the assemblages that surround it, while the latter can be called absolute deterritorialisations because they effectively uproot the assemblage in the process of transforming it into something else. In these cases, Deleuze and Guattari state:

[39] Deleuze and Guattari, *A Thousand Plateaus*, 361. Viewed from a certain perspective, assemblages are not really distinct at all. Deleuze and Guattari write: 'There are only multiplicities of multiplicities forming a single assemblage, operating in the same assemblage' (*A Thousand Plateaus*, 38).

[40] Deleuze and Guattari, *A Thousand Plateaus*, 345.

[41] Deleuze and Guattari, *A Thousand Plateaus*, 63 (translation modified).

> It is no longer adequate to say that there is interassemblage, passage from a territorial assemblage to another type of assemblage; rather, we should say that one leaves all assemblages behind, that one exceeds the capacities of any possible assemblage, entering another plane.[42]

While there are multiple different inter-assemblage lines that escape from an assemblage, it is only those that bring about absolute deterritorialisations that are named as lines of flight. These lines can be taken as primary, because it is only in these cases that all prior organisations of the assemblage are destroyed, allowing for the development of an assemblage that is unconstrained by its previous territorialisations.

Given the complexity of these ideas, it is worth pausing here to consider the activity of absolute deterritorialisation in more detail. Much like the related concept of the line of flight, the concept of absolute deterritorialisation is one that undergoes continuous variations as it moves through Deleuze and Guattari's work. For example, in *Anti-Oedipus* the distinction between relative and absolute deterritorialisation is used to mark the difference between the deterritorialising activity of capitalism, which is relative because all deterritorialisations are immediately recuperated by reterritorialising activities of capture, and the deterritorialisations of schizophrenia, which are absolute, and which therefore threaten to exceed the apparatus of the capitalist machinery.[43] In *What is Philosophy?*, on the other hand, Deleuze and Guattari use the distinction between relative and absolute deterritorialisation to define their practice of geophilosophy. As Craig Lundy has argued, in this text 'relative deterritorialization always concerns a movement from territories towards the earth of which they are all a part', while 'in absolute deterritorialization it is the earth itself that is made relative to a structure of thought'.[44] The continuous line of variation that runs through all of these senses concerns what I have been calling *transformation*. It is the concept of the line of flight that allows us to think these moments of absolute deterritorialisation and it is therefore this concept which is central to Deleuze and Guattari's philosophy of transformation.

There is, however, a second difficulty that we must navigate here. According to Paul Patton, absolute and relative deterritorialisations

42 Deleuze and Guattari, *A Thousand Plateaus*, 359.

43 Deleuze and Guattari, *Anti-Oedipus*, 192.

44 Lundy, 'Deleuze and Guattari's Historiophilosophy', 118.

are distinguished by the fact that 'relative deterritorialization concerns only movements within the actual – as opposed to the virtual – order of things', and as a result of this 'absolute deterritorialization remains an unrealizable or impossible movement, manifest only in and through relative deterritorialization'.[45] This is tantamount to claiming that real processes of transformation are not possible. However, it is important to remember here that for Deleuze and Guattari, the virtual is also real. While absolute deterritorialisations might not be actual, that does not relegate them to the realm of impossibility. Andrew Culp helps us recognise the real possibility of absolute deterritorialisation in his critical response to Manuel DeLanda who, much like Patton, argues that absolute deterritorialisation is nothing but a limit that cannot be reached.[46] According to Culp, absolute deterritorialisation only appears as an impossibility from within the purview of science, which can only investigate what is actual:

> DeLanda claims that he is wary of the 'absolute deterritorialization,' as he says it exists only as a limit, so attention should rather be spent on what can be immediately reterritorialized. Deleuze and Guattari suggest, in contrast, that the inability to perceive absolute deterritorialization is a limitation inherent to a purely scientific approach.[47]

One way to resolve this dispute would be to say that, while Patton and DeLanda are certainly correct to point out that processes of absolute deterritorialisation are not played out before our eyes in actual states of affairs, this does not mean that they are not real. In fact, Deleuze and Guattari's work – and their invention of the concept of the line of flight in particular – is specifically designed to allow us to think these processes of transformation through the use of *philosophy* rather than *science*, which alone is capable of thinking transformation as such.

So far, by exploring the ways in which a rhizomatic or vegetal image of thought is able to map the territorial connections that produce assemblages and define their interactions, I have tried to show that assemblages face in two directions simultaneously, with one deterritorialising edge facing towards consistency and the other reterritorialising edge facing towards organisation. I have also been

[45] Patton, *Deleuzian Concepts*, 52.
[46] DeLanda, *A New Philosophy of Society*, 124.
[47] Culp, 'Philosophy, Science, and Virtual Communism', 102.

able to show what role the concept of the line of flight plays in determining the power relations of this bivalence. However, Deleuze and Guattari also write of lines of relative and absolute deterritorialisation that '[t]he former are stratic or interstratic, whereas the latter concern the plane of consistency and its destratification', and that 'absolute deterritorialization becomes relative only after stratification occurs on that plane or body'.[48] To understand this point we must recognise that assemblages are not in fact bivalent, but tetravalent. While they have a vertical axis determined by the two poles of deterritorialisation and reterritorialisation, they also have a horizontal axis determined by what Deleuze and Guattari call the double articulation of content and expression. The stratifications mentioned here, which relativise deterritorialisations and organise the assemblage according to a hierarchy of strata, are produced by this double articulation. In order to give a comprehensive account of the role played by the concept of the line of flight in *A Thousand Plateaus*, I will now turn to the question of how lines of flight cut across the stratifications of an assemblage as well as its territorial boundaries.

Content, Expression and Stratification

The concepts of the refrain and the territory help to explain how the world is composed of material assemblages that have no identity, but manage to maintain a certain level of stability as they go through constant modifications and occasional transformations. The rhizomatic image of thought gives us a way of thinking with these material assemblages to map the connections that they make, and to explore the different possibilities for transformation within them. However, it is also the case that material assemblages come in different kinds and embody different forms. Most importantly, physical matter differs from organic matter, and both differ from the material of linguistics. In order to understand the differences between the physical, the organic and the linguistic, Deleuze and Guattari must introduce the processes that they call stratification and coding. In the previous sections, we saw how 'substances as formed matters refer to territorialities and degrees of territorialization and deterritorialization'. In this section I am going to look at how 'forms imply a code, modes of coding and decoding'.[49] By combining the two processes of

[48] Deleuze and Guattari, *A Thousand Plateaus*, 62–3.
[49] Deleuze and Guattari, *A Thousand Plateaus*, 46.

de/reterritorialisation and de/recoding together, we will eventually be able to give a comprehensive account of the philosophy of matter that Deleuze and Guattari put forward in *A Thousand Plateaus*. Ultimately, this will allow us to offer a more nuanced definition of the concept of the line of flight as it appears in *A Thousand Plateaus*, one that shows the role that the concept plays on the vertical axis of de/reterritorialisations and on the horizontal axis of content and expression.

As Adkins notes, Deleuze and Guattari's discussion of the relation between content and expression, and their accompanying exploration of the processes of stratification and coding, are intended 'to account for basic differences among things as diverse as rocks, animals, and language', but 'without resorting to a metaphysics of discontinuity, or to any kind of hylomorphism'.[50] Deleuze and Guattari are trying to show how the real differences between physical, organic and linguistic materials are created, without relying on any essential difference between these registers, without blocking off the possibility of their communication, and without relying on the arborescent philosophical image of an inert substance that is given form by an intelligent and willing subject. In contrast to this traditional image, Deleuze and Guattari claim that the differentiation of matter into these kinds relies on the 'double articulation' of content and expression. We saw in the previous two chapters how Hjelmslev's categories of a-signifying semiotics and a-semiotic encodings were so important for Deleuze and Guattari's attack on structural linguistics. This analysis is generalised in *A Thousand Plateaus*, so that the material content of all assemblages does not preclude the possibility of it becoming signifying. Here Deleuze and Guattari argue that it is one and the same material-semiotic content that is expressed as physical matter, organic matter and linguistic matter.[51] The difference between these categories relies not on any essential difference between these orders, but simply on the process of articulation by which any

[50] Adkins, *Deleuze and Guattari's A Thousand Plateaus*, 51.

[51] It could be argued that Deleuze and Guattari's general ontology relies on the schema of general semiology put forward by Hjelmslev. It is also the case that their concept of matter is derived from Hjelmslev's concept of 'matière' (*Prolegomena to a Theory of Language*, 47–60). Deleuze and Guattari's use of the concept does not refer to brute or inert matter, but to 'the unformed, unorganised, nonstratified or destratified body and all its flows; subatomic and submolecular particles, pure intensities, prevital and preindividual free singularities' (*A Thousand Plateaus*, 49).

material-semiotic content comes to be expressed. In order to explain the double articulation by which contents are expressed, Deleuze and Guattari also utilise the traditional philosophical categories of 'substance' and 'form', but in a non-traditional way. Specifically, they argue that every assemblage combines both a content and its expression, and each of these will have its own substance and its own form, so that the distinction between substance and form relates not to the different categories of unformed substance and ideal form, but to the different moments in the articulation of matter.

Deleuze and Guattari introduce their theory of double articulation with the example of the formation of sedimentary rock. According to this analysis there are four distinct moments in the formation of any such rock: first, a number of particles are selected by a flow of water, as in a river; second, the particles become ordered by their size and weight to form levels of silt; third, processes of calcification cause the levels of silt to become fixed; and fourth, this calcification results in a solid mass with relatively static relations between its extensive parts. The first two stages in this process relate to the first articulation of content, while the latter two stages relate to the second articulation of expression. Each of these two articulations have both a substance and a form. In the first articulation, the substance is constituted by the particles, and the process of formation is determined by the way the intensive relations between the weight and speed of these particles creates distinct layers. Generalising this process, Deleuze and Guattari write: 'The first articulation chooses or deducts, from unstable particle-flows, metastable molecular or quasi-molecular units (*substances*) upon which it imposes a statistical order of connections and successions (*forms*).'[52] The second articulation of the sedimentary rock in this example also has both a form and a substance. Here, the process of calcification provides the form and the solidified rock gives us the substance. Once again, moving from the specifics of the rock towards a general theory of articulation, Deleuze and Guattari write: 'The second articulation establishes functional, compact, stable structures (*forms*), and constructs the molar compounds in which these structures are simultaneously actualized (*substances*).'[53]

It is important to note here that Deleuze and Guattari use their theory of double articulation to show that the respective relations

52 Deleuze and Guattari, *A Thousand Plateaus*, 46.
53 Deleuze and Guattari, *A Thousand Plateaus*, 46.

between intensity and extensity, the molecular and the molar, and content and expression do not map on to one another. While it is the case that the first articulation relies on the *intensive* relations between its parts to provide the form, and the second articulation results in *extensive* relations between the parts of an object, Deleuze and Guattari warn that 'it cannot be taken for granted that the distinction between the two articulations is always that of the molecular and the molar'.[54] The reason for this is that the distinction between content and expression is always relative, so that the substance produced by the second articulation in one case can also play the role of the substance of the first articulation in another. To illustrate this point we only need to recognise that the grains of sand that provided the substance to the first articulation in the example above must have been produced by a previous process of double articulation at a lower level.

The final point to make here concerns the relationship between de/reterritorialisation on the one hand, and de/coding on the other. According to the schema of double articulation laid out in *A Thousand Plateaus*, the processes of de/reterritorialisation relate only to the substances of both content and expression, while the processes of de/coding relate to the forms of both content and expression. To return to the case of the sedimentary rock, the substance of content is composed of deterritorialised flows of particles, the form of content is determined by the coding of these flows into layers, the form of expression is provided by the way that calcification overcodes the first coding into something rigid and fixed, and the substance of expression is the reterritorialised stone. This differentiation of the two processes of de/reterritorialisation and de/coding also allows Deleuze and Guattari to strengthen their previous arguments against structuralism. While the binary relations between substance and form might seem to lend themselves to a structuralist analysis, the fact that the substance of content and the substance of expression have their own mode of interaction, while the form of content and the form of expression have another, makes it impossible for any structural analysis to become complete. Deleuze and Guattari write that both articulations 'establish binary relations between their respective segments', so that between the segments of the two articulations 'there are biunivocal relationships obeying far more complex laws'. On the basis of this, the

[54] Deleuze and Guattari, *A Thousand Plateaus*, 46.

authors claim that 'it is an illusion to believe that structure is the earth's last word'.[55] Simply put, the biunivocal relations between substances and the biunivocal relations between forms cannot be given a structuralist interpretation because each is interrupted by the binary relations between substance and form at their respective levels of articulation.

Before returning to the concept of the line of flight, it will be instructive to consider how different processes of double articulation can produce organic and linguistic assemblages and not only physical ones. Once we have explored the differences between these three strata, and once we have seen how they interact to form both machinic assemblages of bodies and collective assemblages of enunciation, we will be in a better position to show exactly what it means to draw a line of flight, and exactly how the absolute deterritorialisations that result are distinguished from relative deterritorialisations. The physical, organic and linguistic are not, according to Deleuze and Guattari, different kinds of entities, but different modes of double articulation. Each of these modes of articulation is supported by an 'abstract machine' and each proceeds in a different way. On the physical stratum the double articulation proceeds by way of what Deleuze and Guattari call 'induction'.[56] This is the process by which a slow build-up of the intensive relations between molecules brings about a transformation in the extended nature of a molar aggregate. The sedimentary rock we considered above is a good example of this: it is by a slow reduction in the relative speed of the particles that they take on a relatively static form. Deleuze and Guattari's other example here, borrowed from Gilbert Simondon's analysis of the processes of individuation, is that of the crystal.[57] What interests Deleuze and Guattari in this case is that because it proceeds by way of induction, a crystal is formed, and continues to grow, only at the limit where it interacts with its outside. One crystal cannot create another crystal, but can only develop by expanding at its surface. The crystal 'expands in all directions, but always as a function of the surface layer of the substance', so that it is 'incapable of formally reproducing and expressing itself; only the accessible

55 Deleuze and Guattari, *A Thousand Plateaus*, 46.

56 Deleuze and Guattari, *A Thousand Plateaus*, 67.

57 Simondon, *L'individu et sa genèse physico-biologique*. For a clear discussion of this process in English, see Sauvanargues, 'Crystals and Membranes: Individuality and Membranes'.

surface can reproduce itself, since it is the only deterritorializable part'.[58]

While the physical abstract machine operates by induction and can only develop by expanding at its surface, the abstract machine that carries out organic stratifications operates by 'transduction'. Transduction is a complex term that is used differently at different points in Deleuze and Guattari's work.[59] In this context, transduction refers to the process by which material is transferred from the interior of one assemblage to the interior of another. In the case of organic matter this transduction is carried out by genetic material, which allows organisms to develop not only through growth, but also via reproduction.[60]

The third stratum, which Deleuze and Guattari variously refer to as 'linguistic' and 'alloplastic', operates neither by induction nor by transduction, but by translation. The first thing to note here is that what defines the linguistic stratum is not its use of signs. According to this analysis, all matter goes by way of the double articulation of content and expression and is governed by a general semiotics of signs. What distinguishes the linguistic stratum is its ability to translate 'all of the flows, particles, codes, and territorialities of the other strata into a sufficiently deterritorialized system of signs'.[61] This process of translation does not refer to the ability of one language to be translated into another, but 'the ability of language, with its own givens on its own stratum, to represent all the other strata'.[62]

In order to understand the uses of the concept of the line of flight in *A Thousand Plateaus* it is not vital to explicate the exact

[58] Deleuze and Guattari, *A Thousand Plateaus*, 67.

[59] In biology, transduction refers to the process by which a virus can transfer genetic material from one organism to another. Simondon uses it to describe any process whereby 'a disparity or a difference is topologically and temporally restructured across some interface' (MacKenzie, *Transductions: Bodies and Machines at Speed*, 25). The concept is also used by Guattari, who defines it as a process that 'is simultaneously representation and production' (*The Anti-Oedipus Papers*, 258), and describes it rather loosely in an interview as 'the idea that, in essence, something conducts itself, something happens between chains of semiotic expression, and material chains' (Seem and Guattari, 'Interview: Félix Guattari', 39).

[60] Deleuze and Guattari have a very particular reading of genetics that relies heavily on the work of the French biologists François Jacob and Jacques Monod. For more on Deleuze and Guattari's use of biological terms, see Marks, 'Molecular Biology in the Work of Deleuze and Guattari', 81–97.

[61] Deleuze and Guattari, *A Thousand Plateaus*, 69.

[62] Deleuze and Guattari, *A Thousand Plateaus*, 69.

mechanisms by which each of these three processes of double articulation operate. It will, however, be useful to recognise two general points concerning their effects. First, Deleuze and Guattari argue that, in the case of the physical stratum, expression is dependent on content, but due to the way in which the organic stratum organises physical matter, in the organic articulation expression becomes independent of content. This means that organisms are able to vary their modes of expression in relation to their milieu, in order to carry out tasks such as the marking of a territory. Because of the way that the abstract machine of the linguistic stratum is able to translate the components of the other strata, Deleuze and Guattari argue that 'in language, not only is expression independent of content, but form of expression is independent of substance'.[63] This simply means that a single form of expression in language can relate to substances that are not linguistic, but organic or physical. The second general point to be made here follows from the first: because of the way that expression becomes more detached from content as we move from the physical to the organic to the linguistic, it is also the case that the level of deterritorialisation available on each stratum increases. To name this phenomenon, Deleuze and Guattari say that on the physical stratum deterritorialisation is *superficial*, on the organic stratum it is *linear*, while on the linguistic stratum it is *superlinear*. This means that language has a higher potential for transformation than either organic or physical matter.

The three processes of double articulation described here are not intended to be thought independently of one another. In reality, each of these processes interacts with the others, and it is possible for the substance of expression of one articulation to be taken up as the substance of content for another articulation of a different order. What this means is that the intermingling of various physical, organic and linguistic assemblages forms larger assemblages. In practice, we are never able to distinguish multiplicities of one order from those of another, and must accept that there are 'only multiplicities of multiplicities forming a single assemblage, operating in the same assemblage'.[64] Deleuze and Guattari build on their theory of the machinic capacities of matter, previously developed in *Anti-Oedipus*, to explain how these amalgamations of the assemblages formed by the three different *abstract machines* of double articulation create

[63] Deleuze and Guattari, *A Thousand Plateaus*, 70.
[64] Deleuze and Guattari, *A Thousand Plateaus*, 38.

both *machinic assemblages of bodies* and *collective assemblages of enunciation*. Assemblages interact so that the contents that produce physical, organic and linguistic assemblages are all machined together in an intensive set of relations. This collection of contents is called a machinic assemblage of bodies and relates to the first articulation of content. All of the different expressions of each of these interacting contents are also machined together in an extensive expression that Deleuze and Guattari call a collective assemblage of enunciation. This means that every assemblage has both 'its segment of expression, the collective assemblage of enunciation as the set of incorporeal transformations' as well as 'the segment of material content where bodies intermingle and interact with one another'.[65] The importance of this distinction becomes apparent at a pragmatic level. We will see in the next chapter, for example, that these terms are essential for Deleuze and Guattari's analysis of political formations. In fact, while each political form is defined in part by the machinic assemblage of bodies that defines its content, our ability to recognise it as a specific political form is determined by the level of stability of its collective assemblage of enunciation. Specifically, when a collective assemblage of enunciation reaches a high enough level of stability it is called a *regime of signs*. We will return to the importance of these regimes in the next chapter when we examine the pragmatic role that the concept of the line of flight plays in bringing about political transformations.

Before we go any further, however, we are now in a position to show how the line of flight relates to the stratification of assemblages. We have seen that rather than being defined merely by the interactions between deterritorialisation and reterritorialisation on a single axis, any assemblage is also stratified on a horizontal axis that splits its content from its expression via a double articulation of matter. It is because of the two directions of each of these two axes that we can say that assemblages are tetravalent. In the last section, we saw that the concept of the line of flight is used to name those inter-assemblage connections that bring about absolute deterritorialisations, but now we must ask how the line of flight relates to stratification as well. The first thing to note here is that while de/reterritorialisation and stratification are distinct processes that operate on different axes of the assemblage, they also interact with each other.[66] We can take as a starting point Deleuze and Guattari's claim that 'absolute

[65] Bell, 'Postulates of Linguistics', 77.
[66] Adkins, *Deleuze and Guattari's A Thousand Plateaus*, 51.

deterritorialization becomes relative only after stratification occurs'.[67] This comment reflects our earlier discussion of the primacy of the line of flight, but adds that it is the process of stratification that relativises the deterritorialisations that the line of flight brings about. Put differently, processes of deterritorialisation are not only working against the processes of reterritorialisation on the vertical axis, but are also crossing the physical, organic and linguistic strata that segment the assemblage on the horizontal axis. Processes of deterritorialisation become relative when they must proceed in segments from one stratum to another. Speaking of what qualifies a process of deterritorialisation as either relative or absolute, Deleuze and Guattari write that it 'is not its speed (some are very slow) but its nature, whether it constitutes epistrata and parastrata and proceeds by articulated segments or, on the contrary, jumps from one singularity to another following a nondecomposable, nonsegmentary line drawing a metastratum'.[68] If we recognise that epistrata and parastrata refer to the spaces above and to the side of the stratifications, then we can see that what defines the line of flight, and allows it to bring about absolute deterritorialisations, is its ability to cut across the strata that would otherwise segment the assemblage into the physical, the organic and the linguistic. This is why Deleuze and Guattari speak of 'a line of flight enabling one to blow apart strata'.[69]

In practice, assemblages are not distinct but always interacting, so that in reality the physical, the organic and the linguistic are always machined together. Now we can see that what separates the absolute deterritorialisation of the line of flight from relative deterritorialisations is that the former deterritorialise specifically by cutting across the strata. In these cases, an assemblage is transformed because a connection is made not only between two assemblages on the same physical, organic or linguistic stratum, but between assemblages on different strata and thus between different levels of the collective assemblage. A connection is made between an object, an organism and a word that brings about an incorporeal transformation in which everything changes. Using Guattari's concept of the transversal, which we discussed in an earlier chapter, it would be possible to say that a line of flight is like a diagonal line that cuts across both the horizontal axis of the strata and the vertical axis of

[67] Deleuze and Guattari, *A Thousand Plateaus*, 64.
[68] Deleuze and Guattari, *A Thousand Plateaus*, 63.
[69] Deleuze and Guattari, *A Thousand Plateaus*, 16.

de/reterritorialisations. In this sense, it is also the line of flight which puts these two different axes into relation with each other.

The Plane of Consistency and the Question of Dimensions

We have now seen how the rhizomatic image of thought allows us to map the many connections that make up an assemblage, and how, on top of the relative deterritorialisations that enact alterations in the assemblage, the line of flight can bring about absolute deterritorialisations of the assemblage by cutting across the strata. One point that we have not yet explored is the question of what is reached when an assemblage is absolutely deterritorialised. According to the terminology of *A Thousand Plateaus*, the answer to this question is the plane of immanence, or the plane of consistency.[70] The plane of consistency is the plane on which stratifications emerge. In fact, the strata are nothing other than 'thickenings on a plane of consistency', which does not rely on the strata but 'is everywhere, always primary and always immanent'.[71] Deterritorialisations are also drawn on this plane. Given the fact that the process of stratification operates by giving form to the substance of both content and expression, we might think that the plane of consistency would be composed of a completely unformed mass, but Deleuze and Guattari claim that it is 'in no way an undifferentiated aggregate of unformed matters, but neither is it a chaos of formed matters of every kind'.[72] Instead, they argue that the plane of consistency '*constructs continuums of intensity:* it creates continuity for intensities that it extracts from distinct forms and substances'.[73] As a field of intensities, the concept of the plane of consistency plays a similar role to that of the depths in *Difference and Repetition* and *Logic of Sense*, as well as the intensive field of desiring-production in *Anti-Oedipus*. In both volumes of the *Capitalism and Schizophrenia* series the plane of consistency is also the site of the direct investment of desire.[74] One difference is that in *A Thousand Plateaus*, given the application of the rhizomatic image

[70] These two terms are interchangeable in *A Thousand Plateaus* and often appear together: 'the plane of consistency or immanence' (297, 313). See also Young, Genosko and Watson, *The Deleuze and Guattari Dictionary*, 239. The French word *plan* can be translated as either plane or plan.

[71] Deleuze and Guattari, *A Thousand Plateaus*, 78.

[72] Deleuze and Guattari, *A Thousand Plateaus*, 78.

[73] Deleuze and Guattari, *A Thousand Plateaus*, 78.

[74] Deleuze and Guattari, *A Thousand Plateaus*, 170, 183–4, 313.

of thought, Deleuze and Guattari are able to offer more insight into the various different processes that happen on this plane. Specifically, and as we have already seen, they are able to define the plane of consistency as a 'continuum of intensities' consisting of a pre-signifying semiotic matter 'of particles or signs-particles', and produced by a 'conjunction of deterritorialized flows'.[75] Deleuze and Guattari name these characteristics as 'the three factors proper to the plane of consistency'.[76]

The plane of consistency is said to account for all the dimensions of all the multiplicities drawn on it. Deleuze and Guattari write:

> Multiplicities are flat, in the sense that they fill or occupy all of their dimensions: we will therefore speak of a *plane of consistency* of multiplicities, even though the dimensions of this 'plane' increase with the number of connections that are made on it.[77]

This insistence that all multiplicities are drawn on a single plane is a way of accounting for the univocity of being and for the immanence of a philosophy able to think this univocity.[78] Deleuze and Guattari's comments concerning the fact that the plane of consistency fills all of its dimensions also show that Deleuze's reading of Riemannian differential geometry remains central to their updated theory of multiplicities.[79] In the first chapter of this book we saw how Riemann had used differential calculus to develop a geometry that was applicable for all curved and non-curved spaces. As Deleuze writes in *Difference and Repetition*, this geometry allows us to think 'an n-dimensional, continuous, defined multiplicity' immanently.[80] Deleuze and Guattari hold on to this point when they write in *A Thousand Plateaus* that the multiple must be made, 'not by always adding a higher dimension, but rather in the simplest of ways, by dint of sobriety, with the number of dimensions one already has

[75] Deleuze and Guattari, *A Thousand Plateaus*, 78.
[76] Deleuze and Guattari, *A Thousand Plateaus*, 78.
[77] Deleuze and Guattari, *A Thousand Plateaus*, 9.
[78] For more on the univocity of being, and Deleuze's refusal of the Oneness of being, see Widder, 'The Rights of Simulacra', 437–53.
[79] Here I refer to Deleuze and Guattari's comments on Riemann's geometry as they appear in the introduction to *A Thousand Plateaus*, and in the tenth plateau. Deleuze and Guattari also discuss Riemann's work extensively in the fourteenth plateau, where they pay special attention to the question of fractals and their fractional number of dimensions.
[80] Deleuze, *Difference and Repetition*, 230.

available—always *n – 1*'.[81] In these cases, we have no external measure of distance and no static grid of orientation against which to judge the position of a line, so that each new connection must provide its own measure and its own dimension. What this means for Deleuze and Guattari at the point of writing *A Thousand Plateaus* is that any new connection drawn in a multiplicity will bring about a transformation in the nature of that multiplicity. This alteration of a multiplicity via the making of new connections is what Deleuze and Guattari have been calling an assemblage: 'An assemblage is precisely this increase in the dimensions of a multiplicity that necessarily changes in nature as it expands its connections.'[82]

This way of conceptualising the assemblage also helps to clarify why it is said that the line of flight is primary in an assemblage, namely because it is only by drawing a line of flight that the necessary inter-assemblage connection can be made, the added dimension can be produced, and the assemblage can come into being. In order to explain this reconceptualisation of the relationship between the line of flight, the multiplicity, the assemblage and the plane of consistency, Deleuze and Guattari write the following:

> The line of flight marks: the reality of a finite number of dimensions that the multiplicity effectively fills; the impossibility of a supplementary dimension, unless the multiplicity is transformed by the line of flight; the possibility and necessity of flattening all of the multiplicities on a single plane of consistency or exteriority, regardless of their number of dimensions.[83]

The fact that Deleuze and Guattari insist on the primacy of the line of flight also helps to explain how they hope to produce a philosophy that can account for the nature of transformation in general. In short, the theory of multiplicities given above shows that thought can never begin with something static and produce transformation, but that transformation is always a prerequisite for what is static. In the terminology of *A Thousand Plateaus*, this is summed up in the comment that all stratifications are nothing other than 'thickenings on a plane of consistency'.[84] It might be the case that lines of flight are defined as 'the maximum dimension after which the multiplicity

[81] Deleuze and Guattari, *A Thousand Plateaus*, 7.
[82] Deleuze and Guattari, *A Thousand Plateaus*, 9.
[83] Deleuze and Guattari, *A Thousand Plateaus*, 10.
[84] Deleuze and Guattari, *A Thousand Plateaus*, 78.

undergoes metamorphosis', but it is also the case that multiplicities are composed of these lines, and are therefore always changing in nature.[85] Because the variations and dimensions of any multiplicity are immanent to it, '*it amounts to the same thing to say that each multiplicity is already composed of heterogeneous terms in symbiosis, and that a multiplicity is continually transforming itself into a string of other multiplicities, according to its thresholds and doors*'.[86] To put this another way, we can say that because assemblages are only produced when the maximum dimension of a multiplicity is reached, 'becoming and multiplicity are the same thing'.[87] Just as the absolute deterritorialisation of the line of flight is primary in the assemblage, so change and transformation are primary on the plane of consistency.

In the next section of this chapter we will push our exploration of the nature of the plane of consistency a little further by looking at Deleuze and Guattari's analysis of painting in *A Thousand Plateaus*. However, before moving on, it will be instructive to pause and consider why Deleuze and Guattari claim that philosophers have previously misrecognised the plane of consistency and therefore why the nature of transformation has remained so elusive to thought. In the tenth plateau, '1730: Becoming-Intense, Becoming-Animal, Becoming-Imperceptible...', Deleuze and Guattari compare 'two planes, or two ways of conceptualizing the plane'.[88] One of these is the plane of consistency that we have just been considering. The other is the 'plan(e) of organization or development'.[89] The plane of organisation is that 'hidden structure necessary for forms' which the dogmatic image of thought takes as the precondition for good sense in thought. This 'hidden structure' is perhaps most clearly exemplified by Plato's famous analogy between the thinker and the butcher, both of whom are required to work by 'dividing things again by classes, where the natural joints are'.[90] What Deleuze and Guattari take issue with is the idea that there are any hidden but necessary 'natural joints' at all. Such an assumption, they argue, is always 'inferred' or 'concluded from its own effects'.[91] The assumption of

85 Deleuze and Guattari, *A Thousand Plateaus*, 23.
86 Deleuze and Guattari, *A Thousand Plateaus*, 275.
87 Deleuze and Guattari, *A Thousand Plateaus*, 275.
88 Deleuze and Guattari, *A Thousand Plateaus*, 292.
89 Deleuze and Guattari, *A Thousand Plateaus*, 297.
90 Plato, *Phaedrus*, 265e.
91 Deleuze and Guattari, *A Thousand Plateaus*, 293.

an always hidden plane that sits behind reality and provides it with a structure is at the core of arborescent thinking. Deleuze and Guattari say that the plane of organisation is both 'teleological' and 'structural' because the apparent design of such a plane – the placement of the joints – 'establishes the proportional relations of a structure' and must be posited by 'the mind of a god, or in the unconscious of life, of the soul, or of language'.[92] Deleuze and Guattari also use the language of dimensions to argue that the plane of organisation introduces transcendence into thought. Once again, Deleuze's previous analysis of Riemannian geometry is useful here. Before the advent of Riemannian geometry, it was only possible to work with curved spaces in geometry by representing these spaces in a non-curved space of a higher dimension. As we saw earlier, the problem with this practice is that it must take for granted the existence of a supplementary space used for analysis alone, which must also be assumed to be flat.[93] In *A Thousand Plateaus*, Deleuze and Guattari condemn the dogmatic image of thought on the same grounds, claiming that the plane of organisation is always assumed to exist 'in a supplementary dimension to that to which it gives rise ($n + 1$)'.[94] The plane of consistency, on the other hand, 'is necessarily a plane of immanence' because the rhizomatic thought that thinks with the plane of consistency never allows for the existence of a supplementary dimension and recognises that dimension added to a multiplicity brings about a change in nature.

The purpose of raising this point here, concerning the difference between the plane of consistency and the plane of organisation, is to show how Deleuze and Guattari can claim that the line of flight is not simply an activity of thought. While the arborescent model for thought always embeds its object in an abstract space, where it is cut off from the rest of reality and made static and unchanging in order to pass judgement upon it, the rhizomatic model for thought thinks with assemblages as they are changing and as they are interacting with other assemblages. What this means is that the concepts that relate to the rhizomatic image of thought, such as

92 Deleuze and Guattari, *A Thousand Plateaus*, 293.

93 Greenberg, *Euclidean and Non-Euclidean Geometries*, 373–4. See Deleuze's comments on philosophies that require a 'fictitious third dimension' (*Difference and Repetition*, 61).

94 Deleuze and Guattari, *A Thousand Plateaus*, 293.

deterritorialisation, stratification and the line of flight, do not exist within thought, waiting to be imposed on matter in an act of judgement. Instead, these concepts concern an immanent thought that cannot be detached from that which it thinks. The line of flight is therefore not simply in the head of the subject who thinks it, or in the object about which it is thought, but on the plane of consistency which refuses to separate the subject from the object, and on which there is only a 'continuum of intensities'.[95]

Multilinear Systems and the Example of Linear Perspective (Again)

Throughout *A Thousand Plateaus*, Deleuze and Guattari develop their many conceptual inventions through analyses of artistic forms.[96] In the tenth plateau, they elaborate on the dynamics of the plane of consistency and the plane of organisation by discussing the many ways that they operate in both music and painting. In each case, Deleuze and Guattari aim to differentiate those forms of music, or of painting, that face towards the plane of organisation from those that face towards the plane of consistency. According to their analysis, the forms of music and of painting that face the plane of organisation are those that form *punctual systems*. Punctual systems are those that create order through the use of vertical and horizontal lines, which create a grid for determining the location of points (i.e. punctual). In these cases, vertical and horizontal lines provide a structure, while diagonals 'play the role of connectors between points'.[97] In these cases: 'The line and the diagonal remain totally subordinated to the point because they serve as coordinates for a point or as localizable connections for two points, running from one point to another.'[98] Deleuze and Guattari state that these systems are 'arborescent, mnemonic, molar, structural; they are systems of

[95] Deleuze and Guattari, *A Thousand Plateaus*, 78.

[96] Perhaps the most comprehensive example of this comes with their analysis of the form of the novella in the eighth plateau, where the concept of the line of flight plays an integral role. Paul Patton uses Deleuze and Guattari's analysis of Fitzgerald's novella to define one outcome of the line of flight as a 'kind of shift towards another quality of life' (Patton, *Deleuze and the Political*, 87).

[97] Deleuze and Guattari, *A Thousand Plateaus*, 325.

[98] Deleuze and Guattari, *A Thousand Plateaus*, 326.

territorialization or reterritorialization'.[99] Punctual systems are also defined as being representational.[100]

According to Deleuze and Guattari, the forms of music and of painting that face towards the plane of consistency are not punctual but multilinear: 'Opposed to the punctual system are linear, or rather multilinear, systems.'[101] Multilinear systems do not rely on an orientating grid of horizontal and vertical lines, they do not define the location of individual points, and thus they do not subordinate lines to points. In this plateau, Deleuze and Guattari suggest that creativity in the arts is always linked to the development of multilinear systems that oppose the historical imposition of punctual systems. They write: 'Free the line, free the diagonal: every musician or painter has this intention.'[102]

However, much like the similar distinction between the arborescent and rhizomatic images of thought, the distinction between punctual and multilinear systems is not simply an opposition. Multilinear systems are never separated from punctual ones, but are like methodologies for undoing the stratified relations between points that punctual systems set up. Punctual systems are not taken as failed attempts at creativity, but as sites, or contexts, waiting to be opened up by an act of creative deformation. In certain cases, artists require a punctual system as the backdrop to their activity. Deleuze and Guattari write that:

> One elaborates a punctual system or a didactic representation, but with the aim of making it snap, of sending a tremor through it. A punctual system is most interesting when there is a musician, painter, writer, philosopher to oppose it, who even fabricates it in order to oppose it, like a springboard to jump from.[103]

Given this relation between punctual and multilinear systems, we are now in a position to explore Deleuze and Guattari's updated comments on linear perspective and their analysis of the role of the line of flight in this context. This is what they write:

[99] Deleuze and Guattari, *A Thousand Plateaus*, 326.

[100] By defining these systems as representational, Deleuze and Guattari are not saying that they are figurative, or that they produce an image of something that they represent, but that they have a systematic way of organising sensation. For Deleuze, artistic forms such as abstract painting escape from figuration, but not from representation (*Francis Bacon*, 8–12).

[101] Deleuze and Guattari, *A Thousand Plateaus*, 326.

[102] Deleuze and Guattari, *A Thousand Plateaus*, 326.

[103] Deleuze and Guattari, *A Thousand Plateaus*, 326.

> There is no falser problem in painting than depth and, in particular, perspective. For perspective is only a historical manner of *occupying* diagonals or transversals, lines of flight in other words, of reterritorializing the moving visual block ... But the lines of flight, the transversals, are suitable for many other functions besides this molar function. Lines of flight as perspective lines, far from being made to represent depth, themselves invent the possibility of such a representation, which occupies them only for an instant, at a given moment. Perspective, and even depth, are the reterritorialization of lines of flight, which alone created painting by carrying it farther.[104]

First, this quotation suggests that linear perspective, as a technique for dealing with the false problem of depth in painting, should be considered as an archetypal punctual system. It takes the vertical and horizontal axis of the canvas as a grid for determining the location of points, and uses diagonals, or converging lines, to connect these points in an attempt to simulate depth. The second thing that this quotation suggests, however, is that despite the stratifying capacity of linear perspective, it is possible to use this system as a springboard towards the multilinear, and towards the plane of consistency. The shift we can see here from Deleuze's earlier comments in *Difference and Repetition* concerns the potentials for creativity or for transformation that lie within linear perspective. Rather than being simply an example of the dangers of representation, in *A Thousand Plateaus* Deleuze and Guattari aim to show how this punctual system can be opposed, namely by recognising the primacy of the line of flight over the perspectival system that captures it. Linear perspective may be a punctual system which tends towards the plane of organisation, but it is the line of flight – resisting representation and running between indiscernible points – which is also the internal point of escape from linear perspective. It is by following lines of flight that linear perspective can be made into a springboard with which to oppose the representational history of painting.

In the first chapter of this book we saw how Deleuze and Guattari's concept of the line of flight relates to the concept of the *ligne de fuite* in the terminology of linear perspective. Briefly put, these are the lines that run between vanishing points and determine the abstract line towards which two parallel planes converge if extended to infinity. However, contrary to this definition, in a translator's note to the long quotation given above, Massumi adds the following comment:

[104] Deleuze and Guattari, *A Thousand Plateaus*, 329.

'*lignes de fuite*: here, the lines in a painting moving toward the vanishing point, or *point de fuite*'.[105] From our analysis, we now know that this note is incorrect. *Lignes de fuite* are not the lines that converge towards the vanishing point, but are instead the lines that run between the vanishing points. This is important because of what it means for the kind of creativity that Deleuze and Guattari are attempting to call for. If the line of flight were like the line that runs towards the vanishing point, then to follow a line of flight would be a kind of 'heading off into the distance', a movement over the horizon. But this is not how the term is used. Rather than being a line that escapes over the horizon, the line of flight *is* the horizon. To draw a new line of flight is therefore an activity of creating a new horizon, or of detaching the horizon from the representational space of the painting. Not of escaping the current organisation of relations by getting outside, or beyond them, but escaping them by reorganising them from within. Deleuze and Guattari write that 'Creations are like mutant abstract lines that have detached themselves from the task of representing a world.'[106] However, they also clarify that they do not detach themselves from representation by escaping reality, but 'precisely because they assemble a new type of reality'.[107] It will be important to keep this form of creative action in mind when we turn to the question of political transformations in the following chapter.

The Body without Organs and the Ethics of Transformation

Drawing lines of flight can lead to absolute deterritorialisation on the plane of consistency. Another way of putting this is to say that drawing a line of flight can bring about a transformation. However, at this point it is reasonable to ask whether such transformations are necessarily an ethically favourable outcome. Or, more to the point, we can ask when such transformations will be ethical, and for whom. Despite Deleuze and Guattari's regular prescriptions to their readers that they should aim to 'extend the line of flight to the point where it becomes an abstract machine covering the entire plane of consistency', they also pepper their book with words of caution.[108]

105 Deleuze and Guattari, *A Thousand Plateaus*, 329.
106 Deleuze and Guattari, *A Thousand Plateaus*, 326.
107 Deleuze and Guattari, *A Thousand Plateaus*, 326.
108 Deleuze and Guattari, *A Thousand Plateaus*, 12.

We are told, for example, that absolute deterritorialisation might be 'overlaid by a compensatory reterritorialization' that would be more despotic than what was deterritorialised.[109] On top of the possibility of the line of flight turning into a segmentary line, we are also warned that the line of flight is 'imbued with such singular despair' relating to the immanent possibility of 'a death, a demolition' that it might bring about.[110] In the final section of this chapter, I want to explore some of these dangers by looking at the concept of the Body without Organs (BwO). I will argue here that it is a mistake to assume that drawing lines of flight, and bringing about transformations, is of ethical value in and of itself. However, by looking at the extent to which Deleuze and Guattari's work builds on the possibility of a Spinozist ethics, I will argue that, while it is not ethically positive to draw a line of flight, ethics is only possible when an adequate knowledge of causes is attained, and that to reach such a form of knowledge it is vital to think rhizomatically and to map the many lines of flight that are primary in the assemblage under consideration. We will see here that there is nothing inherently ethical about drawing lines of flight, but that a true ethics requires the mapping of such lines. Ethics might not be the art of bringing about transformations, but it does involve an understanding of the transformative capacities of the world.

In *Anti-Oedipus*, Deleuze and Guattari used the concept of the BwO to designate the unformed and unorganised state of the body, against which the desiring-machines worked to form connections, disjunctions and conjunctions. We saw in the last chapter how the BwO was given as one end of a continuum, along which bodies become more or less organised. At the other pole of this continuum is the organism. Using the conceptual framework laid out in *A Thousand Plateaus*, we can now say that the BwO plays the role of the plane of consistency specifically for the double articulation and stratification of organic matter. While organisms are created via the selection and formation of an intensive substance of content, which, by way of transduction, results in the formation of an extensive substance of expression, the processes of deterritorialisation that cut across these stratifications lead the organism back towards the BwO. Speaking of such cases, Deleuze and Guattari write: 'In effect, the body without organs is itself the plane of consistency.'[111] We might

[109] Deleuze and Guattari, *A Thousand Plateaus*, 559.
[110] Deleuze and Guattari, *A Thousand Plateaus*, 227.
[111] Deleuze and Guattari, *A Thousand Plateaus*, 45.

think, given the apparently despotic nature of the organisation of the body, that Deleuze and Guattari would take the BwO as a goal – and, indeed, they dedicate a whole plateau to the question, 'How do you make yourself a Body without Organs?' – however, this is the section of the book that contains the highest level of caution. We are told that making oneself a BwO is not easy, that 'you can botch it', and that 'it can be terrifying, and lead you to your death'.[112]

The main technique offered for the deterritorialisation of the body is the act of resisting the normal function of the organs. Instead of 'seeing with your eyes, breathing with your lungs, swallowing with your mouth', the aim will be to 'walk on your head, sing with your sinuses, see through your skin, breathe with your belly'.[113] This demand might not be quite as impossible as it first sounds, as the aim of disorganising the body is not simply to use the wrong organs for each task, but to experiment with the possibilities offered by the body. The idea is not to stop breathing through your mouth and start breathing through your belly, but to experiment with the different possibilities of breathing. In Deleuze's book on the paintings of Francis Bacon, written at the same time as *A Thousand Plateaus* and covering many of the same themes, he clarifies that in making oneself a BwO the aim is not simply to destroy the organs, but to create 'transitory organs'.[114] Taking the act of viewing one of Bacon's paintings as his primary example, Deleuze explains how the eye 'ceases to be organic in order to become a polyvalent and transitory organ' because the possibilities contained in the eye are freed from the prescribed function of feeding visual information to the brain.[115] In the act of the encounter with the intensity of the painting, we also feel the painting with organs other than the eye. It affects us in other ways than the purely visual and 'gives us eyes all over: in the ear, in the stomach, in the lungs'.[116] In the previous section on the role of the line of flight in linear perspective, we saw that to escape from the restrictions of the organised space of perspectival painting the aim was not to draw a line that flees over the horizon, but to detach the horizon from its fixed position in order to put the whole space in variation. Similarly here, in making oneself a BwO the aim

112 Deleuze and Guattari, *A Thousand Plateaus*, 166.
113 Deleuze and Guattari, *A Thousand Plateaus*, 167.
114 Deleuze, *Francis Bacon*, 48–52.
115 Deleuze, *Francis Bacon*, 52.
116 Deleuze, *Francis Bacon*, 52.

is not to escape the body by getting outside it, but to detach an organ from its fixed function and put it into variation with the other organs of the body.

Understandably, this process is not without its dangers. When speaking of composing the BwO, Deleuze and Guattari write that 'there is no assurance that two lines of flight will prove compatible, compossible', and that as a result of this 'there is no assurance that the body without organs will be easy to compose'.[117] Drug addicts, sexual fetishists and anorexics are given as examples of people who have tried to make themselves into a BwO by experimenting with the possibilities of the body, but who have ended up with 'emptied bodies instead of full ones'.[118] By detaching one organ from its assumed function and putting it into variation with the other organs, your new internal relations may become unstable or incompatible, you may empty yourself out. In order to avoid falling into the danger of joining this 'dreary parade of sucked-dry, catatonicized, vitrified, sewn-up bodies', Deleuze and Guattari counsel caution.[119] It is due to the very nature of experimentation that we cannot know in advance what will happen. This is why Deleuze and Guattari like to quote Spinoza's famous claim that 'nobody as yet has determined the limits of the body's capabilities: that is, nobody as yet has learned from experience what the body can and cannot do'.[120] Experimentation is dangerous and always proceeds in small steps. It is also the case that experimentation is never complete. For this reason the BwO is never simply attained, but is always a limit that one approaches.[121] It is a skill that is learned through practice, and in context, rather than in theory. You cannot reach the BwO 'by wildly destratifying' because you must 'keep enough of the organism for it to reform each dawn'.[122] This comment suggests that if all of the organisations of the body are dismantled simultaneously, then there will not be any ground on which to base the reorganisation of its organs.

In one of the most telling passages of the book, given towards the end of the plateau on the BwO, Deleuze and Guattari give the

[117] Deleuze and Guattari, *A Thousand Plateaus*, 226.
[118] Deleuze and Guattari, *A Thousand Plateaus*, 167.
[119] Deleuze and Guattari, *A Thousand Plateaus*, 167.
[120] Spinoza, *Complete Works*, 280.
[121] Deleuze and Guattari, *A Thousand Plateaus*, 166.
[122] Deleuze and Guattari, *A Thousand Plateaus*, 178.

following answer to the question of how to make oneself a body without organs:

> Lodge yourself on a stratum, experiment with the opportunities it offers, find an advantageous place on it, find potential movements of deterritorialization, possible lines of flight, experience them, produce flow conjunctions here and there, try out continuums of intensities segment by segment, have a small plot of new land at all times. It is through a meticulous relation with the strata that one succeeds in freeing lines of flight, causing conjugated flows to pass and escape and bringing forth continuous intensities for a BwO.[123]

This quote brings together many of the practical points we have just explored. First, the process always proceeds by experimentation. You do not yet know what your lines of flight are, or what your possibilities of deterritorialisation are, so it will take some trial and error to find out. Crucially, throughout this process, you must also keep some of the body organised. Without a small area to come back to after each experimentation, it is more likely that the experiments will fail. This quote is also useful for the way that it ties together some of the themes we have already explored in both *Anti-Oedipus* and *A Thousand Plateaus*. Just as it was the schizoanalyst's task in *Anti-Oedipus* to seek out and follow a subject's lines of flight, to find their desiring-machines and to experiment with their possibilities, here one makes oneself a BwO in much the same way. This quote is also useful because it brings back some of the terminology related to the concept of the *refrain*. Specifically, given the practical case of experimenting with the BwO, we can see why the first two stages of the refrain, in which an inside is separated from the outside and becomes a home, are necessary for the third stage of the refrain, in which explorations can be made into the outside.

What remains surprising is the fact that, despite the many words of caution in the text, the concept of the line of flight, and the state of absolute deterritorialisation that it apparently brings about, are often read as being ultimately desirable.[124] This is especially confusing given the fact that Deleuze and Guattari make it explicit that remaining 'stratified—organized, signified, subjected—is not the worst that can happen'. Instead, they claim that 'the worst that can happen is if you throw the strata into demented or suicidal collapse, which brings

[123] Deleuze and Guattari, *A Thousand Plateaus*, 178.
[124] Holland, *Deleuze and Guattari's 'A Thousand Plateaus'*, 56.

them back down on us heavier than ever'.[125] We will return to this danger in the next chapter, when we discuss Deleuze and Guattari's political pragmatics. However, in order to understand the ethics of the line of flight, and the ethical framework of the whole book, it is important to note here how Deleuze and Guattari's ethics draws on the work of Spinoza, and to a lesser extent Nietzsche, and how the ethical principles that it develops are distinct from a morality.

In his earlier work, Deleuze had paid a good deal of attention to the distinction between morality and ethics.[126] Through the work of Spinoza, Deleuze had found a methodology for determining what is ethically good or bad, without any need to rely on an additional category distinction between what is good and what is evil. For Spinoza, what is good in the ethical sense for any specific body is just that which increases that body's capacity to act. If two bodies interact in such a way that they increase each other's capacity to act, then the interaction is good, and it produces the positive affect of joy. If, on the other hand, two bodies interact in such a way that they reduce each other's capacity to act, then the interaction is ethically bad and produces the affect of sadness. These two affects are ultimately distinguished on the basis of their activity or passivity: that which is good and produces joy is active, while that which is bad and produces sadness is passive. What is good and what is bad, according to this simple schema, is not determined by any transcendent moral law, but is discovered on a case-by-case basis depending on the compatibility of bodies and the power contained in them. Consequently, Deleuze writes of Spinoza's philosophy that in it there is 'neither Good nor Evil, there is no moral opposition, but there is an ethical difference'.[127]

The question of how to become an ethical individual now becomes something very distinct from any social or religious obligation to follow a particular moral code. Instead, to become ethical requires the development of a special kind of knowledge that will be able to understand the interaction of bodies, that will be able to explain what causes the affects of joy and sadness, and ultimately will allow for the selection of those interactions that will bring about active

[125] Deleuze and Guattari, *A Thousand Plateaus*, 178.

[126] 'This is how good and evil are born: ethical determination, that of good and bad, gives way to moral judgement' (Deleuze, *Nietzsche and Philosophy*, 121–2).

[127] Deleuze, *Expressionism in Philosophy: Spinoza*, 261. See also Deleuze, *Spinoza: Practical Philosophy*, 17–30.

encounters. Spinoza defines this kind of understanding as the acquisition of 'adequate ideas', and distinguishes it from those ideas that remain 'inadequate'.[128] While a full description of Spinoza's ethics is beyond the reach of this chapter, what is most important here is the thought that while inadequate ideas only relate to effects, adequate ideas enable us to understand causes. Summarising this point in Spinoza, Deleuze writes that with inadequate ideas, 'we have knowledge of effects only; or to put it differently, we know only properties of things. Only adequate ideas, as expressive, give us knowledge through causes, or through a thing's essence.'[129] He adds in clarification that an adequate idea '*is just an idea that expresses its cause*'.[130] What is important for our discussion, and what is carried over into *A Thousand Plateaus*, is the idea that ethical action is not determined by any pre-given, transcendent law, and that to act ethically one must attain knowledge of the kinds of affects produced when bodies interact so that positive and joyous relations can be selected over those that produce the sad passions.

In order to understand the ethical implications of the concept of the line of flight as it appears in *A Thousand Plateaus*, we must recognise that it is operating within this form of Spinozist ethics. Using distinctly Spinozist terminology, in *A Thousand Plateaus* Deleuze and Guattari give the following response to the question of how to produce an ethics:

> We know nothing about a body until we know what it can do, in other words, what its affects are, how they can or cannot enter into composition with other affects, with the affects of another body, either to destroy that body or to be destroyed by it, either to exchange actions and passions with it or to join with it in composing a more powerful body.[131]

The rhizomatic model of thought employed in *A Thousand Plateaus* is selected precisely because it is able to map the connections that

128 For an overview of the relation between ideas and the passions, see LeBuffe, 'The Anatomy of the Passions'. For a discussion of the difference between adequate and inadequate ideas, see McAllister, 'Adequate and Inadequate Ideas in Spinoza'.

129 Deleuze, *Expressionism in Philosophy*, 133–4.

130 Deleuze, *Expressionism in Philosophy*, 133. For Spinoza, this cause is God. However, following more closely from Nietzsche's understanding of the Will to Power as ultimate cause, Deleuze and Guattari will take desire to be the cause in need of expression.

131 Deleuze and Guattari, *A Thousand Plateaus*, 284.

produce bodies and determine their interactions. While the arborescent image of thought remains at the level of effects, seeing only subjects, objects and predicates, the rhizomatic image of thought is able to analyse the forces that cause these effects to be produced. In short, it is the rhizomatic model of thought alone that can provide us with *adequate ideas*, and thus with an understanding of transformation.

Deleuze and Guattari make such a connection between Spinoza's ethics and their concept of the BwO that they are happy to ask: 'is not Spinoza's *Ethics* the great book of the BwO?'[132] Given this Spinozist context, it is now possible to rephrase the question posed at the beginning of this section: Is it ethically positive to draw lines of flight? Do lines of flight, and the absolute deterritorialisation of the body that they bring about, increase that body's capacity to act? This is not a straightforward question to answer. While deterritorialisation does increase the capacities of the body, this relies on the body not becoming emptied of the intensive flows that cross it. As we have seen, the line of flight can lead to death, which inevitably leads to a decrease in the body's capacity to act. It seems then that it is not necessarily ethically positive to draw lines of flight. However, our discussion of Spinoza's ethics also allows us to ask different kinds of questions of the line of flight. If it is the case that the distinction between what is good and what is bad is not given by a transcendent moral law, and is therefore unknowable except by experimentation, then it is not meaningful to ask whether lines of flight will be ethical actions in all cases. It is more reasonable to pose the question from the perspective of knowledge. If it is only via the acquisition of adequate ideas that we are able to understand causes, and if it is only through an understanding of causes that ethical actions may be selected, then the question we should ask is: Does the concept of the line of flight help us to attain adequate ideas? The answer to this question is much more positive. As primary elements of any assemblage, lines of flight are necessary components of the vegetal image of thought. Without this concept at hand, we are unable to understand the dynamics that condition the interaction and production of bodies. While the drawing of lines of flight is not necessarily ethical, the ability to map the various lines of flight that produce our bodies, and the bodies that we are surrounded by, is certainly a necessary requirement for acquiring adequate ideas.

132 Deleuze and Guattari, *A Thousand Plateaus*, 170.

After providing their instructions for the process of experimentation that is required to make oneself a Body without Organs, Deleuze and Guattari claim that if you follow these instructions you will have 'constructed your own little machine, ready when needed to be plugged into other collective machines'.[133] What is interesting about this comment is that it is forward-looking. Mapping the lines of flight that surround you, and exploring the deterritorialisations that pass through you, might not bring about ethical outcomes in and of themselves, but this process provides you with an understanding of your causes – it allows one to conceptualise reality as composed of transformations – so that you will be able to proceed by selecting those connections that will increase your capacity to act.

[133] Deleuze and Guattari, *A Thousand Plateaus*, 179.

6

A Thousand Plateaus and Political Pragmatics

Political Transformations Revisited

Following the analysis of the conceptual positioning of the concept of the line of flight in *A Thousand Plateaus*, in this chapter I will turn my attention to the theory of political economy put forward in the text, and ask what role the newly defined concept of the line of flight plays in this analysis. Ultimately, I will show that the concept of the line of flight is central to the political pragmatics of experimentation that Deleuze and Guattari advocate in the book. In brief, now that Deleuze and Guattari have a more developed metaphysics and ethics of transformation, they are able to return to the question of political transformations with a renewed perspective, namely one that is able to consider political transformations that are not circumscribed by purely capitalist coordinates. My decision to turn to Deleuze and Guattari's politics here – rather than, say, their aesthetics or their epistemology – is intended to provide a rejoinder to the analysis given of their political proclamations in *Anti-Oedipus*.

However, before turning to the modes of political transformation that Deleuze and Guattari discuss, first we need to answer some general questions about the political theory that their pragmatics is based on. In the first section below, I will show how Deleuze and Guattari's new theory of a general semiotics of content and expression challenges structural accounts of both linguistics and anthropology, and lays out a novel account of the difference between historical forms of political economy in terms of *regimes of signs*, along with their *order-words* and the *incorporeal transformations* that these bring about. In the next section I will give an account of the four different regimes of signs that Deleuze and Guattari discuss in the text and analyse the role that the line of flight plays in each of them. Third, I will show how this move towards an analysis of the power dynamics of regimes of signs leads Deleuze and Guattari first to a reformulation of the molar/molecular dyad and then on to a reconceptualisation of their political analysis as a practice of *diagrammatics* or *machinic analysis*. After returning to the role that the concept of the refrain plays here, and after making some brief comments on the way in which Deleuze and Guattari draw on the history of Institutional Analysis to guide their political proclamations, I will end the chapter with a final overview in which I explain where the concept of the line of flight fits into the politics of *A Thousand Plateaus*. By the end of this chapter, we should not only therefore have a clear understanding of how the concept of the line of flight functions in Deleuze and Guattari's political philosophy of transformation, but we will also have used it to explore the practical and political consequences of their major work.

Linguistic Pragmatics

In the 'Postulates of Linguistics' plateau, Deleuze and Guattari describe their approach to language as a 'pragmatics'.[1] In part, this concept is used to point to the fact that they are interested in the material ways in which language works, and to differentiate themselves from thinkers such as Chomsky, who they see as abandoning the importance of context. But Deleuze and Guattari do not only use this word 'pragmatics' to signal their interest in what is outside language. On the contrary, they refer to their work as involving an '*internal pragmatics*' which considers the functions of linguistic statements alongside the variations and transformations that are internal to language.[2] Each statement must therefore be understood according to the way it brings about changes in the state of affairs, and according to the way that it brings about changes in the language of which it is a part. For this reason, Deleuze and Guattari claim that 'Pragmatics is a politics of language.'[3] This mode of analysis is also pragmatic in another sense: as both context and language are in a state of continuous variation, such a practice must shun the idea of discovering a universal system of meaning, and must restrict itself to the practical task of dealing with what is immediately problematic in a situation. In this section I would like to examine the way in which Deleuze and Guattari's linguistics pragmatics is central to both their political analysis and their account of political transformations.

[1] Deleuze and Guattari, *A Thousand Plateaus*, 86.
[2] Deleuze and Guattari, *A Thousand Plateaus*, 100.
[3] Deleuze and Guattari, *A Thousand Plateaus*, 91.

We must begin here by asking how Deleuze and Guattari's theory of stratification – which explains the difference between physical, organic and linguistic matter as a difference in the mode of stratification of content into expression – impacts on their understanding of the different forms of political economy that they studied in *Anti-Oedipus*. If it is the case that physical, organic and linguistic matter are all stratifications on the same plane of consistency, and are all combined in assemblages of power, then we should be able to use this framework to explore some fundamental political questions. For example, how does the arrangement of physical land and physical apparatuses of production relate to the arrangement of the organic bodies that it supports? How does an arrangement of organic bodies relate to what is said, and vice versa? How do each of these interact with the arrangement of physical matter? First, it is important to remember that these three stratifications are not organised hierarchically.[4] It is not the case that physical stratifications lead to organic and then alloplastic or linguistic stratification. As Deleuze and Guattari put it: 'The different figures of content and expression are not stages. There is no biosphere or noosphere, but everywhere the same Mechanosphere.'[5] Second, we must remember that in the double articulation of translation that defines the alloplastic stratum, content and expression become detached in such a way that the form of expression of the alloplastic stratum can take the form of content of any other stratum as its object. What this means is that language operates by overcoding physical and organic bodies and rearranging their respective forms of content.

Because of this power of overcoding, it is only the linguistic stratum that can properly be said to have signs. However, Deleuze and Guattari argue that these signs are not necessarily 'endowed with signifiance'.[6] All physical and organic matter has its own semiotic form of expression and has its own sense; what separates linguistic signs from the other strata must then be understood not in terms of what they *mean*, but in what they can *do*. Taking the example of the way that children learn the rules of language in primary school, Deleuze and Guattari argue that the 'compulsory education machine does not communicate information', but instead 'imposes upon the child semiotic coordinates possessing all of the

[4] Deleuze and Guattari, *A Thousand Plateaus*, 65–75.

[5] Deleuze and Guattari, *A Thousand Plateaus*, 77.

[6] Deleuze and Guattari, *A Thousand Plateaus*, 73.

dual functions of grammar', including the ordering distinctions between 'masculine–feminine, singular–plural, noun–verb, subject of the statement–subject of enunciation'.[7] Language takes the form of orders given by the teacher, which overcode the bodies of the students and subsequently determine the set of possible ways that they can interact with physical matter. In a telling comparison, Deleuze and Guattari write that words are not tools, but that 'we give children language, pens, and notebooks as we give workers shovels and pickaxes'.[8] Just as mining tools organise the body of workers to provide them with a very specific horizon of possibility for acting, the orders of the teacher organise the children into a predetermined set of social practices.

Following this practical analysis of the power of language to overcode bodies, Deleuze and Guattari argue that language is fundamentally illocutionary. This means that it operates not by the representative function assumed in theories of signification or communication, but by performative acts, such as those of promising, ordering, decreeing and commanding. The terminology that Deleuze and Guattari introduce to describe these processes includes both 'order-words' and 'incorporeal transformations'. In short, language operates by the issuing of order-words which overcode an assemblage via the double articulation of translation, which brings about an incorporeal transformation in the semiotic relations of the assemblage, and ultimately determines what that assemblage can do. To take another example, when the officiator at a wedding states 'I now pronounce you man and wife', he or she brings about an incorporeal transformation in the semiotic relations between the couple. The statements of the officiator intervene in the circulation of order-words, such that the couple are transformed from being engaged to being married, and the powers open to them are also transformed: they can adopt a child, apply for a joint mortgage, or share their material wealth without the intervention of state taxation.

For Deleuze and Guattari, order-words are not simply a particular set of statements given in the imperative, but 'the relation of every word or every statement to implicit presuppositions'.[9] What this statement points out is that incorporeal transformations rely on a particular arrangement of bodies to be effective. In the example

[7] Deleuze and Guattari, *A Thousand Plateaus*, 84.
[8] Deleuze and Guattari, *A Thousand Plateaus*, 84.
[9] Deleuze and Guattari, *A Thousand Plateaus*, 87.

above, the priest can only bring about the incorporeal transformation of the wedding given a set of underlying material relations defined by the history of the Church. Subsequently, 'the meaning and syntax of language can no longer be defined independently of the speech acts they presuppose', and because of this, 'pragmatics becomes the presupposition behind all of the other dimensions' of language.[10] Deleuze and Guattari's line of argument here begins with their theory of stratification; it moves from the overcoding nature of language, through an analysis of the pragmatics of that overcoding, to a definition of language that highlights the constantly varying relations between a set of order-words and the arrangement of bodies that these order-words take for granted. They write that 'the only possible definition of language is the set of all order-words, implicit presuppositions, or speech acts current in a language at a given moment'.[11] It is with this definition in mind that we will be able to see how Deleuze and Guattari rework the theory of political economy that they first articulated in *Anti-Oedipus*.

The first thing we notice about this definition of language, and the theory of political economy that it accompanies, is that both are distinctly anti-structuralist. Deleuze and Guattari take great pains to emphasise that a form of content 'is not a signified, any more than a form of expression is a signifier', and that this is true 'for all of the strata, including those on which language plays a role'.[12] What this means is that the relation between the form of expression of the alloplastic stratum and the form of content of the other strata that it overcodes do not form a series of exclusive disjunctions that determine one-to-one relations between a series of signifiers and a series of signifieds.[13] Subsequently, it is not possible to give an account of the political relations of a society simply by assuming that the structural relations of language offer a representation of these interactions. The most obvious example here comes directly from *Anti-Oedipus*: while the despotic overcoding of the signifier does in fact structure desire into oedipal relations of lack and castration, this organisation is contingent on the material forms of the capitalist

[10] Deleuze and Guattari, *A Thousand Plateaus*, 86.
[11] Deleuze and Guattari, *A Thousand Plateaus*, 87.
[12] Deleuze and Guattari, *A Thousand Plateaus*, 74.
[13] This insight follows directly from Deleuze and Guattari's arguments in *Anti-Oedipus* concerning the inclusive disjunctions and transversal connections made between the elements of the code of the unconscious.

mode of production. What is more, desire itself always finds a way to escape this form of capture. At this point in *A Thousand Plateaus*, Deleuze and Guattari recast what they had called the transcendental illusions that accompany the illegitimate use of the three syntheses of the unconscious in *Anti-Oedipus* as 'the illusion constitutive of man', which 'derives from the overcoding immanent to language itself'.[14] They speak here of the 'imperialist pretensions on behalf of language', which derive from the mistaken assumption by which we jump directly from the fact that the linguistic stratum *can* overcode any of the other strata to the conclusion that it *does in fact* overcode all of the strata.[15] On the contrary, while order-words may intervene in any state of affairs, this state of affairs must necessarily contain physical and organic articulations of matter that remain outside the linguistic stratum.

Unlike some of Guattari's claims in *Psychoanalysis and Transversality* and some of Deleuze and Guattari's claims in *Anti-Oedipus*, what marks out this theory of illocutionary language put forward in *A Thousand Plateaus* is that it no longer subjugates linguistics to a more basic realm of intensive material processes. In previous chapters I showed how, based on Guattari's Marxist reformulation of Lacanian structuralism, Deleuze and Guattari had begun to map the distinction between the machinic and intensive process of the unconscious and the linguistic structure of conscious thought on to the distinction that Marx formulates between the material base of a society and the legal and cultural superstructure to which it gives rise.[16] However, given their new analysis of the way in which order-words can bring about incorporeal transformations in assemblages composed of physical and organic strata as well as linguistic ones, Deleuze and Guattari now claim not only that 'content and expression are never reducible to signified–signifier', but that 'neither are they reducible to base–superstructure'.[17] Crucially, this means that one can 'no more posit a primacy of content as the determining factor than a primacy of expression as a signifying system'.[18] If it is the case that the only difference between physical, organic and linguistic matter is the form of double articulation by which

[14] Deleuze and Guattari, *A Thousand Plateaus*, 71.
[15] Deleuze and Guattari, *A Thousand Plateaus*, 70.
[16] See Chapter 2.
[17] Deleuze and Guattari, *A Thousand Plateaus*, 76.
[18] Deleuze and Guattari, *A Thousand Plateaus*, 76.

content relates to expression, then all of these articulations share the same plane of consistency. This means that linguistic expressions are not simply molar statistical aggregates arising from unconscious molecular processes.[19] In a practical sense, what this means is that organisations of power are 'in no way located within a State apparatus but rather are everywhere, effecting formalizations of content and expression, the segments of which they intertwine'.[20] At the point of writing *Anti-Oedipus*, Deleuze and Guattari had defined each of the three major forms of political economy in their systematic analysis in relation to the state. So-called 'primitive' societies were said to ward off the state via a process of coding, 'despotic' regimes were said to institute the state via a process of overcoding, while 'capitalist' societies were supposedly defined by the way that they constantly decoded and recoded social strata in relation to the power of the state. Given the flat plane of consistency which linguistic strata share with the physical and the organic, it will no longer be possible to define each of these modes of political economy purely in terms of their relation to the state, neither will it be possible to see them each as molar products of underlying molecular processes.

According to the theory of content and expression put forward in *A Thousand Plateaus*, each form of political economy is defined not simply by its mode of production, nor by its relation to the state (although these are still important factors), but by the relative stability of a particular organisation of order-words. If any semiotic field, comprising the forms of expression of all contents in a given assemblage, is normally composed of a constant variation of order-words and collective assemblages of enunciation, then, to quote from *A Thousand Plateaus*: 'To the extent these variables enter at a given moment into determinable relations, the assemblages combine in a *regime of signs*.'[21] Each regime of signs is simply a relative stabilisation of the dynamic interplay of order-words in a given situation. As Deleuze and Guattari clarify: 'We call any specific formalization of expression a regime of signs', and therefore a 'regime of signs

[19] Deleuze and Guattari explicitly state that the molar/molecular distinction only corresponds to the expression/content distinction for the physical articulation of induction. In the case of the organic articulation of transduction or the alloplastic articulation of translation, molar aggregates may be taken as contents: 'The double articulation sometimes coincides with the molecular and the molar, and sometimes not' (Deleuze and Guattari, *A Thousand Plateaus*, 49).

[20] Deleuze and Guattari, *A Thousand Plateaus*, 76.

[21] Deleuze and Guattari, *A Thousand Plateaus*, 92.

constitutes a semiotic system'.[22] It is important to note here that a regime of signs is not simply a collection of words, even a collection of order-words. Instead, a regime of signs is 'a set of statements arising in a social field considered as a stratum'.[23]

According to the theory of the double articulation of content and expression, the physical, the organic and the alloplastic are each stratifications on the plane of consistency. The world is composed of physical stratifications, organic stratifications and social stratifications. A form of political economy is nothing other than a form of social stratification, namely an organisation of asymmetric power relations in a society. Here Deleuze and Guattari draw heavily on Foucault's work in *Discipline and Punish*, which had analysed the particular relation between content and expression in a prison.[24] As Ronald Bogue notes, it is Foucault's work that 'makes evident that alloplastic stratification not only codes, territorialises, controls, restricts and rigidifies, but also effectuates asymmetrical power relations'.[25] It is these asymmetrical power relations that become relatively solidified in a regime of signs, and it is these asymmetrical power relations that define a form of political economy. Each of these determinable forms is not defined 'in the last instance' by either its content or its expression, but by the way in which a regime of signs captures the relations of content and expression in a regular and repeatable system of relations.[26] In the next section we will see that Deleuze and Guattari discuss four different regimes of signs in *A Thousand Plateaus*. Each of these regimes has its own distinct set of power relations and also has its own use for the concept of the line of flight.

The Four Regimes and their Lines of Flight

The four different regimes of signs that Deleuze and Guattari discuss in *A Thousand Plateaus* are each defined by their respective relations to signification. These four are the pre-signifying regime, the signifying regime, the counter-signifying regime and the post-signifying regime. This list is not intended to be exhaustive, and Deleuze and

22 Deleuze and Guattari, *A Thousand Plateaus*, 123.
23 Deleuze and Guattari, *A Thousand Plateaus*, 74.
24 Deleuze and Guattari, *A Thousand Plateaus*, 74–5.
25 Bogue, 'Who the Earth Thinks It Is', 59.
26 Deleuze and Guattari, *A Thousand Plateaus*, 76.

Guattari explicitly state that there are undoubtedly many others.[27] Given the fact that these four regimes are not supposed to correspond with a historical progression, and given the central importance of the regime of signification, it will be easiest to begin with a characterisation of this regime. The signifying regime of signs refers to any case in which there is a despotic takeover of all linguistic functioning by the role of the signifier. The 'simple general formula' by which we may recognise the signifying regime is that here, 'every sign refers to another sign, and only to another sign, ad infinitum'.[28] Signifying regimes of signs are those in which there is a master signifier of excess and lack and in which all meaning is captured by a constant process of sliding from signifier to signifier in an enclosed semiotic field.

What Deleuze and Guattari are describing here is quite simply the subject matter of structural linguistics, and they make this clear by stating that signifying regimes of signs relate to 'the situation Levi-Strauss describes' in his structuralist anthropology.[29] By describing the signifying regime of signs in these terms, Deleuze and Guattari do not completely jettison structuralism, but give it a designated and delineated space within a much larger theory of semiotics.[30] Rather than being an absolute condition for meaning, the signifying regime of signs is only instantiated in situations where the social stratification of power is despotic or imperialist. Because of the dynamics of signification, in the signifying regime 'the network of signs is infinitely circular', leading to a semiotics based on a 'multiplicity of the circles or chains', in which the centre of the circle becomes an always-implicit centre of power.[31] According to Deleuze and Guattari, the signifying regime upholds this circular asymmetry of power relations through the use of paranoia. Because of the constant slippage of the signifier, and because every sign will always refer to yet another sign, meaning is constantly held one step out of reach, creating a situation of generalised anxiety. In brief, a signifying regime of signs can be found wherever there is a despotic capture of all semiotic

[27] The plateau in which the regimes are discussed is titled 'On Several Regimes of Signs'. For more on the selection of the four regimes, see Adkins, *Deleuze and Guattari's A Thousand Plateaus*, 83.

[28] Deleuze and Guattari, *A Thousand Plateaus*, 124.

[29] Deleuze and Guattari, *A Thousand Plateaus*, 124.

[30] This is similar to the move that Deleuze and Guattari make in *Anti-Oedipus* when they show how signification sits alongside a number of other processes of a-signifying semiotics and a-semiotic encodings.

[31] Deleuze and Guattari, *A Thousand Plateaus*, 125.

functions, and wherever this despotism operates via a generalised sense of paranoia.

As each regime is nothing other than the semiotic expression of a concrete assemblage, and as every assemblage is partially composed of lines of flight, we can ask how each of the different regimes relates to its lines of flight. Because the signifying regime is a form of capture, in which all semiotic functions are organised in concentric circles around the body of the despot, lines that escape this circular format will pose a great danger to the regime. Deleuze and Guattari write that where a semiotic system is signifying, 'the system's line of flight is assigned a negative value, condemned as that which exceeds the signifying regime's power'.[32] Put simply, when social relations are all defined in relation to a despot, any social connections that escape the despotic interior and connect with an outside pose a threat to the ultimate power of the ruler and will therefore be deemed intolerable. Because all movements of deterritorialisation and reterritorialisation within a signifying regime are measured in relation to the position of the despot, Deleuze and Guattari also state that the line of flight in signifying regimes is a *relative* line. The stock example in *A Thousand Plateaus* of a negative and relative line of flight in a signifying regime of signs is that of a scapegoat. A scapegoat escapes the interiority of a despotic society, but only relative to the despot, and this escape is considered a negative casting-out, not a positive exploration of the outside.

In contrast to the signifying regime, the pre-signifying regime is defined as the expression of a social stratification that actively wards off the possibility of a despotic and signifying regime taking hold. In pre-signifying regimes there are multiple forms of expression, including 'corporeality, gesturality, rhythm, dance, and rite', which 'coexist heterogeneously with the vocal form'.[33] This pluralism, or polyvocality, is designed to prevent the power takeover by a despotic form of signification that would reduce all expression to linguistic expression. In pre-signifying regimes, the different semiotic orders, or different forms of expression, are actively kept separate from one another through the use of ritual and tradition. This process of coding the different forms of expression in a society is key to the pre-signifying regime. Despite the fact that Deleuze and Guattari refer to this regime as 'primitive', they are keen to note that it does not

[32] Deleuze and Guattari, *A Thousand Plateaus*, 129–30.
[33] Deleuze and Guattari, *A Thousand Plateaus*, 130.

operate 'by ignorance, repression, or foreclosure of the signifier', but 'is animated by a keen presentiment of what is to come', namely the 'already-present threat' of the power of the signifier.

One of the ways that the pre-signifying regime wards off the possibility of despotism is by making sure that chains of signification can come to an end, rather than becoming infinite and circular.[34] As a result of this, the pre-signifying regime is composed of multiple lines of descent that cross one another, stop, or begin again according to the rites of social life. Due to the different forms of social stratification that the signifying and pre-signifying regimes bring about, they also have different relationships with their respective lines of flight. Much like in the signifying regime, lines of flight that escape the pre-signifying regime are deemed negative because they threaten the coding of the different forms of expression that serve to ward off signification, and thus threaten the collapse of the regime. However, unlike in signifying regimes, where all deterritorialisation is measured relative to the position of the despot, here the line of flight is an *absolute* line. What this means is that the escape of the line is not an escape from a specified centre, but an escape that cuts across all the multilinear systems of polyvocality used to ward off the emergence of a centre.

It should be obvious by this point that the presentations of the pre-signifying regime and the signifying regime in *A Thousand Plateaus* are basic reformulations of the primitive and despotic social machines that Deleuze and Guattari discussed in *Anti-Oedipus*. The only real difference between the way that these societies are characterised across the two books is that in *Anti-Oedipus* the central concern was the material apparatus of the state, and the use of signifying language was seen as a secondary effect of the state itself. Here, on the other hand, Deleuze and Guattari reverse the direction of importance: it is signification itself that institutes the state and not the reverse. Following the schema of *Anti-Oedipus*, we might expect there to be only one final regime of signs to act as the correlate of the 'civilised' capitalist form of society discussed in that text. However, in *A Thousand Plateaus*, Deleuze and Guattari discuss two more regimes of signs, neither of which correlates directly with capitalism.[35]

[34] Deleuze and Guattari take the example of cannibalism, in which the name that defines the line of descent of the one who is eaten comes to an end.

[35] While Deleuze and Guattari do not define capitalism as a particular regime of signs, they do define it as the conjunction of three different strata, two of which

The first of these is the counter-signifying regime of signs. This regime is defined by its use of a mixed semiotic based on 'arithmetic and numeration'.[36] While numbers are used in the signifying regime in order to organise the interior space of the state, the counter-signifying regime is based on the use of a special kind of number that Deleuze and Guattari call the 'numbering number'.[37] What makes this semiotic specific is that it uses number to mark 'a mobile and plural distribution, which itself determines functions and relations, which arrives at arrangements rather than totals, distributions rather than collections, which operates more by breaks, transitions, migration, and accumulation than by combining units'.[38] It will be easier to understand what Deleuze and Guattari aim to conceptualise here by looking at the form of social stratification that accompanies the counter-signifying regime. In contrast to the sedentary nature of the state form defined by the signifying regime, the social form that relates to the counter-signifying regime is said to be nomadic.[39] The animal-raising nomads of the steppe are said to use numerical signs to create an open and distributed space that is in constant variation. To do this they use numerical signs in a way that is 'not produced by something outside the system of marking it institutes'.[40] What this means is that they utilise an ordinal and not a cardinal number system in order to define the space that they inhabit as a continuous, rather than a discrete, spatial multiplicity. The counter-signifying regime is therefore the expression of a nomadic form of social stratification, defined by its process of *smoothing* space. Under this interpretation, nomadism is not defined as a process of moving through an otherwise fixed space, but of constructing a space that is in constant variation. What is key here is the recognition that this activity is based on a

correlate with the signifying and post-signifying regimes of signs. The third is the organic stratification of the individual person.

36 Deleuze and Guattari, *A Thousand Plateaus*, 131.

37 Deleuze and Guattari, *A Thousand Plateaus*, 131. The concept of the numbering number comes from Aristotle, and Deleuze first uses it in a text on Bergson, to whom he credits the idea that 'difference itself has a number, a virtual number, a numbering number' (*Desert Islands*, 34). Deleuze and Guattari develop this concept further in the twelfth plateau (*A Thousand Plateaus*, 429–30).

38 Deleuze and Guattari, *A Thousand Plateaus*, 131.

39 Deleuze and Guattari are more specific than this: while the pre-signifying regime relates to nomads of the 'hunter' type, the counter-signifying regime relates to nomads of the 'fearsome, warlike, and animal-raising' type (*A Thousand Plateaus*, 131).

40 Deleuze and Guattari, *A Thousand Plateaus*, 131.

counter-signifying semiotic in which signs are used to create variable distributions of matter, rather than to represent matter in a fixed, or striated, space.

Deleuze and Guattari give over the twelfth plateau to a detailed description of the functioning of this counter-signifying, nomadic semiotic, which they name nomadology. They are particularly interested in the way in which nomadic social forms utilise their lines of flight to expand their territories. They are also interested in showing what happens when this deterritorialising activity of nomadic societies comes up against the reterritorialising effects of the state. Deleuze and Guattari claim that nomadic societies operate by assembling their many lines of flight into special assemblages known as 'war machines'.[41] War machines do not necessarily have war as their object, but simply operate by overcoming spatial boundaries and creating smooth spaces out of striated space. Only when these war machines come up against the stratifying power of the signifying regime of signs, and the state form that it expresses, do they take war as their object and become destructive.[42] With their analysis of the war machine, Deleuze and Guattari show that in counter-signifying regimes of signs, lines of flight can be understood as positive, in the sense that they are active in creating smooth spaces, but that they can become relative when they are turned against the state or are appropriated by the state.[43] Summarising the role played by the line of flight in the counter-signifying regime of signs, Deleuze and Guattari write that 'the imperial despotic line of flight is replaced by a line of abolition that turns back against the great empires, cuts across them and destroys them, or else conquers them and integrates with them to form a mixed semiotic'.[44] In this sense, it is not only that counter-signifying regimes utilise their lines of flight in a different way, but that they are specifically defined by their uses of lines of flight.

The fourth and final regime of signs that Deleuze and Guattari discuss in *A Thousand Plateaus* is the post-signifying regime. This regime of signs is said to operate by a 'passional or subjective'

[41] This term is borrowed from Kleist. Deleuze and Guattari, *A Thousand Plateaus*, 27.

[42] Deleuze and Guattari, *A Thousand Plateaus*, 460.

[43] Deleuze and Guattari give a detailed description of how war machines are co-opted by the state to create armies: 'What we call a military institution, or army, is not at all the war machine in itself, but the form under which it is appropriated by the State' (*A Thousand Plateaus*, 461).

[44] Deleuze and Guattari, *A Thousand Plateaus*, 131.

semiotics in which signs operate primarily via processes of subjectification.[45] The post-signifying regime is said to arise from the signifying regime in the following way: a line of flight escapes from the circular signifying semiotic; however, unlike in the case of the scapegoat, this line is no longer taken to be negative, but instead 'receives a positive sign' and becomes 'occupied and followed by a people who find in it their reason for being or destiny'.[46] The most salient example given by Deleuze and Guattari of this form of regime is the story of the birth of the Jewish people. Expelled from the despotic Egyptian state, Moses accepts this line of flight as his destiny and follows the line into the desert.[47] The negative line is transformed into a positive line in relation to a people defined by their passion. Describing the way that this acceptance of the line of flight acts as a form of subjectification, Deleuze and Guattari explain the defining experience of the Jewish people in the following way: 'It is we who must follow the most deterritorialised line, the line of the scapegoat, but we will change its sign, we will turn it into the positive line of our subjectivity, our Passion, our proceeding or grievance.'[48]

While Deleuze and Guattari claim that the social stratification of post-signifying regimes is defined by a line of flight, this line is said to be segmented. After the initial break from the signifying regime is affirmed and accepted as a subjectifying trait, the linear proceeding taken up by the society eventually 'runs its course, at which point

[45] Deleuze and Guattari, *A Thousand Plateaus*, 134.

[46] Deleuze and Guattari, *A Thousand Plateaus*, 134.

[47] It is unclear here whether societies defined by the post-signifying regime should be considered as nomadic. While they are not sedentary, they do create a form of mobile interiority which preserves the power of the state. By transporting the ark through the desert, the Jewish people maintained their covenant with God and thus upheld the law of interiority which gives the state its power. It would therefore be more accurate to conceptualise post-signifying regimes as a combination of the forces in the signifying and counter-signifying regimes, but with an anti-nomadic intention. Perhaps the best way to explain this situation is to say that both pre-signifying and counter-signifying regimes of signs rely on multilinear systems, while both signifying and post-signifying regimes rely on punctual systems. When Deleuze and Guattari state that 'smooth or nomad space lies between two striated spaces: that of the forest, with its gravitational verticals, and that of agriculture, with its grids and generalized parallels' (*A Thousand Plateaus*, 424), the latter of these striations can be understood as the farmland of the signifying regimes, while the forests can be understood as the wilderness of the post-signifying regimes.

[48] Deleuze and Guattari, *A Thousand Plateaus*, 135.

a new proceeding begins'.[49] Eventually, the post-signifying regime becomes a regularly segmented line of flight that is nothing other than a '*linear and temporal succession of finite proceedings*'.[50] In the case of the history of the Jewish people, Deleuze and Guattari note that the two stages of the destruction of the Temple form the first two segments of the social formation.[51]

The post-signifying regime of signs is particularly interesting for our study of the role of the line of flight in Deleuze and Guattari's political philosophy because it is a concrete example of one of the explicit dangers of lines of flight. While lines of flight can be blocked by signifying regimes of signs, and can therefore fail to escape at all, they can also succeed in their attempt to escape, only to fall into the subsequent danger of segmentation. Deleuze and Guattari refer to the first danger as that of running up against a 'white wall', and they refer to the second as that of being sucked into a 'black hole'.[52] The first danger is that of signification and relates to the instantiation of a signifying regime of signs, while the second is that of subjectification and relates to the instantiation of a post-signifying regime of signs. One of the clearest examples given in *A Thousand Plateaus* of this second danger is that of the drug addict. While drugs can, theoretically, be used as a line of flight along which the body can escape the despotic organisation to which it is continually subjected, this escape becomes segmented and ultimately gets sucked into the black hole of addiction: 'the line of flight ... of drugs is constantly being segmentarized under the most rigid of forms, that of dependency, the hit and

49 Deleuze and Guattari, *A Thousand Plateaus*, 133.

50 Deleuze and Guattari, *A Thousand Plateaus*, 133.

51 The title of the fifth plateau contains two dates, 587 BC and AD 70, which refer to these two incorporeal transformations.

52 These two dangers are explored in some depth in the Faciality Plateau (*A Thousand Plateaus*, 185). The transformation of the head into a face, and therefore the transformation of the body into a point of signification, is the central power structure that upholds the signifying regime of signs. In signifying regimes of signs the face is always seen from the front as a flat white space on which all signification is inscribed. In the post-signifying regime, 'faciality undergoes a profound transformation' because 'averted faces, in profile, replace the frontal view of the radiant face'. It is this 'double turning away that draws the positive line of flight' (*A Thousand Plateaus*, 136). The subsequent authoritarian tendency of the passional and subjective line of flight is thus defined not by the surface of the white face, but by the black hole of the eye. The different forms of faciality discussed in the seventh plateau can thus be read as the ways in which the signifying and post-signifying regimes interact.

the dose, the dealer'.[53] Contrary to what we might have expected, the post-signifying regime of signs is therefore not a viable alternative to the domination of the signifying regime of signs. Both have their own dangers. Ultimately, despite the fact that the post-signifying regime of signs begins with a positive affirmation of a line of flight, it is also defined by the way that it controls this line. In the post-signifying regime the line of flight is positive, and even considered absolute in its full escape from signification, and yet it is constantly segmented and therefore sucked into the black hole of subjectivity.

The four regimes of signs discussed here are given as examples of different ways in which the expression of a linguistic, or alloplastic, stratification of matter can reformulate the contents of the physical and organic strata with which it forms a concrete assemblage. As each of these regimes is nothing other than the semiotic expression of a concrete assemblage, and as every assemblage is, by definition, partially composed of lines of flight, it is possible to define these four regimes as different ways in which lines of flight are controlled. In both pre-signifying regimes and signifying regimes, lines of flight are characterised as negative and are systematically blocked because of the way they threaten to bring down the whole social structure of which they are a part. In the case of pre-signifying regimes, this occurs when a line of flight cuts across the different, polyvocal forms of expression and reduces everything to linguistic signification. In the case of signifying regimes, this occurs when a line of flight escapes the absolute centre and connects with an outside that can challenge the ultimate power of the despot. With counter-signifying regimes of signs, lines of flight run into a different set of dangers. They are arranged into a war machine that deterritorialises the land, but this machine can become appropriated by the state, whereupon it takes war as its object and becomes a kind of death machine. Post-signifying regimes are also defined by their relation to a line of flight, which in this instance is made positive. However, as we have seen, this positive line is prone to segmentation, in which the subject defined by the line is sucked into a black hole of abolition.

In the next section, we will see how Deleuze and Guattari's positive political project in *A Thousand Plateaus* is not attached to any of these four regimes. Instead, via an analysis of the way that regimes of signs can interact and transform into one another, Deleuze and

[53] Deleuze and Guattari, *A Thousand Plateaus*, 314.

Guattari hope to find a way of freeing lines of flight that will not be captured, relativised or segmented by any of these four regimes.

Becoming Molecular

After having completed their analysis of the three modes of double articulation, and after having completed their analysis of the four regimes of signs, Deleuze and Guattari are now in a position to use these categories to describe the contemporary context of power which we inhabit. They name the three 'principal strata binding human beings' as 'the organism, signifiance and interpretation, and subjectification and subjection'.[54] The first of these relates to the specific double articulation of organic matter by which the organs of human bodies are arranged into the human organism. The second relates to the way in which the signifying regime of signs raises the signifier to the level of an abstract universal and arranges all linguistic acts in a circle around the face of the despot. The third relates to the post-signifying regime of signs, which makes passional subjects of us all, each heading towards his or her own black hole. Taken together, these three stratifications, the first of which is organic, the second and third of which are alloplastic, 'are what separates us from the plane of consistency and the abstract machine, where there is no longer any regime of signs, where the line of flight effectuates its own potential positivity'.[55]

At this point, having named these three strata, Deleuze and Guattari shift their mode of analysis. The methods they have used up until now have only been able to name these strata, but if we want to understand how they are produced, and how we might be able to escape from them, we will need to begin our whole process of analysis again from a different perspective. One way to explain the limitations of the technique used so far would be to say that, while our previous analysis has shown the ways in which society has historically tended towards particular planes of organisation, we have not yet analysed the processes of becoming that effectuated these tendencies. Even while Deleuze and Guattari have repeatedly stated that regimes of signs are not related to one another historically, and even while they have maintained that regimes of signs are never completely distinct from one another, the analysis up to this

[54] Deleuze and Guattari, *A Thousand Plateaus*, 148.
[55] Deleuze and Guattari, *A Thousand Plateaus*, 148.

point has treated these regimes *as if they were historical* and *as if they were distinct*. What we need instead is to conduct our analysis from the perspective of *becoming*.

Perhaps the clearest way to distinguish becoming from history is through the observation that historical thinking is a way of relating different events together and ordering them in a series, while thinking with becoming is a way of explaining the production of events. As Deleuze and Guattari put it, 'history can think only in terms of relationships (between A and B), not in terms of production (from A to x)'.[56] The concept of becoming, first developed by Deleuze in his books on Nietzsche and Bergson, attempts to grasp the kind of movement that occurs in processes of transformation. Rather than assuming that becoming is somehow secondary to being, because it only occurs between one being and another, Deleuze and Guattari take becoming to be primary, with any being fulfilling the role of an interruption in the process of becoming.[57]

At the end of the fifth plateau, 'On Several Regimes of Signs', Deleuze and Guattari lay out a four-stage process for the analysis of political power. Developing the notion of 'pragmatics' that they had developed in linguistics, they refer to this four-stage process simply as 'Pragmatics'.[58] The first two stages of this process take a historical perspective on power, whereas the latter two take the perspective of becoming. These four stages are the *generative*, *transformational*, *diagrammatic* and *machinic* components of any analysis. The generative component involves a practice of tracing; specifically it is the tracing of the different regimes of signs in a concrete, mixed semiotic. Deleuze and Guattari's naming of the four different regimes of signs completed this task. The transformational component traces the lines of flight in each of these regimes of signs to show how they relate to one another and how they can pass into one another. We saw this in Deleuze and Guattari's analysis of the different kinds of lines of flight that exist in each regime of signs. The two components of analysis that we have not yet touched on are the diagrammatic and the machinic. Because each regime of signs only exists as a stratification of matter into content, expression, substance and form, the

[56] Deleuze and Guattari, *A Thousand Plateaus*, 258.

[57] 'Becoming' is one of the central concepts that connects Deleuze's earlier work to his work with Guattari in *A Thousand Plateaus*. See Deleuze's essay 'Control and Becoming', in *Negotiations*, 169–74.

[58] Deleuze and Guattari, *A Thousand Plateaus*, 160.

diagrammatic component of analysis goes beyond the representation of regimes of signs in their particular expressions to the continuums of intensity and the tensors that effectuate these stratifications. These continuums of intensity and tensors on the plane of consistency are said to diagram the abstract machines.[59] The fourth and final stage of analysis suggested by Deleuze and Guattari is the machinic component. The machinic component consists in 'the study of the assemblages that effectuate abstract machines'.[60] What this means is that the fourth component looks at how abstract machines produce events.[61]

In a moment I will turn to the final two stages of this four-part analysis in a little more detail, and explain the role that the concept of the line of flight plays here. However, it is worth pausing briefly to clarify two things. First, the difference between the historical approach of the first two stages and the approach of becoming used in the second two stages is aligned with the difference between the molar and the molecular regimes of analysis that we explored in our analysis of *Anti-Oedipus*. Second, the difference between the first two stages and the second two stages is also said to correspond to the distinction between the quantitative and the qualitative. In previous chapters, we saw how Deleuze and Guattari argued in *Anti-Oedipus* that is was possible to analyse political formations according to two distinct regimes. When taken from the perspective of its molecular elements, any political formation is made up of a-historical flows of desire. When taken from the perspective of the large statistical molar aggregates that these molecules compose, the same political

59 For a full description of the role of tensors and flows of intensity in relation to diagrams, see Deleuze and Guattari, *A Thousand Plateaus*, 156. Brent Adkins also gives a clear explication of this stage of political analysis in *Deleuze and Guattari's A Thousand Plateaus*, 92.

60 Deleuze and Guattari, *A Thousand Plateaus*, 162.

61 *A Thousand Plateaus* can be read as a movement through these four stages: the first five plateaus are *generational* because they trace the different regimes and explain how they are produced; plateaus six, seven and eight then carry out the *transformational* component, using the BwO, faciality and the three lines of signification to show how regimes of signs can be transformed; plateaus nine, ten and eleven then move to the *diagrammatic* moment and use the concepts of micro-politics, becoming and the refrain to map the abstract machines; finally, in plateaus twelve, thirteen and fourteen, Deleuze and Guattari complete the *machinic* analysis by looking at how these abstract machines are effectuated by different assemblages of power, namely the nomads and the state.

formation is made up of structures that form a linear history.[62] In *A Thousand Plateaus* this schema is made more complex by the introduction of the theory of stratification. While the distinction between the molecular and the molar only aligns with the distinction between content and expression in the case of the double articulation of the induction of physical matter, and not in the cases of the transduction and translation of organic and alloplastic matter, it is still the case that on the plane of consistency, on which each of these stratifications is nothing but a coagulation, there are only molecular flows. In short, the plane of consistency has no history and thus it is molecular, while each of the three stratifications of matter produces a history and is therefore connected to the molar. With this in mind, we can also see the movement from the generational and transformative components of analysis to the diagrammatic and machinic components as a move from a molar to a molecular analysis.

Finally, Deleuze and Guattari are clear in *A Thousand Plateaus* that the molar relates to what is qualitative, what can be sensed, while the molecular relates precisely to the quantitative. For this reason, they say that the diagrammatic and machinic components of analysis must move from an analysis of qualitative elements to their underlying 'quanta'.[63] Echoing their work in *Anti-Oedipus*, they write in *A Thousand Plateaus*: 'Beliefs and desires are the basis of every society, because they are flows and as such are "quantifiable"; they are veritable social Quantities, whereas sensations are qualitative and representations are simple resultants.'[64] To summarise, we can say that, by concentrating on the three stratifications of matter and the four regimes of signs, the generational and transformative components of political analysis concentrated too much on the molar aggregates of politics and their historical relationships. The diagrammatic and machinic components of analysis, on the other hand, will make the shift from history to becoming, will find the molecular flows of quanta below the qualitative molar aggregates, and will enable us to think becoming.

62 The direction of the flow of time is reversible in the modelling of molecular physics, but is unidirectional in the modelling of thermodynamic systems at a molar scale.

63 Deleuze and Guattari, *A Thousand Plateaus*, 239.

64 Deleuze and Guattari, *A Thousand Plateaus*, 241.

Diagrammatics, Machinic Analysis and Micropolitics

What does it mean to say that, after we have analysed the different regimes of signs, and after we have looked at how they can be transformed into one another, we must locate their abstract machines? As we have just seen, what distinguishes an abstract machine from the regime of signs is that for an abstract machine there is no distinction between content and expression and no distinction between form and substance. What then can we say about an abstract machine? Deleuze and Guattari state that an abstract machine 'operates by *matter*, not by substance; by *function*, not by form'.[65] This suggests that below the extended representation of a regime of signs, or even a mixed semiotic of multiple regimes of signs, it is possible to find the intensities that produce this extension. Crucially, this site of intensity will make no distinction between bodies and words and is therefore both proto-material and proto-semiotic. Because the abstract machine does not have extensive parts it is not possible to trace its outline; however, it is possible to *diagram* the productive capacities of its intensities. As Ray Brassier notes, the process of diagramming is a 'cognitive operation carried out with a view to effectuating certain practical imperatives under specific material constraints'.[66] It is 'akin to engineering' in that it 'lets us see to what extent a line of flight is liberatory *for us*'.[67] What this looks like in practice is a shift towards abstraction.[68] While regimes of signs cannot be understood as completely detached from the historical context in which they are effectuated, abstract machines have no relation to history and can thus be understood completely in the abstract.

In order to make this stage of the analysis more comprehensible, let us take one example. We saw previously that any regime of signs is defined by its order-words. However, Deleuze and Guattari also say that the only reason we have for studying linguistics, and for analysing the circulation of order-words, is 'to transform the compositions of order into components of passage'.[69] Because any

[65] Deleuze and Guattari, *A Thousand Plateaus*, 156.

[66] Brassier, 'Concrete Rules and Abstract Machines', 270.

[67] Brassier, 'Concrete Rules and Abstract Machines', 270.

[68] Although, as Adkins notes, here abstraction is used 'in the sense opposed to discrete not opposed to concrete' (*Deleuze and Guattari's A Thousand Plateaus*, 92).

[69] Deleuze and Guattari, *A Thousand Plateaus*, 122.

assemblage is tetravalent, each order-word has its own degree of deterritorialisation. Each word has a 'twofold nature' by which it can either order or pass.[70] While the generational analysis of regimes of signs picks out the ordering components of words within a regime, it is also possible to 'push the order-words themselves to the point of deterritorialization, to the point of becoming musical'[71] and to find the 'pass-words beneath order-words'.[72] As such, regimes of signs are not overcome simply through an analysis of their order-words. They are also not overcome by finding ways of transforming one regime of signs into another. Instead, Deleuze and Guattari claim that we must act 'not by fleeing, but by making flight act and create'.[73] We must not only look at the ways in which lines of flight are blocked in regimes of signs, but also at the ways in which lines of flight are relativised or segmented in the transformations between regimes. We must diagram the lines of flight that work at the level of the abstract machine, we must intervene here and experiment with the possibilities for creation that these lines contain.

The many different kinds of becoming that Deleuze and Guattari study in *A Thousand Plateaus*, such as the becoming-woman and the becoming-animal, are simply various ways of diagramming the abstract machines that effectuate the regimes of signs that we find ourselves within. The process of becoming-woman is not the same as the activity of altering the relation between your extensive parts in order to move from the molar formation of 'man' to the molar formation of 'woman'. Instead, it is about finding the molecular and intensive flows that escape from the binary gender opposition in order to experiment with new possibilities of the body that would not be defined by their relation to the universal category of 'man'. Ultimately, in order to combat the three principal strata – namely those of the organism, signifiance and subjectification – Deleuze and Guattari advocate three corresponding processes of becoming, namely becoming-imperceptible, becoming-indiscernible and becoming-impersonal. The process of becoming-imperceptible is a technique for overcoming the primary activity of the organic mode of stratification, which is the constant regulation of the inside and the

[70] Deleuze and Guattari, *A Thousand Plateaus*, 122.
[71] Bell, 'Postulates of Linguistics', 81.
[72] Deleuze and Guattari, *A Thousand Plateaus*, 122.
[73] Deleuze and Guattari, *A Thousand Plateaus*, 122.

outside via processes of transduction.[74] Becoming-indiscernible works to undercut the signifying regime of signs by detaching signs from their stratum and making them escape from their capture by the face of the despot.[75] Finally, becoming-impersonal is a process of combating the subjectifiying capacities of the post-signifying regime of signs through the dissolution of the subject into a collective assemblage of enunciation. By analysing 'the relation between the (anorganic) imperceptible, the (asignifying) indiscernible, and the (asubjective) impersonal', Deleuze and Guattari aim to equip the reader of *A Thousand Plateaus* with the tools to escape from the three principal strata that bind the contemporary lives of human beings.[76]

This diagrammatic moment of abstraction would, however, be completely useless for any political analysis if it was not accompanied by the final stage of *machinic* analysis. While the diagrammatic component allows us to reach the molecular flows that remain uncaptured by the strata, there would be no reason to find these flows if we were not able to use them to restructure the molar aggregates that we inhabit: 'molecular escapes and movements would be nothing if they did not return to the molar organizations to reshuffle their segments, their binary distributions of sexes, classes, and parties'.[77] If the first two components of analysis allowed us to analyse the molar formations of the strata that bind us, and if the third component allowed us to diagram the molecular flows of the abstract machine that produces such molar formations, then the fourth, machinic component of analysis allows us to 'locate a "power center" at the border between the two'.[78] This power centre is defined 'by the relative adaptations and conversions it effects between the line and the flow'.[79] The point that Deleuze and Guattari seem to be making here is that the relationship between molecular flows and molar aggregates is not a natural one, neither is it one of representation. The molar aggregates on the strata need to be extracted from the

[74] The example given is the camouflage fish and its capacity to 'world' with its environment (*A Thousand Plateaus*, 308–9).

[75] The example given is the Ostrogoths, those barbarians who shifted away from the state towards the nomads (*A Thousand Plateaus*, 245).

[76] Deleuze and Guattari, *A Thousand Plateaus*, 308.

[77] Deleuze and Guattari, *A Thousand Plateaus*, 238–9. The three distributions of sexes, classes and parties map on to the three principal strata of the organism, signifiance and subjectification.

[78] Deleuze and Guattari, *A Thousand Plateaus*, 239.

[79] Deleuze and Guattari, *A Thousand Plateaus*, 239.

molecular flows by assemblages of power. The two examples that Deleuze and Guattari give of such power centres are financial capital and the Church. Each of these institutions of power manages the formation of molar aggregates by taking up the task of 'making the segments correspond to the quanta, of adjusting the segments to the quanta'.[80] It is by locating these power centres, and intervening in their operation, that it will be possible to extract different molar organisations from the many potentialities of the molecular abstract machines that underpin them.

According to their analysis of such power centres, Deleuze and Guattari state that every central power has three different aspects or zones. The first is its 'zone of power', or its ability to organise a 'solid rigid line'; the second is its 'zone of indiscernibility' by which it is diffused in a micropolitical or molecular context; and the third is its 'zone of impotence', which relates to those flows and quanta that it cannot 'control or define'.[81] We have to remember here that these power centres, including the institutions of financial capital and religion, are not omnipotent powers but assemblages of power. Just like all other assemblages, they are defined as much by their lines of flight as by what they capture. The purpose of the fourth moment of analysis is therefore to experiment with these power centres to find their zones of impotence. Each of these zones of impotence will be nothing other than an 'abstract machine of mutation' operating within the power centre, where it has the power to completely alter the way in which molar segments are arranged out of molecular flows.

With this conceptualisation of analysis in mind, we can now understand the political analysis that Deleuze and Guattari conducted in *Anti-Oedipus* in new terms. In *Anti-Oedipus*, they aimed to show how the power centre of capitalism is made up of different zones, one of which operates by a process of decoding. This decoding aspect of capital is its zone of impotence which, if properly utilised, could push capitalism beyond the internal limit that it constantly tries to push outside itself, and ultimately bring about a post-capitalist future. In *A Thousand Plateaus*, on the other hand, Deleuze and Guattari have shifted their point of attack away from capitalism towards the two major regimes of signs that define and constrict contemporary life, namely the signifying and the post-signifying regimes. The analyses

80 Deleuze and Guattari, *A Thousand Plateaus*, 240.
81 Deleuze and Guattari, *A Thousand Plateaus*, 249.

that they carry out in plateau twelve and plateau thirteen, of nomadism and of apparatuses of capture respectively, can be read precisely as attempts to find the zones of impotence within the power centres that produce these two regimes.[82]

It is important to recognise the changing role that the concept of the line of flight plays in the political analysis of power centres. While it is true that the zones of impotence in each power centre are composed of lines of flight, the concept is being used here in a slightly different way than it was in our previous analysis of the four different regimes of signs. From the perspective of a regime of signs, a line of flight can never be anything other than an escape and can never appear as anything other than a threat from the outside, even if the regime operates precisely by relativising or by segmenting this threat. The reason that lines of flight held this ephemeral position in our discussion of regimes of signs is that this discussion was still in the generative and transformational stages of analysis, and was still treating these regimes from the position of the molar aggregates that they form. In our movement to a diagrammatic and machinic analysis of abstract machines, on the other hand, we are now able to conceptualise lines of flight not only as fleeting escapes, but as integral components of an abstract machine of consistency.

Finally, it is important to reiterate that this analysis does not simply treat lines of flight as ethically positive or as politically expedient. Speaking of the different kinds of lines drawn by the three different zones of the power centres, Deleuze and Guattari write: 'We cannot say that one of these three lines is bad and another good, by nature and necessarily. The study of the dangers of each line is the object of pragmatics or schizoanalysis.'[83] In the previous chapter we

[82] One of the major changes that accompanies this shift towards a machinic analysis of power centres is a recognition that the language of the 'plane of consistency' and the 'plane of organisation' can only take us so far. In their analysis of abstract machines, Deleuze and Guattari will see that these were only 'two ways of conceptualizing the plane' (*A Thousand Plateaus*, 292) and that the difference is between three different abstract machines: 'There are different types of abstract machines that overlap in their operations and qualify the assemblages: *abstract machines of consistency*, singular and mutant, with multiplied connections; *abstract machines of stratification* that surround the plane of consistency with another plane; and *axiomatic or overcoding* and *abstract machines* that perform totalizations, homogenizations, conjunctions of closure' (*A Thousand Plateaus*, 566).

[83] Deleuze and Guattari, *A Thousand Plateaus*, 250.

saw how lines of flight are not ethically positive in themselves, but that the rhizomatic model of thought, which has brought us to this machinic analysis of power and has allowed us to conceptualise the line of flight, does have its own ethical value. The analysis of lines of flight allows us to experiment with new possible assemblages of bodies and thus to increase our potential to act; this experimentation is therefore ethical in itself. However, such experimentation is accompanied by its own dangers. Speaking of the different dangers that accompany the three different kinds of lines drawn by the three zones of the power centres, Deleuze and Guattari identify the most dangerous possibility in the line of flight, which they say is like 'a war one risks coming back from defeated, destroyed, after having destroyed everything one could'.[84] Unlike with the other dangers, Deleuze and Guattari are careful to give a clear definition of this threat, which is associated only with the line of flight. They define this danger in the following way: 'the line of flight crossing the wall, getting out of the black holes, but instead of connecting with other lines and each time augmenting its valence, *turning to destruction, abolition pure and simple, the passion of abolition*'.[85] The specific danger discussed here is explicitly differentiated from the previous problems of the line of flight either being blocked by the white wall or being trapped in a black hole. In this case we have 'the line of flight crossing the wall, getting out of the black holes', only to turn to its own destruction.[86]

This danger of pure abolition is not faced by the regimes of signs, seen from the perspective of a generative or transformative analysis; instead, it is a danger recognised by the diagrammatic and machinic analysis of the abstract machines that effectuate these regimes of signs. Because of this, it might not be surprising to discover that the discussion of this danger only appears in earnest in *A Thousand Plateaus*. In *Anti-Oedipus*, Deleuze and Guattari write that the 'schizo is not revolutionary, but the schizophrenic process—in terms of which the schizo is merely the interruption, or the continuation in the void—is the potential for revolution'.[87] In *A Thousand Plateaus*, via their diagrammatic analysis of abstract machines of power, Deleuze and Guattari are now able to assess the specific danger of the schizo in

[84] Deleuze and Guattari, *A Thousand Plateaus*, 253.
[85] Deleuze and Guattari, *A Thousand Plateaus*, 253.
[86] Deleuze and Guattari, *A Thousand Plateaus*, 253.
[87] Deleuze and Guattari, *Anti-Oedipus*, 374.

abstract terms. In *A Thousand Plateaus*, they speak of 'the paradox of those emptied and dreary bodies' which had '*emptied themselves of their organs* instead of looking for the point at which they could patiently and momentarily dismantle the organization of the organs we call the organism'.[88] This is what happens when you escape too fast; you do not reach the plane of consistency but simply the plane of pure abolition.

In response to this problem, Deleuze and Guattari offer two different solutions, the first conservative and the other creative. The conservative response, which we considered in the last chapter when discussing Deleuze and Guattari's ethics, is that in the destratification of the organic strata, you must 'keep enough of the organism for it to reform each dawn'.[89] The same call for caution is repeated with the two strata of the signifying and post-signifying regimes, where 'you have to keep small supplies of signifiance and subjectification, if only to turn them against their own systems when the circumstances demand it'.[90] However, this *ethical* shift towards a more cautious and pragmatic approach to the art of drawing lines of flight is now accompanied by a more positive, creative and *political* response as well. Quite simply, the positive response to this problem is the creation of the concept of the refrain.

As we saw previously, the concept of the refrain allows Deleuze and Guattari to explain the creation of territorial assemblages, and it is these assemblages that allow us to avoid the specific danger of the line of flight '*turning to destruction, abolition pure and simple*'.[91] The construction of a refrain operates by finding resonances in chaos and using them to define an inside, or a plot of land. The refrain 'jumps from chaos to the beginnings of order in chaos' and is what provides consistency to the plane of consistency.[92] Via the repetition of a rhythmic difference, the refrain produces an inside from which it is possible to experiment. In the most abstract terms, we can say that the project of *A Thousand Plateaus* attempts to provide us with the tools to produce a BwO on the plane of consistency, and that the refrain and the line of flight are two of the central tools in such an endeavour. The line of flight allows us to destratify the three

88 Deleuze and Guattari, *A Thousand Plateaus*, 178.
89 Deleuze and Guattari, *A Thousand Plateaus*, 178.
90 Deleuze and Guattari, *A Thousand Plateaus*, 178.
91 Deleuze and Guattari, *A Thousand Plateaus*, 253.
92 Deleuze and Guattari, *A Thousand Plateaus*, 343.

principal strata that bind us, and the refrain allows us to maintain a positive and creative relation with the plane of consistency.

As Deleuze and Guattari's political prescriptions concerning the line of flight and the refrain are given in purely abstract terms, it can be difficult to know what such a practice would look like in any given, concrete assemblage. In what follows, I will try to give an indication of what such a practice would look like in concrete terms by situating Deleuze and Guattari's comments within both the political climate in which their book was published, and the working context of Institutional Psychotherapy.

Institutional Analysis, Transformation and Lines of Flight

In his translator's introduction to *A Thousand Plateaus*, Brian Massumi notes that the *Capitalism and Schizophrenia* series was produced, at least in part, as a response to the 'disintegration of the Left into dogmatic "groupuscules"'.[93] Deleuze and Guattari were aware that such an 'amoeba-like proliferation' of different schools of thought was politically problematic, as it resulted in inactivity – each small, leftist cult working for its own ends like a group of miniature Stalinist parties.[94] The need to produce a discourse that escaped the dominant regimes of signification and subjectification was palpable, but it was also the case that these escapes were not enough on their own because they had no way of dealing with the danger of abolition that we have just explored. Fleeing from the state and fleeing from capitalism is one thing, but producing a creative, productive and collaborative practice outside these regimes is another.[95] In *Anti-Oedipus*, Deleuze and Guattari had put forward a political programme of molecular politics that would connect various minoritarian struggles, each seen as a line of flight from contemporary capitalism, without totalising them. It is my contention that the concept of the refrain is introduced in *A Thousand Plateaus* specifically to allow

[93] Deleuze and Guattari, *A Thousand Plateaus*, 568.

[94] Deleuze and Guattari, *A Thousand Plateaus*, 568.

[95] Another way to describe this problem is in relation to *sense:* if a practice becomes totally detached from the orienting context of a social life, then there is no longer any sense to that which a group is fighting for. The dissolution of sense could otherwise be called melancholy or postmodern malaise, a regular enemy of leftist politics. For more on this problem as it relates to the French context in the second half of the twentieth century, see Mathy, *Melancholy Politics: Loss, Mourning, and Memory in Late Modern France*.

for the possibility of constructing the shared territorial assemblage required for such a molecular revolution. The concept of the refrain, designed to combat the specific danger of the complete dissolution of the ground for political action, is therefore not only an abstract term that relates to the diagrammatic analyses of abstract machines, but a heavily politicised concept.

In *The Machinic Unconscious*, which contains many of Guattari's first experiments with concepts that would later become central to *A Thousand Plateaus*, the concept of the refrain is provided as a tool for political cohesion. There Guattari argues that 'every individual, every group, every nation' is '"equipped" with a basic range of incantatory refrains'.[96] These refrains are used by political groups to 'affirm their social identity, their territory, and their internal cohesion'.[97] The example that Guattari gives here is also telling. He writes of the trade corporations of ancient Greece which 'possessed their own kind of sonorous seal, a short melodic formula called "*nomos*"'.[98] This passage is particularly interesting because it allows us to link the largely theoretical project of *A Thousand Plateaus* with Guattari's practical work in Institutional Psychotherapy and Institutional Analysis. To summarise this connection, we could say that every political project requires a refrain to determine the cohesion or consistency of a group. In the specific case of the anti-capitalist struggle that Deleuze and Guattari saw their work as a part of, this refrain should take the form of a *nomos*. Such a *nomos*, or nomadic refrain, is like a 'customary, unwritten law' that is 'inseparable from a distribution of space'.[99] The reason that the use of a nomadic refrain is distinctly anti-capitalist is explained by Guattari in *The Machinic Unconscious*. He claims there that capitalistic societies rely on the 'pure' separation and specialisation of different activities of production, and that it is 'the heterogeneous, mixed, the fuzzy, and the dissymmetrical' that challenge this purity.[100] In contrast to this, the refrain provides 'the consistency of a fuzzy aggregate'.[101]

In order to combat the tendency towards abstraction here, and to bring our analysis back to a concrete political situation, it will be

96 Guattari, *The Machinic Unconscious*, 107.
97 Guattari, *The Machinic Unconscious*, 107.
98 Guattari, *The Machinic Unconscious*, 107.
99 Deleuze and Guattari, *A Thousand Plateaus*, 344.
100 Guattari, *The Machinic Unconscious*, 108.
101 Deleuze and Guattari, *A Thousand Plateaus*, 420.

useful to take the publication of *A Thousand Plateaus* as an example of a political act. By using the tools of Institutional Analysis to examine the act of writing and publishing this book, we will be able to see what it might mean in practice to draw lines of flight, and we will also be able to see how the use of a refrain can provide the consistency required to stop these lines of flight 'turning to destruction' and thus leading to the death of any budding molecular revolution.[102]

In the second chapter of this book we saw how the production of subject groups was a central activity in the work of Institutional Psychotherapy that Guattari developed at La Borde. We also saw how, outside the psychiatric hospital, Guattari applied the same process of subject-group formation in political contexts through the discipline of Institutional Analysis. The defining characteristic of a subject group, which differentiated it from a subjugated group, was that its consistency was produced internally via the relation between its members, rather than being determined by a shared relation with an external factor. At the point of writing *Psychoanalysis and Transversality*, Guattari was clear that subject groups are able to take up a praxis and are able to speak. In his preparatory work for *A Thousand Plateaus*, however, Guattari writes that it is the *refrain* that produces 'the collective and asignifying subject of the enunciation'.[103] What this means is that it is the resonance produced by the repetition of a rhythmic difference among a group of elements that creates a group and allows it a voice. We also saw in our previous analysis that Guattari aimed to produce the conditions for such a group by increasing the 'coefficient of transversality' among its members.[104] By drawing a transversal or diagonal line across the different discourses that would otherwise stratify a group into a social hierarchy, Guattari aimed to produce a shared language for a group so that they could work towards a shared goal. What I want to suggest here is that, armed with the framework of Institutional Analysis, along with the two concepts of the line of flight and the refrain, it is possible to read *A Thousand Plateaus* as an attempt to produce a subject group.

A Thousand Plateaus is a book which uses 'a complex technical vocabulary drawn from a wide range of disciplines in the sciences, mathematics, and the humanities', and yet Deleuze suggests

102 Deleuze and Guattari, *A Thousand Plateaus*, 253.
103 Guattari, *The Machinic Unconscious*, 107.
104 Guattari, *Psychoanalysis and Transversality*, 113.

that one should read it 'as you would listen to a record'.[105] The apparent oddity of trying to read a technical book as if it were a record can come to sound very reasonable if we recognise that the different plateaus in the text do not relate to one another like the chapters of a normal book. Instead of treating each chapter as an argumentative step that builds on the previous chapters and is governed by an external logic which relates them all together, Deleuze and Guattari make it clear that their book, like any other, is 'made of variously formed matters', such that there are 'lines of articulation or segmentarity, strata and territories; but also lines of flight'.[106] What Deleuze and Guattari do in *A Thousand Plateaus* is threefold: first, they map the lines of flight that escape from any number of discourses; second, through the repetition of differences they produce a refrain that puts each of these lines into resonance with one another; and third, they make these various lines of flight connect to form a transversal line that cuts across all of the various discourses and opens the possibility of the formation of an interdisciplinary subject group.

Let us quickly take each of these three steps in turn. Initially, using the technique of tracing, Deleuze and Guattari carry out a generational and transformative analysis of a whole range of different regimes of speech. In the fields of biology, art, literature, linguistics, politics and history, among others, they find the powers that are escaping the traditional bounds of the discourse. Next, in order to avoid the possibility that each of these lines of flight should become a line of pure abolition and do nothing but 'turn in the void', they shift to a diagrammatic and machinic analysis which uses a technique of mapping. Here Deleuze and Guattari are able to find resonances between the different lines of flight. From the chaos of these various escapes, a refrain provides 'the beginnings of order in chaos' in the form of a plane of consistency on which the different lines of flight can meet.[107] Finally, by connecting these lines of flight on the plane of consistency, a transversal line is produced which connects biologists, artists, novelists, linguists, political theorists and historians in a single group. These different disciplinary activities are no longer related to one another negatively, through their opposition or through their shared relation to some higher organising power. Instead, they relate

[105] Deleuze and Guattari, *A Thousand Plateaus*, ix.
[106] Deleuze and Guattari, *A Thousand Plateaus*, 4.
[107] Deleuze and Guattari, *A Thousand Plateaus*, 343.

to one another via an internal resonance and take on the consistency of a subject group.[108]

In what sense can it be said that this is a political activity? To see how this is not merely an intellectual project but a practical one, it is enough to recognise that the difference between academic disciplines is not only produced by their different methodologies or their different subject matters, but by the very real fact that they do not speak the same language, and as such they do not speak to one another. This is manifested practically in the physical separation of schools. This is true for different academic groupings just as it is true for different political groups: despite the possibility for fruitful collaboration, groups are stratified by the different languages that they speak and therefore cannot take on the consistency of a subject group. In *Anti-Oedipus*, Deleuze and Guattari speak of the possibility of finding an 'active point of escape where the revolutionary machine, the artistic machine, the scientific machine, and the (schizo) analytic machine become parts and pieces of one another'.[109] They state here that by putting these different machines in contact with one another it will be possible to produce a 'new land'.[110] In *A Thousand Plateaus*, they attempt to fulfil this promise via the dual use of the concept of the line of flight and the concept of the refrain. First we must map the lines of flight that escape each of these domains, then we must use the refrain to create a resonance between them. The 'new land' that is produced is not intended to be a final, utopian resting point, but is precisely the 'small plot of land' that we are told to hold 'at all times', in order to continue experimenting without producing a complete dissolution of the self.[111]

108 One of the things that makes *A Thousand Plateaus* such a complex book is that it both explains the process by which philosophy can become a project of diagrammatics that works to draw transversal lines that cut across different domains of speech, and simultaneously enacts this process. For most of this chapter I have focused on the way in which the text describes this possibility. Here, I am attempting to show how it enacts it. We could also add here that while the descriptive task of the book unfolds chapter by chapter, the enactive task has no beginning or end, and is expressed through the resonance that exists between the chapters.

109 Deleuze and Guattari, *Anti-Oedipus*, 354.

110 Deleuze and Guattari, *Anti-Oedipus*, 354.

111 Deleuze and Guattari, *A Thousand Plateaus*, 178. The question remains as to whether Deleuze and Guattari's attempt to use this method to create a subject group was, or will be, successful. Deleuze was doubtful on this point, stating that while *A Thousand Plateaus* was 'the best that we have done together, Felix

Before closing this chapter, I want to make one final point about the art of drawing lines of flight as it is put forward in *A Thousand Plateaus*, in relation to the way that the concept was used in *Anti-Oedipus*. In Chapters 3 and 4 of this book I argued for a reading of *Anti-Oedipus* in which there are four distinct uses of the concept of the line of flight. Of these four uses, the first two were said to relate to the transformation of desiring-machines and the latter two to the transformation of social machines. The four senses of the line of flight were given as follows: 1) those processes of desire witnessed by the psychoanalyst that refuse to be captured by Oedipus; 2) the lines traced by the legitimate uses of the syntheses of the unconscious, namely the transverse connections and inclusive disjunctions between heterogeneous chains of code that form the multiplicity of desiring-production; 3) the decoded social flows that threaten primitive and despotic regimes of power as an external limit and that are internalised by capitalism; and 4) the absolute limit of capitalism that can be reached when the decoded flows released by capital cannot be recaptured and reterritorialised by it. In this case, the first and third uses of the concept of the line of flight both focus on the fact that these lines escape from a given assemblage, seen from a molar standpoint. Whether it is through the analysis of an individual on the psychoanalyst's couch, or the analysis of a particular form of political economy, the line of flight is seen in these cases as something that flees. The second and fourth uses of the line of flight begin from a different perspective. Here, through an analysis of the molecular flows that produce any molar aggregate, the lines of flight are seen as primary and as integral to the constitution of the assemblage under consideration.

The uses of the concept of the line of flight in *A Thousand Plateaus* follow a similar trajectory. Deleuze and Guattari begin by mapping the lines of flight that escape from a given assemblage. In the cases of the four regimes of signs under consideration, this mode of analysis involves finding the ways in which each regime relates to that which escapes from it. Pre-signifying regimes treat lines of flight as absolute and negative, and continually work to block the possibility of these escapes. Signifying regimes take their lines of flight to be negative but relative, and always assess the danger of such a line in relation to the

and me' and that it was 'the best of all that I have done', ultimately it was not a success because 'The book was too long, perhaps. And what is more, the time had passed.' Eribon, 'Le "Je me souviens" de Gilles Deleuze', 114.

body or face of the despot. Counter-signifying regimes use their lines of flight to build a war machine that is positive, but still taken as relative in relation to the state against which such a machine would react. Finally, post-signifying regimes lodge themselves directly on a line of flight that is positive and absolute, but proceed to segment that line. In all of these cases, Deleuze and Guattari begin with the molar aggregates of the regime and then explore the lines of flight that escape them. At this stage of their analysis in *A Thousand Plateaus*, the concept of the line of flight is being used as it was in the first and third sense given in *Anti-Oedipus*. After this analysis is complete, Deleuze and Guattari make a shift towards a diagrammatic mode of analysis in which they aim to explore the abstract machines that effectuate these regimes of signs. Here, they find that 'from the viewpoint of micropolitics, a society is defined by its lines of flight, which are molecular'.[112] This is, in many ways, equivalent to the shift from the molar to the molecular moments of their analysis in *Anti-Oedipus*. Here, Deleuze and Guattari discover the 'lines of flight that are primary' in an assemblage and constitute its 'cutting edges of creation'.[113] It is with this move to the diagrammatic and machinic analysis of regimes of signs that Deleuze and Guattari are able to bring together the many lines of flight they have previously discovered and produce a refrain that puts them into contact with one another. In this way, the many lines of flight form a transversal line that cuts across the different plateaus of the text to open the possibility of a new and revolutionary mode of philosophical analysis taken up by an interdisciplinary subject group. The perspective that Deleuze and Guattari take here in relation to the line of flight is equivalent to the second and fourth uses of the concept of the line of flight as it appears in *Anti-Oedipus*.

The fact that Deleuze and Guattari take these different perspectives across different sections of their *Capitalism and Schizophrenia* project does not lead them into self-contradiction, because each of the perspectives is taken up within a broader pragmatics of transformation. The molar analysis and the molecular analysis are both required if we are to think the possibility of such transformations. Following a rhizomatic model of thought leads us through a number of stages of analysis which are related to one another pragmatically, and while the concept of the line of flight is utilised in a different

[112] Deleuze and Guattari, *A Thousand Plateaus*, 238.
[113] Deleuze and Guattari, *A Thousand Plateaus*, 585.

way at each of these stages, it retains a level of consistency of its own, and is a key element that links each stage of this pragmatics to the next. More specifically, it is the concept of the line of flight that connects these stages and constitutes them as moments in a process of philosophical transformation.

Conclusion: Deleuze and Guattari's Transformation of Philosophy

Philosophy and the Creation of Concepts

> What unity remains for philosophies, it will be asked, if concepts constantly change?
>
> Gilles Deleuze and Félix Guattari, *What is Philosophy?*[1]

Throughout this book I have attempted to offer a picture of Deleuze and Guattari's work that pays close attention to their novel approach to philosophical concepts, and that tries to account for the way in which a particular concept – namely the 'line of flight' – might not only exist despite of, but even be constituted by, the variations that it undergoes in the collective writings of these two thinkers. In this conclusion I aim to turn these reflections outwards, and to consider the ways in which such a philosophical methodology might affect the disciplinary boundaries of philosophy itself.

In order to carry out this task, I will turn to Deleuze and Guattari's final collaborative work, *What is Philosophy?* In a certain sense, this text can be read as a kind of postscript to the *Capitalism and Schizophrenia* series. It is a work in which Deleuze and Guattari look back on their collaborations and ask the question, *what were we doing when we wrote together?* In my reading of the text, I show not only that Deleuze and Guattari's work can be read as a philosophical exploration of the nature of transformation, but that, in the process of carrying out this philosophical work, the pair also provided philosophy with a new image of itself, one that characterises philosophical thought as a permanent movement of conceptual transformation.[2] In brief, I will argue that as well as producing a

1 Deleuze and Guattari, *What is Philosophy?*, 8.

2 The reading I offer here is not intended as an exhaustive account of the purpose and technique of *What is Philosophy?* There are two such books available, namely Butler, *Deleuze and Guattari's What is Philosophy?*, and Bell, *Deleuze and Guattari's What is Philosophy? A Critical Introduction and Guide*, the latter of which pays close attention to the relevance of *transformation* in the text.

philosophy of transformation – in the sense that their work attempts to think about transformative processes – their collective writings can be seen as a *transformation of philosophy.* As an additional outcome of this analysis, we will also see that, rather than taking Deleuze and Guattari to be anomalies in the history of philosophy due to their novel treatment of concepts, we can take their techniques of conceptual creation as a rubric for the reinterpretation of philosophy, one which points both to the power of those thinkers who came before them and to the possibilities of future philosophical exploration.

In order to make this argument, I will first lay out a brief analysis of Deleuze and Guattari's answer to their eponymous question in *What is Philosophy?* To do this we will need to examine the specific set of terms for defining philosophical activity that they use in this text. There are three key pieces of terminology here:

> Philosophy presents three elements, each of which fits with the other two but must be considered for itself: *the prephilosophical plane it must lay out (immanence), the persona or personae it must invent and bring to life (insistence), and the philosophical concepts it must create (consistency).*[3]

It is the interaction of these three elements – the plane, the persona and the concept – that Deleuze and Guattari claim is the defining feature of philosophical activity. Let us start with the *concept* and its relationship with the *plane.* In a broader attempt to distinguish philosophy from science and art, Deleuze and Guattari claim that 'philosophy is the art of forming, inventing, and fabricating concepts' and that 'more rigorously, philosophy is the discipline that involves *creating* concepts'.[4] For Deleuze and Guattari, philosophy is activated when someone encounters a problem, and when they must create a new concept to express this problem. A philosophical concept does not represent the world, nor does it define an abstract component of the world; instead it responds to the world by expressing a problem.[5] However, the expression of a new problem by way of

[3] Deleuze and Guattari, *What is Philosophy?*, 76–7.

[4] Deleuze and Guattari, *What is Philosophy?*, 2, 5.

[5] Much has been written on Deleuze and Guattari's novel analysis of concepts. For example, in *Sleights of Reason*, Mary Beth Mader shows how, for Deleuze and Guattari, each concept is composed of heterogeneous elements that are related to one another in the concept, and that this allows the concept to be self-referential (5–6). What I would like to add to this account is an analysis of how these elements are changeable. That is to say, the concept transforms over time, or depending on context, as different elements are brought into or cast out of its

a new concept does not leave the rest of thought untouched. Deleuze and Guattari describe it something like this: concepts all interact in a mutually upholding web of interrelations; this web of concepts determines a field of thought, which regulates what it is possible to think; when, in an attempt to pose a new problem, a philosopher is forced to create a new concept, the introduction of this new concept into the conceptual field effects a reorientation of the whole web of interrelations. The name that Deleuze and Guattari give to the pre-conceptual field of concept-relations is the 'plane of immanence'.[6] They explain that 'the plane of immanence is not a concept that is or can be thought but rather the image of thought, the image thought gives itself of what it means to think, to make use of thought, to find one's bearings in thought'.[7] On this account, each philosopher is defined by the concept (or concepts) that they create, which in turn produces a new plane of immanence, which we might also call a new field of problems for thought. As they write: 'Philosophy is at once concept creation and instituting of the plane. The concept is the beginning of philosophy, but the plane is its instituting.'[8] Deleuze and Guattari are forthcoming with examples of concepts from the history of philosophy: 'Aristotle's substance, Descartes's cogito, Leibniz's monad, Kant's condition, Schelling's power, Bergson's duration'.[9] Whether the word chosen is already in common use or whether it is a new coinage, in each case the concept in question is understood by Deleuze and Guattari as the expression of a problem that was previously inexpressible, and the creation of this concept effectively reorientates philosophy around a new set of problems.

The third term in Deleuze and Guattari's new explanatory trio is the *conceptual persona*. This term is necessary because the creation of concepts always requires the philosopher to speak and to think from a particular point of view. The authors explain that 'conceptual personae constitute points of view according to which planes of immanence are distinguished from one another', and that these conceptual personae 'also constitute the conditions under which each

orbit. This insight is in line with Paul Patton's long-standing project that seeks to show the mobility of Deleuze's concepts. See, for example, the opening chapter of Patton's *Deleuzian Concepts*. In this chapter I am trying to point towards what such mobility might mean for the disciplinary nature of philosophy.

6 Deleuze and Guattari, *What is Philosophy?*, 37.

7 Deleuze and Guattari, *What is Philosophy?*, 37.

8 Deleuze and Guattari, *What is Philosophy?*, 41.

9 Deleuze and Guattari, *What is Philosophy?*, 7.

plane finds itself filled with concepts'.[10] If philosophical thought is activated by an encounter with a problem, then it is always *someone* who encounters this problem. This *someone* is not, however, a person in the social sense, but something akin to an intellectual perspective:

> The conceptual persona is the becoming or the subject of a philosophy ... In everyday life speech-acts refer back to psychosocial types who actually attest to a subjacent third person: 'I decree mobilization as President of the Republic,' 'I speak to you as father,' and so on. In the same way, the philosophical shifter is a speech-act in the third person where it is always a conceptual persona who says 'I': 'I think as Idiot,' 'I will as Zarathustra,' 'I dance as Dionysus,' 'I claim as Lover.'[11]

Again, Deleuze and Guattari supply a list of examples. For Kant to create the concept of 'conditions', he must think from the perspective of the conceptual persona of 'the judge', and in doing so he institutes a new plane of immanence named 'the tribunal of reason'.[12] For Nietzsche to create the concept of 'bad conscience', it was necessary to invent a new conceptual persona of 'the priest' and a new plane, namely 'the will to power understood from the point of view of nihilism'.[13] What is important here is that part of the creative act of doing philosophy involves taking up a new perspective, or a new position, that has never previously been taken up. It is because the list of possible perspectives on any given phenomenon is infinite that philosophy always has new problems to express and thus needs new concepts to express them: 'The list of conceptual personae is never closed and for that reason plays an important role in the evolution or transformations of philosophy.'[14]

This picture of philosophy raises a number of questions about how we should interpret the history of philosophy and how we should understand the interactions between different philosophical points of view. I will turn to some of these questions in more depth in the next two sections, but before I do so I want to note the way in which Deleuze and Guattari's analysis of the relationship between concepts, planes of immanence and conceptual personae might connect with their previous uses of the concept of the line of

[10] Deleuze and Guattari, *What is Philosophy?*, 75.
[11] Deleuze and Guattari, *What is Philosophy?*, 64.
[12] Deleuze and Guattari, *What is Philosophy?*, 72.
[13] Deleuze and Guattari, *What is Philosophy?*, 83.
[14] Deleuze and Guattari, *What is Philosophy?*, 5.

flight. Deleuze and Guattari characterise each plane of immanence in spatial terms and also refer to it as a 'field' and as a 'ground'.[15] A plane of immanence is like the landscape of thought, seen from the perspective of a specific conceptual persona. The difference between two conceptual personae – and thus between two different planes of immanence – is not a question of 'spatiotemporal coordinates' but of movement.[16] It is by moving in a different way, or according to a different rhythm, that the landscape not only moves but becomes a new landscape altogether. As Deleuze and Guattari explain it, in the instituting of a new plane of immanence, 'it is the horizon itself that is in movement', and not only 'the relative horizon' but 'the absolute horizon'.[17] Returning to the development of the concept of the line of flight from Deleuze's initial analysis of depth and linear perspective in *Difference and Repetition*, we can say that the line of flight is this absolute horizon; it is the vanishing line that gives the plane depth and allows it to escape from itself. According to this analysis, we could say that the inventive act of creating a new concept is equivalent to the act of tracing a line of flight. If each plane of immanence is an assemblage of problems, then the line of flight is the line that escapes from one assemblage and connects to another. We might then speak, to take one example from the history of philosophy, of Kant tracing a *line of flight* from the Cartesian plane of immanence of *scepticism*, and escaping the perspective of *the Idiot* to take on the new perspective of *the Judge* by inventing the concept of *conditions*, and in so doing instituting a new plane of immanence named the *tribunal of reason*.

Towards the end of this conclusion I will offer a new analysis of Deleuze and Guattari's *Capitalism and Schizophrenia* series, one which uses the definition of philosophy provided in *What is Philosophy?* to assess it as a work of philosophy. However, before I do this, it will be useful to lay out more clearly how Deleuze and Guattari's account of philosophy as the creation of concepts has broader implications for our understanding of the relationship between those different modes of thought that characterise the history of philosophy. To do this I will provide a brief account of what they call 'geophilosophy'.

[15] Deleuze and Guattari, *What is Philosophy?*, 7.
[16] Deleuze and Guattari, *What is Philosophy?*, 37–8.
[17] Deleuze and Guattari, *What is Philosophy?*, 38.

Geophilosophy

One of the main aims of Deleuze and Guattari's novel approach to defining philosophy is to show that philosophy does not develop along a teleological or strictly historical trajectory, but that each philosopher – or more strictly, each conceptual persona – introduces genuine novelty into thought. Their critique is explicitly aimed at Hegel and Heidegger, who they claim 'remain historicists inasmuch as they posit history as a form of interiority in which the concept necessarily develops or unveils its destiny'.[18] The problem with such an approach, according to Deleuze and Guattari, is that 'the unforeseeable creation of concepts is thus poorly understood'.[19] In brief, we can say that Deleuze and Guattari want to show that philosophy is a discipline of change, of heterogeneity and of transformation, and that each philosophical innovation makes a genuine break with the historical trajectory that leads up to it.

In order to avoid the tendency of historical thought to serialise past events into a lineage, which presents itself as a necessary unfolding, Deleuze and Guattari draw on geographical thinking, and especially on the work of geographer and historian Fernand Braudel, to speak of *geophilosophy*. They say that 'philosophy is a geophilosophy in precisely the same way that history is a geohistory from Braudel's point of view'.[20] Braudel was a historian by training who wanted to show how the trajectory of historical events can only be understood by taking into account the geographical and geological conditions of any age, including the geographical relations between different societies.[21] Just as Deleuze and Guattari had argued in *Anti-Oedipus* that the development towards capitalism,

[18] Deleuze and Guattari, *What is Philosophy?*, 95.

[19] Deleuze and Guattari, *What is Philosophy?*, 95.

[20] Deleuze and Guattari, *What is Philosophy?*, 95.

[21] Guilherme Ribeiro offers a concise account of Braudel's concept of geohistory: 'It is a tool capable of examining how the environment and built space were part of the long-term historical process that transformed the earth's surface into an ecumene – which means excavating its effects on the composition of social life ... It is from the ties between societies and their spaces that Braudel learns the different rhythms of history. In other words, a change in scale can also be a change in temporality. That is why its geohistory is multiscalar, as space is synonymous with diversity, connection, intertwined networks – notions that call into question linear time and the philosophies of progress' (*A arte de conjugar tempo e espaço*, 608). For more on Deleuze and Guattari's use of Braudel, see DeLanda, 'Molar Entities and Molecular Populations in Human History'.

through what they called savagery and despotism, was driven not by a necessary process of the sublation of internal contradictions – as in the orthodox Marxist view – but by encounters with external factors, in *What is Philosophy?* they draw on the work of Braudel to argue that the history of philosophy has been driven by a series of contingent encounters with an outside. It is for this reason that in a book that is explicitly about the nature of philosophy, Deleuze and Guattari offer a detailed sociopolitical analysis of ancient Greece, the apparent birthplace of philosophy. This analysis is not an intellectual history but a geohistorical account of the forces both internal and external to Greek society that provided the contingent conditions for the creation of a new mode of thought. Similarly, the analysis that Deleuze and Guattari provide in the book about contemporary capitalism – and in a broader sense the analysis of the relations between philosophy, science and art – is intended to provide the reader with a map of the contemporary forces that condition thought, and within and against which contemporary philosophy must position itself.

Deleuze and Guattari draw on geography as a discipline because they argue that geography 'wrests history from the cult of necessity in order to stress the irreducibility of contingency. It wrests it from the cult of origins in order to affirm the power of a "milieu" ... It wrests it from structures in order to trace the lines of flight.'[22] In brief, we can say that geophilosophy replaces the history of philosophy for Deleuze and Guattari because it offers an account of the relationship between different thinkers which recognises their influence on one another, but without ignoring the various other social, political, psychological and geographical factors that influence the perspective from which a new problem presents itself. To take up the example given in the previous section, we might say that Kant's institution of a new plane was not determined in advance by some internal contradiction in Descartes' work that Kant was required to overcome, but that a contingent set of social and geographical factors – including his encounter with Hume, but also the political context of his native Prussia, his social life in Königsberg, the intellectual conflict between religion and science, and the colonial conquests going on around him – all came together in a specific milieu to influence his work.

Such an account does not do away with history all together, but only with a historicist model of interpretation. Building on the language of physical geography, and on their characterisation of the

[22] Deleuze and Guattari, *What is Philosophy?*, 96.

plane of immanence as a kind of landscape, Deleuze and Guattari write that 'philosophy is becoming, not history; it is the coexistence of planes, not the succession of systems'.[23] The plane of immanence that is instituted by one conceptual persona is not summoned into existence from nowhere. Instead, each plane of immanence draws on, develops or cuts across previous planes: 'Mental landscapes do not change haphazardly through the ages: a mountain had to rise here or a river to flow by there again recently for the ground, now dry and flat, to have a particular appearance and texture.'[24] What is crucial about this characterisation is that while the temporal succession has a direction (in that thinkers cannot influence the thought of those who came before them), it does not have a strict or deterministic order. One conceptual persona may combine or cross various planes from radically different times: 'It is true that very old strata can rise to the surface again, can cut a path through the formations that covered them and surface directly on the current stratum to which they impart a new curvature.'[25] Deleuze and Guattari explain this model of influence by claiming that philosophical time is a 'time of coexistence that does not exclude the before and after but superimposes them in a stratigraphic order'.[26]

According to the terminology developed in *What is Philosophy?*, we can say that philosophical thought is transformative because it performs topological transformations on the field of what it is possible to think. In philosophy, the plane of immanence – that pre-conceptual transcendental field of thought[27] – is expanded, contracted, twisted, spliced or folded.[28]

[23] Deleuze and Guattari, *What is Philosophy?*, 59. In this conclusion I have chosen to focus on the concept of the 'concept' in *What is Philosophy?* in order to draw attention to the lessons it provides for the previous analysis of the development of the concept of the 'line of flight'. However, a very similar argument could be made by way of an analysis of 'becoming'. As Deleuze and Guattari say: 'Becoming is the concept itself' (*What is Philosophy?*, 110).

[24] Deleuze and Guattari, *What is Philosophy?*, 58–9.

[25] Deleuze and Guattari, *What is Philosophy?*, 58–9.

[26] Deleuze and Guattari, *What is Philosophy?*, 59.

[27] We can think of the plane of immanence as *transcendental* in the same sense that Deleuze speaks of the transcendental nature of *sense* in *Logic of Sense* (112–14). The plane of immanence is thus offered as an overcoming of Sartre's account of the 'impersonal or pre-personal' transcendental field, by removing it from the field of consciousness. See Sartre, *The Transcendence of the Ego*.

[28] Deleuze and Guattari do not explicitly call these transformations topological, and my aim here is not to set parameters on the type of transformations that

A Philosophical Image of Thought

How does the definition of philosophy offered in *What is Philosophy?* reflect back on the work that Deleuze and Guattari had completed before this book? A close look at certain passages in *Difference and Repetition* and in Deleuze and Guattari's own comments on their *Capitalism and Schizophrenia* series will help us to see how this definition is carefully constructed to account for the explicitly *philosophical* nature of their shared project. What we will find is that the characterisation of philosophy as the creation of concepts, the instituting of a plane and the invention of a conceptual persona offers a recapitulation of both *Anti-Oedipus* and *A Thousand Plateaus* as philosophical texts.

However, before we can turn to the *Capitalism and Schizophrenia* series, it will be useful to consider the way in which some of the terminology of *What is Philosophy?* reworks certain ideas that are central to Deleuze's *Difference and Repetition.* Deleuze's approach to the history of philosophy in *Difference and Repetition* differs in many respects from the approach taken with Guattari in *What is Philosophy?* However, both of these texts draw on a distinction between *subjective* presuppositions and *objective* presuppositions, first introduced in the third chapter of *Difference and Repetition*, titled 'The Image of Thought'.[29] In the earlier book, Deleuze had argued that the discipline of philosophy has always defined itself by the activity of doing away with presuppositions: By inspecting their own thoughts, dispelling any unjustified beliefs and by taking nothing for granted, the philosopher tries to attain knowledge which is certain. Unfortunately, according to Deleuze, while philosophers have been busy expelling their explicit or objective presuppositions, they have failed to recognise a hidden set of implicit or subjective presuppositions. Specifically, Deleuze claims, philosophers have always taken for granted, as a kind of *common sense*, a certain number of

can be performed on a plane of immanence (topological transformations are by definition continuous, or homeomorphic, such that two figures are topologically equivalent if one can be hypothetically stretched into the other without tearing).

[29] Deleuze's critique of subjective presuppositions was heavily influenced by Feuerbach's critique of Hegel's presuppositionless logic. This point is made by Somers-Hall, who argues that 'Feuerbach's claim that "every system is only an expression or image of reason" can be seen as a forerunner of Deleuze's own claim that representational thinking rests on an "image of thought"' ('Feuerbach and the Image of Thought', 264).

presuppositions about what it means to be a thinking agent. Taking Descartes' *Meditations* as his major example, Deleuze writes that the innovation of Descartes' *cogito* can be seen in his avoidance of any scholastic, objective presuppositions: if we define man as a rational animal, then we must presuppose the meanings of the concepts 'man' and 'rational'. The *cogito* avoids any such explicit presuppositions but, according to Deleuze, it faces other issues:

> [Descartes] does not escape presuppositions of another kind – subjective or implicit presuppositions contained in opinions rather than concepts: it is presumed that everyone knows, independently of concepts, what is meant by self, thinking, and being.[30]

For Deleuze, 'a subjective or implicit presupposition' is any proposition that takes the form 'Everybody knows...'[31] Here Deleuze is not concerned with specific empirical claims that philosophers have taken for granted, but with methodological claims that concern the philosopher's intimacy with thinking: we know what thinking is like, we know when we are thinking, once we have reached a conclusion we will be able to recognise it. What the philosopher takes for granted in their implicit or subjective presuppositions is therefore 'not a particular this or that but the form of representation or recognition in general'.[32] For this reason, Deleuze writes that 'conceptual philosophical thought has as its implicit presupposition a pre-philosophical and natural Image of thought, borrowed from the pure element of common sense'.[33]

Overall, Deleuze outlines eight specific postulates that make up the most common implicit presuppositions of conceptual thinking.[34] Taken together, these postulates compose what Deleuze names the 'Image of Thought', which is nothing other than the specific set of presuppositions which Western philosophy has failed to expel. As Deleuze explained in an interview published in the same year as *Difference and Repetition*, the problem that we face as philosophers is that 'we live with a particular image of thought, that is to say,

[30] Deleuze, *Difference and Repetition*, 164.

[31] Deleuze, *Difference and Repetition*, 165.

[32] Deleuze, *Difference and Repetition*, 166.

[33] Deleuze, *Difference and Repetition*, 167.

[34] Namely the postulates of 'the principle', 'the ideal', 'the model', 'the element', 'the negative', 'logical function', 'modality' and 'the end' (*Difference and Repetition*, 207).

before we begin to think, we have a vague idea of what it means to think'.[35] In a move that commentators have viewed variously as brilliant or naïve,[36] Deleuze then sets himself the task of producing 'a philosophy which would be without any kind of presuppositions', which would find 'its true beginning, not in an agreement with the *pre-philosophical* Image but in a rigorous struggle against this Image'.[37] This is what Deleuze calls a 'thought without image' and it is this which he attempts to produce in the latter half of *Difference and Repetition*.[38]

As we have seen, in *What is Philosophy?*, Deleuze and Guattari break from Deleuze's earlier work and reconceptualise the 'image of thought' – as it is presented in *Difference and Repetition* – as a 'plane of immanence' of concepts, stating that 'the plane of immanence is not a concept that is or can be thought but rather the image of thought'.[39] In this text, in direct opposition to Deleuze's claims in *Difference and Repetition*, Deleuze and Guattari argue that philosophy can never do away with implicit presuppositions: '[philosophy] proceeds by presupposing or by instituting the plane of immanence' and this plane of immanence 'is presupposed not in the way that one concept may refer to others but in the way that concepts themselves refer to a nonconceptual understanding'.[40] As Miguel de Beistegui has noted, in this respect,

> *What is Philosophy?* seems to mark a shift from a fundamental aspect of *Difference and Repetition*, in so far as Deleuze and Guattari are now claiming that philosophy – including their own – can never quite shake off or determine entirely its own image: a purely imageless thought is but an illusion.[41]

We can understand this change of perspective as a move from the history of philosophy to a geophilosophy. If philosophy works by performing topological transformations on the field of thought,

[35] Deleuze, *Desert Islands*, 139.

[36] For example, compare Alberto Toscano's celebration of 'Deleuze's revolutionary project of a thought without an image' ('Everybody Thinks', 12) with James Williams's characterisation of this goal as an 'impossible target' (*Gilles Deleuze's Difference and Repetition*, 116).

[37] Deleuze, *Difference and Repetition*, 167.

[38] Deleuze, *Difference and Repetition*, 168.

[39] Deleuze and Guattari, *What is Philosophy?*, 37.

[40] Deleuze and Guattari, *What is Philosophy?*, 42, 40.

[41] De Beistegui, *Immanence: Deleuze and Philosophy*, 10.

then in a certain sense this field of thought must be presupposed. Philosophical practice is thus measured by the extent to which it works on that pre-philosophical plane of thought that must be presupposed in order to think.

To continue with the example used earlier in this chapter, we can look again at Kantian philosophy. What is it about Kant's work that characterises it *as philosophy*? While Deleuze criticises Kant in *Difference and Repetition* for relying on certain subjective presuppositions concerning the collaboration of the faculties, in *What is Philosophy?* Deleuze and Guattari speak of Kant's work in positive terms. Addressing Kant's response to Descartes, Deleuze and Guattari claim that Kant's novelty was in his 'introduction of a new component into the cogito, the one Descartes repressed – time'; in doing this they claim that 'Kant constructs a "transcendental" plane that renders doubt useless and changes the nature of the presuppositions once again'.[42] Again, according to this analysis of Kant, what makes his work philosophical is not the fact that it avoids all presuppositions. On the contrary, what makes his work philosophical is the fact that he *transforms* the pre-philosophical image of thought. By taking up a new perspective on thought (the invention of a conceptual persona), he is able to express a new problem (the creation of concepts), and thus transform what it means to think (the institution of a new plane of immanence). According to Deleuze and Guattari's final collaborative book, philosophy *just is* the process of bringing about such transformations.

Capitalism and Schizophrenia *as Philosophy*

As we saw in Chapter 5, Deleuze and Guattari claim that their work in the *Capitalism and Schizophrenia* series institutes a new plane of immanence by utilising the image of the rhizome to create a 'vegetal model of thought'.[43] In that chapter I quoted Deleuze's own analysis of the connections between his work in *Difference and Repetition*

[42] Deleuze and Guattari, *What is Philosophy?*, 31. I have argued elsewhere that Deleuze and Guattari's analysis of Kantian presuppositions could be improved if they were to pay closer attention to the form of the transcendental arguments that Kant uses to justify his presuppositions. See Thornton, 'The Kantian Image of Thought'.

[43] Deleuze, *Difference and Repetition*, xvii.

and his later work with Guattari. It will be useful here to give the quote in full:

> [I]n [*Difference and Repetition*] it seemed to me that the powers of difference and repetition could be reached only by putting into question the traditional image of thought ... It is therefore the third chapter which now seems to me the most necessary and the most concrete, and which serves to introduce subsequent books up to and including the research undertaken with Guattari where we invoked a vegetal model of thought: the rhizome in opposition to the tree, a rhizome-thought instead of an arborescent thought.[44]

This self-analysis on the part of Deleuze raises a number of questions about the philosophical methodology at play in his work with Guattari. Deleuze claims that his work with Guattari constitutes an intervention into philosophy via its institution of a new image of thought, but should we take all of the pair's collaborations as a single philosophical system, or as a series of experiments, each of which constitutes its own philosophy? Is there a single image of thought in the *Capitalism and Schizophrenia* series, or a multiplicity of planes? If we are to treat them as distinct – so that, for example, *Anti-Oedipus* and *A Thousand Plateaus* each have their own plane of immanence, their own conceptual personae and their own concepts – then how are we to understand the relationship between them?

This is a question that Deleuze and Guattari raise themselves in *What is Philosophy?*, where they note that, 'when comparing particular cases it is no doubt difficult to judge whether there is a single plane or several different ones', giving as their example the specific case of ancient Greek thought: 'do the pre-Socratics have the same image of thought, despite the differences between Heraclitus and Parmenides?'[45] Their own answer to this question concerns what we might call the metaphysical parameters of *an* image of thought. We might not be surprised, given their broader metaphysical project, to find that Deleuze and Guattari do not treat each image of thought as a standalone or individual entity. Working with the metaphysical category of the multiplicity, they put their position as follows: '*The* plane of immanence is *interleaved*.'[46] Planes of immanence, or images of thought, cannot be treated as individuals

[44] Deleuze, *Difference and Repetition*, xv.
[45] Deleuze and Guattari, *What is Philosophy?*, 50.
[46] Deleuze and Guattari, *What is Philosophy?*, 50.

or as groups of individuals, but must be considered as multiplicities. This, then, is how Deleuze and Guattari suggest that we read their previous collaborations, namely as a multiplicity of philosophical experiments, which are neither unified nor completely distinct but interleaved. They note that it is not uncommon for us to 'find several philosophies in the same author' because 'philosophers are always recasting and even changing their concepts'.[47] With this in mind, we can take *Anti-Oedipus* and then each of the plateaus in *A Thousand Plateaus* as different experimental moments in Deleuze and Guattari's project of transforming the pre-philosophical image of thought of their age.

Each of these moments can be discerned using the terminology of *persona*, *concept* and *plane* introduced in *What is Philosophy?* In *Anti-Oedipus*, for example, Deleuze and Guattari speak from the perspective of the schizophrenic. Here, 'the schizophrenic is a conceptual persona who lives intensely within the thinker and forces him to think', and is not, as the schizophrenic is so often forced to be in contemporary life, 'a psychosocial type who represses the living being and robs him of his thought'.[48] The concept that is created when this perspective is taken up is that of 'desiring-production' and the image of thought that results is that of 'schizoanalysis'. The trajectory of *Anti-Oedipus* can thus be read as follows: the work begins with the invention of *the concept of desiring-production*; this is followed by a longer account of the *conceptual persona of the schizophrenic*; and the book concludes with a description of the *plane of immanence of schizoanalysis*. Each of the chapters in *A Thousand Plateaus* can then be read as renewing this creative and transformative process. To a certain extent, each plateau expresses a new problem, arising from a singular encounter, which requires both a new concept and a new conceptual persona, and which results in the institution of a new plane.

Of course, each of these transformations is not completely distinct, and the question of whether they should be taken together is isomorphic to the question of whether the pre-Socratics share the same plane. At certain moments a plateau will become more individuated. For example, the 'Geology of Morals' plateau develops the specific conceptual persona of Professor Challenger who introduces a specific set of new concepts, such as 'strata' and 'double articulation', which

[47] Deleuze and Guattari, *What is Philosophy?*, 51, 21.
[48] Deleuze and Guattari, *What is Philosophy?*, 70.

institute the plane they name 'the Mechanosphere, or rhizosphere'.[49] However, at other moments a concept is developed or reworked over a series of plateaus. For example, the problem of the organisation of the body and the accompanying concept of the Body without Organs is reworked at a number of different points in the book. In the chapter titled 'How Do You Make Yourself a Body Without Organs?' this problem is approached most directly, and a series of conceptual personae are tried out as possible perspectives from which the problem could be adequately expressed: the hypochondriac, the paranoiac, the schizo and the masochist.[50] My purpose here is not to offer a specific rubric for the interpretation of each plateau, but instead to try to show that the conceptual architecture of *What is Philosophy?* can be used to investigate the specifically philosophical nature of Deleuze and Guattari's previous collaborations. *Anti-Oedipus* and *A Thousand Plateaus* show themselves as explicitly philosophical texts when we begin to apply this conceptual architecture, and when we begin to see the various ways in which these texts express new problems by creating new concepts, taking up the perspectives of new conceptual personae, and thus instituting new planes of immanence.

Philosophy and Transformation

The constantly evolving terminology of Deleuze and Guattari's respective and collaborative projects has led readers of these works to take up different positions concerning the degree to which this collective oeuvre can be read as expressing a systematic or coherent body of work. I would like to bring this conclusion to a close with one final reflection on this question. My hope here is that by combining the analysis of *What is Philosophy?* given above with my broader project of examining the way that the concept of the 'line of flight' transforms itself throughout Deleuze and Guattari's work, I can show that their philosophical project is neither systematic nor coherent, but that it has what we might call a machinic consistency.

In his book *Deleuze and Language*, Jean-Jacques Lecercle offers a close reading of Deleuze's philosophical methodology as it arises in his writings on language.[51] Lecercle describes Deleuze as 'a coherent

49 Deleuze and Guattari, *A Thousand Plateaus*, 74.

50 Deleuze and Guattari, *A Thousand Plateaus*, 150.

51 While his book only names Deleuze in the title, Lecercle's analysis covers sections of both *Anti-Oedipus* and *A Thousand Plateaus*.

philosopher, [who] does not claim to be a systematic one'.[52] For Lecercle, Deleuze utilises a 'system of concepts' which is nevertheless unsystematic because it always relies on a correlation or cross-reference between two series of concepts. The two series of concepts do not form one system, but are related by a 'connective synthesis'.[53] We could say that, according to Lecercle, Deleuze has a coherent method for drawing insights from the synthesis of multiple systems of concepts. He is thus coherent, in the sense of *making sense*, without having a philosophical system of his own.

Joe Hughes is one of those who disagree with this analysis. In his book *Deleuze and the Genesis of Representation*, Hughes aims to show that beneath the apparent diversity of content in what he calls 'Deleuze's middle period' – comprising *Logic of Sense*, *Difference and Repetition* and *Anti-Oedipus* – there is an attempt to build a systematic account of the genesis of representation. Flipping Lecercle's claim on its head, Hughes argues that 'Deleuze's philosophy is systematic, but incoherent'.[54] For Hughes, Deleuze is incoherent because, 'while a relatively stable structure persists throughout all three books, the technical terms used to describe that structure change', and yet he is systematic because, 'in spite of the changing senses and changing names, there is still a relatively stable structure'.[55] Interestingly, this thesis is defended and expanded in Rex Butler's guide to *What is Philosophy?* Here Butler argues that,

> although the terms *What is Philosophy?* uses are not the same as in others of their writings, its overall subject matter is. And this is to say that, although the particular terms used in *What is Philosophy?* are different, the role they play within Deleuze and Guattari's argument is comparable to that in others of their books.[56]

More specifically, Butler defends Hughes's claim that all of Deleuze's work is an allegorical attempt to explain the process of genesis, but adds that 'the question of genesis is the explicit subject of *What is Philosophy?* in a way it is not in others of Deleuze's and Deleuze and Guattari's books'.[57]

52 Lecercle, *Deleuze and Language*, 16.
53 Lecercle, *Deleuze and Language*, 16.
54 Hughes, *Deleuze and the Genesis of Representation*, 154.
55 Hughes, *Deleuze and the Genesis of Representation*, 154.
56 Butler, *Deleuze and Guattari's What is Philosophy?*, 28.
57 Butler, *Deleuze and Guattari's What is Philosophy?*, 183.

In a sense, Lecercle and Hughes share the same problem, but offer different resolutions to it. They are both aware that Deleuze and Guattari's concepts seem to change their meanings between different texts, and sometimes even within a single text, and yet they are both keen to recognise the existence of some kind of continuing project that crosses the many works. Lecercle aims to resolve this conundrum by showing that Deleuze has a coherent methodology that we can discern as operating below the explicit content of the work. For Hughes, the unity of Deleuze's project is to be found not in a question of method, but in the construction of a unified philosophical system, which, once again, we can see only by looking below the explicit claims of Deleuze's writing. Thus, while Hughes sets up his account as being 'exactly the opposite' of the one put forward by Lecercle, in fact these two readers both search for a hidden unity in Deleuze's work below the apparent diversity of the writing. The account that I have attempted to offer in this book differs from both of these perspectives. Because each of Deleuze and Guattari's texts is instigated by the encounter with a novel problem, both new methods and new systems are required each time. In this sense, we should say that Deleuze and Guattari's work is both incoherent and unsystematic.

Does this not leave us once again in a philosophical no man's land, where we are forced to ask that same question: 'What unity remains for philosophies ... if concepts constantly change?'[58] If the constant transformation of concepts in Deleuze and Guattari's writings leads to a set of works that are incoherent and unsystematic, then how are we to read them as part of the same philosophical project? How are we to read them at all? What I hope to have shown in this conclusion is that our worry here is misplaced, because systematicity and coherence are not the only categories against which we can judge a philosophy. When Hughes lets slip that the apparent systematicity of Deleuze's work is based only on the '*relatively* stable structure' that undergirds his writings, he inadvertently points to what is really going on.[59] Following the analysis I offered at the end of Chapter 2 concerning Guattari's machinic anti-structuralism,[60] we can say that Deleuze and Guattari's writings have a machinic consistency.

58 Deleuze and Guattari, *What is Philosophy?*, 8.
59 Hughes, *Deleuze and the Genesis of Representation*, 154 (my emphasis).
60 See also Thornton, 'The Rise of the Machines'.

There may be a *relatively* stable structure of conceptual relations between these texts (and between others written by Deleuze, Guattari, or Deleuze and Guattari), but this apparent structure is never completely stable. The conceptual terminology changes in each book (or even in each plateau) because Deleuze and Guattari are tackling different problems in each text. The terminology changes because new concepts are being created, new personae are speaking, and new planes are being instituted. *Anti-Oedipus* is not a philosophical attempt to explain genesis, or a philosophical tract on the nature of transformation; it is an attempt to respond to the rise of fascism and the impasse of the fall of communism. *What is Philosophy?* is not yet another concealed study of the concept of 'genesis', or of 'life', or of 'transformation'; it is an attempt to answer the titular question. Here we should take Deleuze and Guattari at their word. Their works operate as an assemblage that is constituted specifically by the way it is constantly undoing its own structure. With each new piece of writing, the apparently underlying 'structure' of Deleuze and Guattari's oeuvre is also in motion. In this sense the creation and transformation of concepts is like the machinic element that animates and gives rise to the structure.

We might say that Deleuze and Guattari's project gains its consistency from the transformations that it undergoes. Just as the species 'wasp' is constituted by the very fact that it is constantly undergoing mutations, just as the concept of the line of flight gains its consistency from the many transformations that it undergoes in Deleuze and Guattari's act of writing it, just as any desiring-machine functions by breaking down, and just as any assemblage is constituted in part by the lines of flight that escape it, Deleuze and Guattari's philosophy shows itself as *a* philosophy by way of its continual retransformation. It is a philosophy in constant transformation, and as such it offers a model for the transformation of philosophy.

Bibliography

Adkins, Brent, *Deleuze and Guattari's A Thousand Plateaus: A Critical Introduction and Guide* (Edinburgh: Edinburgh University Press, 2015).

Alberti, Leon Battista, *On Painting*, trans. John R. Spencer (New Haven, CT: Yale University Press, 1966).

Althusser, Louis, and Balibar, Étienne, *Reading Capital*, trans. Ben Brewster (London: NLB, 1970).

Anderson, Thomas C., *Sartre's Two Ethics: From Authenticity to Integral Humanity* (Chicago: Open Court, 1993).

Ansell-Pearson, Keith, *Germinal Life: The Difference and Repetition of Deleuze* (London: Routledge, 1999).

Aristotle, *Metaphysics*, ed. W. D. Ross (Oxford: Clarendon Press, 1981).

Badiou, Alain, 'The Fascism of the Potato', in *The Adventure of French Philosophy*, ed. Bruno Bosteels (London: Verso, 2012), 191–201.

Balzac, Honoré de, *The Wrong Side of Paris*, trans. Jordan Stump (London: Random House, 2003).

Bell, Jeffrey, *Deleuze and Guattari's What is Philosophy? A Critical Introduction and Guide* (Edinburgh: Edinburgh University Press, 2016).

Bell, Jeffrey, 'Postulates of Linguistics', in Henry Somers-Hall, Jeffrey Bell and James Williams (eds), *A Thousand Plateaus and Philosophy* (Edinburgh: Edinburgh University Press, 2018), 64–82.

Bell, Jeffrey, and Colebrook, Claire (eds), *Deleuze and History* (Edinburgh: Edinburgh University Press, 2009).

Bell, S. D., and Criddle, B., *The French Communist Party in the Fifth Republic* (Oxford: Clarendon Press, 1994).

Bergson, Henri, *Time and Free Will: An Essay on the Immediate Data of Consciousness*, trans. F. L. Pogson (London: Allen and Unwin, 1971).

Bogue, Ronald, *Deleuze and Guattari* (London: Routledge, 2004 [1989]).

Bogue, Ronald, *Deleuze on Literature* (New York: Routledge, 2003).

Bogue, Ronald, *Deleuze's Way: Essays in Transverse Ethics and Aesthetics* (Aldershot: Ashgate, 2007).

Bogue, Ronald, 'Who the Earth Thinks It Is', in Henry Somers-Hall, Jeffrey Bell and James Williams (eds), *A Thousand Plateaus and Philosophy* (Edinburgh: Edinburgh University Press, 2018), 46–63.

Bonta, Mark, and Protevi, John, *Deleuze and Geophilosophy: A Guide and Glossary* (Edinburgh: Edinburgh University Press, 2004).

Boundas, Constantin, 'Virtual/Virtuality', in Adrian Parr (ed.), *The Deleuze Dictionary*, rev. edn (Edinburgh: Edinburgh University Press, 2010), 300–2.

Brassier, Ray, 'Concrete Rules and Abstract Machines: Form and Function', in Henry Somers-Hall, Jeffrey Bell and James Williams (eds), *A Thousand Plateaus and Philosophy* (Edinburgh: Edinburgh University Press, 2018), 260–79.

Buchanan, Ian, *Deleuze and Guattari's 'Anti-Oedipus': A Reader's Guide* (London: Continuum, 2008).

Buchanan, Ian, 'Deleuze, Gilles and Félix Guattari' in M. Groden et al. (eds), *The Johns Hopkins Guide to Literary Theory and Criticism*, 2nd edn (Baltimore, MD: Johns Hopkins University Press, 2005), 247–50.

Butler, Rex, *Deleuze and Guattari's What is Philosophy?* (London: Bloomsbury, 2016).

Catalano, Joseph S., *A Commentary on Jean-Paul Sartre's Critique of Dialectical Reason* (Chicago: University of Chicago Press, 1986).

Clisby, Dale, 'Deleuze's Secret Dualism? Competing Accounts of the Relationship between the Virtual and the Actual', *Parrhesia*, 24 (2015), 127–49.

Colebrook, Claire, 'Introduction', in Jeffrey Bell and Claire Colebrook (eds), *Deleuze and History* (Edinburgh: Edinburgh University Press, 2009), 1–32.

Coombs, Nathan, *History and Event: From Marxism to Contemporary French Theory* (Edinburgh: Edinburgh University Press, 2016).

Culp, Andrew, 'Philosophy, Science, and Virtual Communism', *Angelaki*, 20.4 (2015), 91–107.

Damisch, Hubert, *The Origins of Perspective*, trans. John Goodman (Cambridge, MA: MIT Press, 1994).

De Beistegui, Miguel, "A book? What book?' or Deleuze and Guattari on the Rhizome', in Henry Somers-Hall, Jeffrey Bell and James Williams (eds), *A Thousand Plateaus and Philosophy* (Edinburgh: Edinburgh University Press, 2018), 9–27.

De Beistegui, Miguel, *Immanence: Deleuze and Philosophy* (Edinburgh: Edinburgh University Press, 2010).

DeLanda, Manuel, *Intensive Science and Virtual Philosophy* (London: Bloomsbury, 2013).

DeLanda, Manuel, 'Molar Entities and Molecular Populations in Human History', in Jeffrey Bell and Claire Colebrook (eds), *Deleuze and History* (Edinburgh: Edinburgh University Press, 2009), 225–36.

DeLanda, Manuel, *A New Philosophy of Society: Assemblage Theory and Social Complexity* (London: Continuum, 2006).

DeLanda, Manuel, 'Space: Intensive and Extensive, Actual and Virtual', in Ian Buchanan and Gregg Lambert (eds), *Deleuze and Space* (Edinburgh: Edinburgh University Press, 2005), 80–8.

De Toledo, Sandra Alvarez (ed.), *Maps and Wander Lines – Fernand Deligny* (Paris: L'arachneen, 2013).
Deleuze, Gilles, *Bergsonism*, trans. Hugh Tomlinson and Barbara Habberjam (New York: Zone Books, 1991).
Deleuze, Gilles, *Desert Islands and Other Texts, 1953–1974*, ed. David Lapoujade (New York: Semiotext(e), 2004).
Deleuze, Gilles, *Dialogues II* (with Claire Parnet), trans. Hugh Tomlinson and Barbara Habberjam (New York: Columbia University Press, 2007).
Deleuze, Gilles, *Différence et répétition* (Paris: Presses Universitaires de France, 1968).
Deleuze, Gilles, *Difference and Repetition*, trans. Paul Patton (London: Continuum, 2004).
Deleuze, Gilles, 'Entretien 1980', interview with Catherine Clement, *L'Arc*, 49 (1980), 99.
Deleuze, Gilles, *Expressionism in Philosophy: Spinoza*, trans. Martin Joughin (New York: Zone Books, 1992).
Deleuze, Gilles, *The Fold*, trans. Tom Conley (London: Continuum, 2006).
Deleuze, Gilles, *Foucault*, trans. Sean Hand (London: Continuum, 2006).
Deleuze, Gilles, *Francis Bacon: The Logic of Sensation*, trans. Daniel W. Smith (London: Continuum, 2003).
Deleuze, Gilles, *Instincts et institutions* (Paris: Hachette, 1953).
Deleuze, Gilles, *Lettres et autres textes*, ed. David Lapoujade (Paris: Les Éditions de Minuit, 2015).
Deleuze, Gilles, *Logic of Sense*, trans. Mark Lester and Charles Stivale (London: Continuum, 2004).
Deleuze, Gilles, *Logique du sens* (Paris: Les Editions Minuit, 1969).
Deleuze, Gilles, *Negotiations*, trans. Martin Joughin (New York: Columbia University Press, 1995).
Deleuze, Gilles, *Nietzsche and Philosophy*, trans. Hugh Tomlinson (London: Continuum, 2006).
Deleuze, Gilles, Review of Gilbert Simondon's *L'individu et sa genese physico-biologique* (1966), *Pli*, 12 (2001), 43.
Deleuze, Gilles, *Spinoza: Practical Philosophy*, trans. Robert Hurley (San Francisco: City Lights Books, 1988).
Deleuze, Gilles, *Two Regimes of Madness: Texts and Interviews 1975–1995* (Paris: Semiotext(e), 2007).
Deleuze, Gilles, and Félix Guattari, *Anti-Oedipus*, trans. Robert Hurley, Mark Seem and Helen R. Lane (London: Continuum, 2012).
Deleuze, Gilles, and Guattari, Félix, 'La Synthèse Disjonctive', *L'Arc*, 43 (1971), 54–62.
Deleuze, Gilles, and Félix Guattari, *A Thousand Plateaus*, trans. Brian Massumi (London: Continuum, 2004).
Deleuze, Gilles, and Félix Guattari, *What is Philosophy?*, trans. Hugh Tomlinson and Graham Burchill (London: Verso, 2003).

Deligny, Fernand, *The Arachnean and Other Texts*, trans. Drew S. Burk and Catherine Porter (Minneapolis, MN: Univocal Publishing, 2015).
Descartes, René, *Discourse on Method, Optics, Geometry, and Meteorology* (Cambridge: Hackett, 2001).
Descartes, René, *Meditations on First Philosophy*, in *The Philosophical Works of Descartes*, trans. Elizabeth Haldane (Cambridge: Cambridge University Press, 1911).
Dosse, F., *Gilles Deleuze and Félix Guattari: Intersecting Lives* (New York: Columbia University Press, 2010).
Eco, Umberto, *Semiotics and the Philosophy of Language* (Bloomington, IN: Indiana University Press, 1984).
Eribon, Didier, 'Le 'Je me souviens' de Gilles Deleuze', *Le Nouvel Observateur*, 16–22 November 1995, 114–15.
Euclid, *The Thirteen Books of Euclid's Elements* (New York: Dover Publications, 1956).
Evans, Dylan, *An Introductory Dictionary of Lacanian Psychoanalysis* (London: Routledge, 1996).
Feldstein, Richard, Fink, Bruce, and Jaanus, Maire (eds), *Reading Seminars I and II: Lacan's Return to Freud* (New York: SUNY Press, 1996).
Fink, Bruce, 'The Nature of Unconscious Thought or Why No One Ever Reads Lacan's Postface to the 'Seminar on 'The Purloined Letter''', in Bruce Fink, Maire Jaanus and Richard Feldstein (eds), *Reading Seminars I and II: Lacan's Return to Freud* (New York: SUNY Press, 1996), 173–90.
Foucault, Michel, *Discipline and Punish*, trans. A. M. Sheridan Smith (New York: Vintage, 1975).
Foucault, Michel, *The Order of Things* (London: Routledge, 2002).
Freud, Sigmund, 'Beyond the Pleasure Principle' (1920), in *The Penguin Freud Reader*, ed. Adam Phillips (London: Penguin, 2006), 132–95.
Freud, Sigmund, 'An Outline of Psychoanalysis' (1940), in *The Penguin Freud Reader*, ed. Adam Phillips (London: Penguin, 2006), 1–63.
Freud, Sigmund, 'The Unconscious' (1915), in *The Standard Edition of the Complete Psychological Works of Sigmund Freud, Volume XIV*, trans. James Strachey (London: Hogarth Press, 1957), 159–95.
Gardner, Sebastian, *Sartre's 'Being and Nothingness': A Reader's Guide* (London: Continuum, 2009).
Genosko, Gary, *Félix Guattari: An Aberrant Introduction* (London: Continuum, 2002).
Genosko, Gary, *Félix Guattari: A Critical Introduction* (London: Pluto Press, 2009).
Genosko, Gary, *The Guattari Reader* (Oxford: Blackwell, 1996).
Genosko, Gary, 'The Life and Work of Félix Guattari', in Félix Guattari, *The Three Ecologies* (London: Bloomsbury, 2000), 106–60.
Goffey, Andrew, 'Guattari and Transversality: Institutions, Analysis and Experimentation', *Radical Philosophy*, 195 (2016), 38–47.

Greenberg, M. J., *Euclidean and Non-Euclidean Geometries: Development and History*, 2nd edn (San Francisco: W. H. Freeman, 1980).

Guattari, Félix, *The Anti-Oedipus Papers*, trans. Kelina Gotman (New York: Semiotext(e), 2006).

Guattari, Félix, *Chaosophy: Texts and Interviews 1972–1977* (New York: Semiotext(e), 2008).

Guattari, Félix, *The Machinic Unconscious: Essays in Schizoanalysis*, trans. Taylor Adkins (Los Angeles: Semiotext(e), 2011).

Guattari, Félix, *Molecular Revolution: Psychiatry and Politics* (London: Penguin, 1984).

Guattari, Félix, *Psychanalyse et transversalité: Essai d'analyse institutionnelle* (Paris: Editions La Découverte, 2003).

Guattari, Félix, *Psychoanalysis and Transversality: Texts and Interviews 1955–1971*, trans. Ames Hodges (New York: Semiotext(e), 2015).

Halliwell, J. R., Pérez-Mercader, J., and Zurek, W. H. (eds), *Physical Origins of Time Asymmetry* (Cambridge: Cambridge University Press, 1994).

Hallward, Peter, *Out of This World: Deleuze and the Philosophy of Creation* (London: Verso, 2006).

Hardt, Michael, *Gilles Deleuze: An Apprenticeship in Philosophy* (Minneapolis, MN: University of Minnesota Press, 2002).

Hjelmslev, Louis, *Prolegomena to a Theory of Language*, trans. Francis J. Whitfield (Madison, WI: University of Wisconsin Press, 1969).

Holland, Eugene, *Deleuze and Guattari's Anti-Oedipus: Introduction to Schizoanalysis* (New York: Routledge, 1999).

Holland, Eugene, *Deleuze and Guattari's 'A Thousand Plateaus': A Reader's Guide* (London: Bloomsbury, 2013).

Hughes, John, *Deleuze and the Genesis of Representation* (London: Continuum, 2008).

Jackson, George, *Soledad Brother: The Prison Letters of George Jackson* (Chicago: Chicago Review Press, 1994).

Kant, Immanuel, *Critique of Pure Reason*, trans. Paul Guyer and Allen Wood (Cambridge: Cambridge University Press, 1998).

Kazarian, Edward P., 'Line of Flight', in Victor E. Taylor and Charles E. Winquist (eds), *Encyclopaedia of Postmodernism* (London: Routledge, 2001), 219–20.

Kline, Morris, *Mathematics in Western Culture* (Harmondsworth: Pelican, 1982).

Koerner, Michelle, 'Line of Escape: Gilles Deleuze's Encounter with George Jackson', *Genre* 44.2 (2011), 157–80.

Lacan, Jacques, *Écrits: The First Complete Edition in English*, trans. Bruce Fink (New York: W. W. Norton, 2006).

Lacan, Jacques, *Le séminaire, livre XVIII: D'un discours qui ne serait pas du semblant* (Paris: Seuil, 2006).

Lacan, Jacques, *The Seminar of Jacques Lacan: Freud's Papers on Technique: 1953–1954 Book I*, trans. John Forrester (New York: W. W. Norton, 1991).

Lacan, Jacques, *The Seminar of Jacques Lacan, Book II 1954–1955: The Ego in Freud's Theory and in the Technique of Psychoanalysis*, ed. Jacques-Alain Miller, trans. Sylvana Tomaselli (New York: W. W. Norton, 1988).

Lacan, Jacques, *The Seminar of Jacques Lacan, Book III 1955–1956: The Psychoses*, ed. Jacques-Alain Miller, trans. Russell Grigg (London: Routledge, 1993).

Lacan, Jacques, *The Seminar of Jacques Lacan, Book VIII: Transference*, ed. Jacques-Alain Miller (London: Polity, 2015).

Lacan, Jacques, *The Seminar of Jacques Lacan, Book XI: The Four Fundamental Concepts of Psychoanalysis*, ed. Jacques-Alain Miller (New York: W. W. Norton, 1998).

Lacan, Jacques, *The Seminars, Book XVII: The Other Side of Psychoanalysis*, trans. Russell Grigg (New York: W. W. Norton., 2008).

Lamarre, Thomas, 'Diagram, Inscription, Sensation', in Brian Massumi (ed.), *A Shock to Thought: Expression After Deleuze and Guattari* (London: Routledge, 2002), 149–70.

Land, Nick, *Fanged Noumena: Collected Writings 1987–2007* (Falmouth: Urbanomic, 2012).

LeBuffe, Michael, 'The Anatomy of the Passions', in Olli Koistinen (ed.), *The Cambridge Companion to Spinoza's Ethics* (Cambridge: Cambridge University Press, 2009), 188–222.

Lecercle, Jean-Jacques, *Deleuze and Language* (Basingstoke: Palgrave Macmillan, 2002).

Lundy, Craig, 'Deleuze and Guattari's Historiophilosophy: Philosophical Thought and its Historical Milieu', *Critical Horizons*, 12.2 (2011), 115–35.

Lundy, Craig, 'Emerging from the Depths: On the Intensive Creativity of Historical Events', *Journal of French and Francophone Philosophy*, 18.1 (2010), 67–85.

Lundy, Craig, 'Why Wasn't Capitalism Born in China? – Deleuze and the Philosophy of Non-Events', *Theory and Event*, 16.3 (2013), 1–6.

MacKenzie, Adrian, *Transductions: Bodies and Machines at Speed* (London: Continuum, 2002).

Mader, Mary Beth, *Sleights of Reason: Norm, Bisexuality, Development* (New York: SUNY Press, 2011).

Marks, John, 'Molecular Biology in the Work of Deleuze and Guattari', *Paragraph*, 29.2 (2006), 81–97.

Marx, Karl, *Capital: A Critique of Political Economy, Volume One*, trans. Ben Fowkes (Harmondsworth: Penguin, 1982).

Marx, Karl, 'A Contribution to a Critique of Political Economy', in *Marx-Engels Collected Works*, vol. 29 (London: Lawrence and Wishart, 1987), 257–313.

Marx, Karl, *Grundrisse: Introduction to the Critique of Political Economy*, trans. Martin Nicolaus (London: Penguin, 1993).
Marx, Karl, and Engels, Friedrich, *The German Ideology* (New York: Prometheus Books, 1998).
Mathy, Jean-Philippe, *Melancholy Politics: Loss, Mourning, and Memory in Late Modern France* (University Park, PA: Penn State University Press, 2011).
May, Todd, *Gilles Deleuze: An Introduction* (Cambridge: Cambridge University Press, 2005).
McAllister, Blake, 'Adequate and Inadequate Ideas in Spinoza', *History of Philosophy Quarterly*, 31.2 (2014), 119–36.
McLuhan, Marshall, *Counterblast* (London: Rapp and Whiting, 1970).
Merleau-Ponty, Maurice, 'Eye and Mind', in *The Merleau-Ponty Aesthetics Reader: Philosophy and Painting*, ed. Galen A. Johnson (Evanston, IL: Northwestern University Press, 1993), 121–50.
Merleau-Ponty, Maurice, *The Prose of the World* (Evanston, IL: Northwestern University Press, 1973).
Merleau-Ponty, Maurice, *The Visible and the Invisible*, trans. Alphonso Lingis (Evanston, IL: Northwestern University Press, 1968).
Miller, Jacques-Alain, 'An Introduction to Seminars I and II', in Bruce Fink, Maire Jaanus and Richard Feldstein (eds), *Reading Seminars I and II: Lacan's Return to Freud* (New York: SUNY Press, 1996), 3–38.
Morris, Meaghan, *Identity Anecdotes: Translation and Media Culture* (London: Sage, 2006).
Mullarkey, John, *Bergson and Philosophy* (Edinburgh: Edinburgh University Press, 1999).
Nietzsche, Friedrich, *The Anti-Christ, Ecce Homo, Twilight of the Idols*, trans. Judith Norman (Cambridge: Cambridge University Press, 2005).
Nietzsche, Friedrich, *On the Genealogy of Morality*, trans. Carol Diethe (Cambridge: Cambridge University Press, 2006).
Panofsky, Irwin, *Perspective as Symbolic Form*, trans. Christopher S. Wood (New York: Zone Books, 1991).
Patton, Paul, *Deleuze and the Political* (London: Routledge, 2000).
Patton Paul, *Deleuzian Concepts: Philosophy, Colonization, Politics* (Stanford, CA: Stanford University Press, 2010).
Plato, *Phaedrus*, trans. Robin Waterfield (Oxford: Oxford University Press, 2002).
Plato, *The Republic*, trans. Benjamin Jowett (New York: Random House, 1973).
Protevi, John, Review of Peter Hallward's *Out of This World*, *Notre Dame Philosophical Reviews* (2007), http://ndpr.nd.edu/news/23058/?id=10564 (accessed 4 January 2018).
Rabate, Jean-Michel, *Crimes of the Future: Theory and its Global Reproduction* (London: Bloomsbury, 2014).

Ragland, Ellie, 'An Overview of the Real, with Examples from Seminar 1', in Bruce Fink, Maire Jaanus and Richard Feldstein (eds), *Reading Seminars I and II: Lacan's Return to Freud* (New York: SUNY Press, 1996), 192–211.

Rakov, Vladimir A., and Uman, Martin A., *Lightning: Physics and Effects* (Cambridge: Cambridge University Press, 2006).

Ribiero, Guilherme, 'A arte de conjugar tempo e espaço: Fernand Braudel, a geo-história e a longa duração. História, Ciências, Saúde', *Manguinhos*, 22.2 (2015), 605–39, https://www.scielo.br/j/hcsm/a/XPqsqDS9R4Fng3CkzPjhzBN/?lang=pt (accessed 24 September 2024).

Riemann, Bernard, 'On the Hypotheses which Lie at the Foundation of Geometry', trans. Henry S. White, in David Eugene Smith (ed.), *A Source Book in Mathematics* (New York: McGraw-Hill, 1929), 411–25.

Rigby, S. H., *Marxism and History: A Critical Introduction*, 2nd edn (Manchester: Manchester University Press, 1998).

Rovelli, Carlo, *Seven Brief Lessons on Physics*, trans. Simon Carnell and Erica Segre (London: Penguin, 2014).

Russell, Bertrand, *An Essay on the Foundations of Geometry* (London: Routledge, 1996).

Santori, R. E., *Sartre on Violence: Curiously Ambivalent* (University Park, PA: Penn State University Press, 2003).

Sartre, Jean-Paul, *Being and Nothingness: An Essay on Phenomenological Ontology*, trans. Hazel E. Barnes (London: Methuen, 1958).

Sartre, Jean-Paul, *Critique of Dialectical Reason: Volume One, Theory of Practical Ensembles*, trans. Alan Sheridan Smith (London: Verso, 2004).

Sartre, Jean-Paul, *The Transcendence of the Ego* (New York: Noonday Press, 1957).

Sartre, Jean-Paul, *What is Subjectivity?*, trans. David Broder and Trista Selous (London: Verso, 2016).

Sauvagnargues, Anne, 'Crystals and Membranes: Individuality and Membranes', in Arne De Boever, Alex Murray, Jon Roffe and Ashley Woodward (eds), *Gilbert Simondon: Being and Technology* (Edinburgh: Edinburgh University Press, 2012), 57–71.

Schuster, Aaron, *The Trouble with Pleasure: Deleuze and Psychoanalysis* (Cambridge, MA: MIT Press, 2016).

Seem, Mark D., and Guattari, Félix, 'Interview: Félix Guattari', *Diacritics*, 4.3 (1974), 38–41.

Seigworth, Gregory, 'Little Affect: Hallward's Deleuze', *Culture Machine* (2007), http://www.culturemachine.net/index.php/cm/article/view/166/147 (accessed 4 January 2018).

Sholtz, Janae, *The Invention of a People: Heidegger and Deleuze on Art and the Political* (Edinburgh: Edinburgh University Press, 2015).

Sibertin-Blanc, Guillaume, *State and Politics: Deleuze and Guattari on Marx*, trans. Ames Hodges (South Pasadena, CA: Semiotext(e), 2016).

Simondon, Gilbert, *L'individu et sa genèse physico-biologique (l'individuation à la lumière des notions de forme et d''information)* (Paris: Presses Universitaires de France, 1964).

Smith, Daniel W., 'From the Surface to the Depths: On the Transition from Logic of Sense to Anti-Oedipus', *Symposium: The Canadian Journal of Continental Philosophy*, 10.1 (2006), 135–53.

Soler, Colette, 'The Symbolic Order (I) and The Symbolic Order (II)', in Bruce Fink, Maire Jaanus and Richard Feldstein (eds), *Reading Seminars I and II: Lacan's Return to Freud* (New York: SUNY Press, 1996), 39–55.

Somers-Hall, Henry, 'Deleuze and Merleau-Ponty: The Aesthetics of Difference', in Constantin V. Boundas (ed.), *Gilles Deleuze: The Intensive Reduction* (London: Continuum, 2009), 123–30.

Somers-Hall, Henry, *Deleuze's Difference and Repetition* (Edinburgh: Edinburgh University Press, 2013).

Somers-Hall, Henry, 'Feuerbach and the Image of Thought', in Daniella Voss and Craig Lundy (eds), *At the Edges of Thought: Deleuze and Post-Kantian Philosophy* (Edinburgh: Edinburgh University Press, 2015), 253–71.

Somers-Hall, Henry, *Hegel, Deleuze, and the Critique of Representation* (New York: SUNY Press, 2012).

Somers-Hall, Henry, Bell, Jeffrey, and Williams, James (eds), *A Thousand Plateaus and Philosophy* (Edinburgh: Edinburgh University Press, 2018).

Spinoza, Baruch, *Complete Works*, trans. Samuel Shirley, ed. Michael L. Morgan (Indianapolis, IN: Hackett, 2002).

Thornton, Edward, 'Deleuze and Guattari's Absent Analysis of Patriarchy', *Hypatia: A Journal of Feminist Philosophy*, 34.2 (2019), 348–68.

Thornton, Edward, 'The Kantian Image of Thought: Beyond Deleuze and Guattari's Analysis of Presuppositions', *Plí: The Warwick Journal of Philosophy*, 32 (2020), 12–36.

Thornton, Edward, 'On Lines of Flight: The Theory of Political Transformation in *A Thousand Plateaus*', *Deleuze and Guattari Studies*, 14.3 (2020), 433–56.

Thornton, Edward, 'The Rise of the Machines: Deleuze's Flight from Structuralism', *The Southern Journal of Philosophy*, 55.4 (2017), 454–74.

Thornton, Edward, 'Thinking and Writing Together: Institutional Pedagogy and Félix Guattari', *Deleuze and Guattari Studies*, 17.2 (2023), 252–68.

Toscano, Alberto, 'Everybody Thinks: Deleuze, Descartes and Rationalism', *Radical Philosophy*, 162 (2010), 8–17.

Watson, Janell, *Guattari's Diagrammatic Thought: Writing Between Lacan and Deleuze* (London: Continuum, 2009).

White, John, *Perspective in Ancient Drawing and Painting* (London: The Society for the Promotion of Hellenic Studies, 1956).

Widder, Nathan, 'The Mathematics of Continuous Multiplicities: The Role of Riemann in Deleuze's Reading of Bergson', *Deleuze and Guattari Studies*, 13.3 (2019), 309–458.

Widder, Nathan, *Political Theory after Deleuze* (London: Continuum, 2012).
Widder, Nathan, 'The Rights of Simulacra: Deleuze and the Univocity of Being', *Continental Philosophy Review*, 34.4 (2001), 437–53.
Williams, James, *Gilles Deleuze's Difference and Repetition: A Critical Introduction and Guide* (Edinburgh: Edinburgh University Press, 2013).
Wood, Christopher S., Review of *The Origin of Perspective* and *Le Jugement de Pâris* by Hubert Damisch, *The Art Bulletin*, 77.4 (1995), 677–82.
Young, Eugene, Genosko, Gary, and Watson, Janell, *The Deleuze and Guattari Dictionary* (London: Bloomsbury, 2013).
Zepke, Stephen, *Art as Abstract Machine: Ontology and Aesthetics in Deleuze and Guattari* (London: Routledge, 2005).
Žižek, Slavoj, *Organs Without Bodies: On Deleuze and Consequences* (New York: Routledge, 2003).

Index

EU Authorised Representative:
Easy Access System Europe Mustamäe tee 50, 10621 Tallinn, Estonia
gpsr.requests@easproject.com

Printed and bound by CPI Group (UK) Ltd, Croydon, CR0 4YY
29/09/2026
02224986-0009

PLATEAUS • NEW DIRECTIONS IN DELEUZE STUDIES

Series Editors Ian Buchanan and Claire Colebrook

'A masterful genealogy of one of the leitmotifs of Deleuze and Guattari's philosophy. Thornton demonstrates with lucidity and erudition the double genesis of the line of flight in the works of both Deleuze and Guattari, developing in the process a compelling reading of their work as a whole.'
Henry Somers-Hall, Royal Holloway, University of London

'Thornton's bold hypothesis is that Deleuze and Guattari initiated a great thaw in attempting to unfreeze Western philosophy. He cogently shows how they put philosophy into a state of continuous variation by developing a philosophy that requires perpetual conceptual change. True to transformation, Thornton seeks consistencies rather than frosting over mutations.'
Gary Genosko, Ontario Tech University

Recognises *Capitalism and Schizophrenia* as the fulcrum of Deleuze and Guattari's philosophical project concerning the problem of transformation

Edward Thornton reveals the metaphysical underpinnings of Deleuze and Guattari's philosophy and shows how, beneath the many references to specific moments of transformation, they provide a complex philosophical framework, particularly designed to treat transformative processes as constitutive of reality.

Central to this study is an examination of the concept of the 'line of flight' (*ligne de fuite*). By showing how this concept allows Deleuze and Guattari to theorise processes of radical change – from the evolutionary developments of biological species to the revolutionary breaks of political change – Thornton challenges readers with a novel vision of Deleuze and Guattari's oeuvre as a methodical response to a philosophical problem of transformation.

Edward Thornton is a researcher and historian of philosophy whose work concerns the broad question of how different systems of thought interact with power.

Cover image: Robert Challens, @mysingleline
Cover design: riverdesignbooks.com

EDINBURGH
University Press
edinburghuniversitypress.com

ISBN 978-1-3995-4807-6

9 781399 548076